D0963178

SHORTLIST

Amsterdam
2008
WHAT'S NEW | WHAT'S ON | WHAT'S BEST

www.timeout.com/amsterdam

Contents

Amsterdam by Area

Essentials

Published by Time Out Guides Ltd
Universal House
251 Tottenham Court Road
London W1T 7AB
Tel: + 44 (0)20 7813 3000
Fax: + 44 (0)20 7813 6001
Email: guides@timeout.com
www.timeout.com

Managing Director Peter Fiennes
Editorial Director Ruth Jarvis
Deputy Series Editor Dominic Earle
Business Manager Gareth Garner
Editorial Manager Holly Pick
Accountant Ija Krasnikova

Time Out Guides is a wholly owned subsidiary of Time Out Group Ltd.

© Time Out Group Ltd
Chairman Tony Elliott
Financial Director Richard Waterlow
Time Out Magazine Ltd MD David Pepper
Group General Manager/Director Nichola Coulthard
Managing Director, Time Out International Cathy Runciman
Time Out Communications Ltd MD David Pepper
Production Director Mark Lamond
Group Marketing Director John Luck
Group Art Director John Oakey
Group IT Director Simon Chappell

Time Out and the Time Out logo are trademarks of Time Out Group Ltd.

This edition first published in Great Britain in 2007 by Ebury Publishing
A Random House Group Company
Company information can be found on www.randomhouse.co.uk
10 9 8 7 6 5 4 3 2 1

For further distribution details, see www.timeout.com

ISBN 13: 9781846700422
ISBN 10: 1-84670-042-6

A CIP catalogue record for this book is available from the British Library

Printed and bound by Firmengruppe APPL, aprinta druck, Wemding, Germany

The Random House Group Limited makes every effort to ensure that the papers used in
our books are made from trees that have been legally sourced from well-managed and
credibly certified forests. Our paper procurement policy can be found on
www.randomhouse.co.uk

Amsterdam Shortlist

This **Time Out Amsterdam Shortlist** is one of a new series of guides drawing on Time Out's background as a magazine publisher to keep you current with what's going on in town. As well as the city's key sights and the best of its eating, drinking and leisure options, it picks out the most exciting venues to have opened in the last year and gives a full calendar of events from September 2007 to December 2008. It also includes features on the important news, trends and openings, all compiled by locally based editors and writers. Whether you're visiting for the first time in your life or a regular on the city streets, you'll find the *Time Out Amsterdam Shortlist* contains all you need to know in a completely portable and easy-to-use format.

This guide divides the city into seven areas, each featuring listings for Sights & Museums, Eating & Drinking, Shopping, Nightlife and Arts & Leisure, and maps showing their locations. At the front of the book are chapters rounding up these scenes city-wide, and giving a shortlist of our overall picks. We also include itineraries for days out, plus essentials such as transport information and details for hotels.

Our listings give phone numbers as dialled within the city. The international code for the Netherlands is 31. To call from outside the country, follow this number with the code for Amsterdam, 020, dropping the inital '0'. Some listed numbers are mobiles, indicated as such.

We have noted differing price categories by using one to four € signs (€-€€€€), representing budget, moderate, expensive and luxury respectively. Major credit cards are accepted unless otherwise stated, and we also indicate when a venue is NEW .

All of our listings are double-checked, but places do suddenly sometimes close or change their hours or prices, so it's a good idea to phone a venue before visiting. While every effort has been made to ensure accuracy, the publishers cannot accept responsibility for any errors that this guide may contain.

Venues are located and marked on the maps in this guide using symbols numbered according to their order within the chapter and are colour-coded for convenience as follows:

❶ Sights & Museums
❶ Eating & Drinking
❶ Shopping
❶ Nightlife
❶ Arts & Leisure

Map key	
Selected House Number	*463*
Major Sight or Landmark	▢
Hospital or College	▢
Pedestrianised Street	▢
Railway Station	▢
Metro Station	Ⓜ
Area Name	**LEIDSEPLEIN**

Time Out Shortlist | Amsterdam 2008 **5**

Time Out Amsterdam Shortlist 2008

EDITORIAL
Editors Steve Korver, Kim Renfrew
Deputy Editor Cyrus Shahrad
Copy Editor Jonathan Derbyshire
Researcher Petra Timmerman
Proofreader Patrick Mulkern

DESIGN
Art Director Scott Moore
Art Editor Pinelope Kourmouzoglou
Senior Designer Henry Elphick
Graphic Designer Gemma Doyle
Junior Graphic Designer Kei Ishimaru
Digital Imaging Simon Foster
Ad Make-up Jodi Sher
Picture Editor Jael Marschner
Deputy Picture Editor Tracey Kerrigan
Picture Researcher Helen McFarland

ADVERTISING
Sales Director/Sponsorship Mark Phillips
International Sales Manager Fred Durman
International Sales Consultant
    Ross Canadé
Advertising Sales (Amsterdam)
    Boom Chicago
Advertising Assistant Kate Staddon

MARKETING
Marketing Manager Yvonne Poon
Sales & Marketing Director,
    North America Lisa Levinson
Marketing Designer Anthony Huggins

PRODUCTION
Production Manager Brendan McKeown
Production Co-ordinator Caroline Bradford
Production Controller Susan Whittaker

CONTRIBUTORS
This guide was researched and written by Joost Baaij, Georgina Bean, Willem de Blaauw, Dara Colwell, Shyama Daryanani, Angelique van Engelen, Monique Gruter, Karina Hof, Kate Holder, Luuk van Huét, Cecily Layzell, Steve Korver, Steven McCarron, Kim Renfrew, Marinus de Ruiter and Mark Wedin.

PHOTOGRAPHY
Photography by Olivia Rutherford, except: pages 3(bottom left), 15, 16, 41, 42, 45, 110, 140 Gemma Day; pages 7, 37 Peer Reed; page 12 Photo Artis; page 19 www.blowverbod-amsterdam.com; pages 23, 71 ABC Books; pages 32, 150, 154 Netherlands Board of Tourism and Conventions; page 34 Rene den Engelsman; pages 39, 62, 68, 112, 135, 147 Heloise Bergman; page 64 Svenja Kaufmann; page 102 Steve Korver; page 133 Franck Hakkert; page 188 Michelle Grant.

The following images were provided by the featured establishments/artists:
pages 29, 30, 47, 49, 84, 87, 94, 107, 121, 132, 141, 142, 168, 169, 171, 173.

Cover photograph: Borneo/Sporenburg bridge. Credit: Olivia Rutherford.

MAPS
JS Graphics (john@jsgraphics.co.uk). Amsterdam transport map by Studio Olykan.

About Time Out

Founded in 1968, Time Out has expanded from humble London beginnings into the leading resource for those wanting to know what's happening in the world's greatest cities. As well as our influential what's-on weeklies in London, New York and Chicago, we publish more than a dozen other listings magazines in cities as varied as Beijing and Mumbai. The magazines established Time Out's trademark style: sharp writing, informed reviewing and bang up-to-date inside knowledge of every scene.

Time Out made the natural leap into travel guides in the 1980s with the City Guide series, which now extends to over 50 destinations around the world. Written and researched by expert local writers and generously illustrated with original photography, the full-size guides cover a larger area than our Shortlist guides and include many more venue reviews, along with additional background features and a full set of maps.

Throughout this rapid growth, the company has remained proudly independent, still owned by Tony Elliott nearly four decades after he started Time Out London as a single fold-out sheet of A5 paper. This independence extends to the editorial content of all our publications, this Shortlist included. No establishment has been featured because it has advertised, and no payment has influenced any of our reviews. And, for our critics, there's definitely no such thing as a free lunch: all restaurants and bars are visited and reviewed anonymously, and Time Out always picks up the bill.

For more about the company, see www.timeout.com.

Don't Miss
2008

De Waag p53

Sights & Museums

If you're looking for the unholy trinity of sex, drugs and/or rock 'n' roll, you will find everything you need in Amsterdam without having to undertake even the slightest bit of preparation – whatever you're looking for will leap out at you. But this town is also dense with plenty of pursuits of the higher, nobler and/or brainier sort. And while it manages to pack the cultural punch of a metropolis, Amsterdam is a remarkably convenient size: most things are within half an hour's walk away from each other, and the excellent network of trams provides back-up for those low on energy. You can also slipstream the locals and saddle up on a bike (though beware of trams and cycle thieves); better still, beg or borrow a boat to really absorb the city from the angle from which it was truly meant to be viewed – gazing up from a canal. In the city centre are Amsterdam's old port (and quickly developing waterfront, p110), its medieval buildings, the red lights that denote the central business district of the world's oldest trade, the grand 17th-century merchants' houses, the high spires of ancient religious institutions, the earliest and prettiest canals and also many of its most famous sights. Except to stroll to Museumplein, with its three most famous art museums and world-class concert hall, few visitors to the city go beyond the confines of *grachtengordel*, that calming concentric belt of Golden Age canals – likened by Albert

Camus in his novel *The Fall* to the circles of Hell – that ensnare the fascinating and historic Old Centre. Be sure not to make that mistake: while primarily residential areas, the Jordaan and the Pijp are also hugely attractive places.

Changes, what changes?

While Amsterdam remains a city in flux – especially with the building of the Noord-Zuidlijn metro line and the massive building projects both around Centraal Station and directly across the IJ in Amsterdam Noord – a big part of Amsterdam's charm is in how little it has changed. Most of the more appealing sights have been around for many decades or, more usually, for centuries. You should, however, be aware that two of the city's most prominent museums are undergoing major changes. The Stedelijk Museum of Modern Art (p129) is now temporarily housed in Post CS near Centraal Station, while its usual home on Museumplein is being massively renovated. This has been a blessing in disguise, since its temporary location appears to have breathed new vitality into the ageing institution, thanks to the fact that it's now in a building filled with smaller gallery spaces, young creative industries and studios. The renovation of the Rijksmuseum, home to Rembrandt's *Night Watch*, is also a blessing of sorts: their notoriously massive collection is so overwhelming that the present exhibition of its top 100 pieces (in the Philips Wing) is actually all one can reasonably expect to absorb over the course of a single visit.

Museum hopping

While most Amsterdam museums charge for admission, prices are reasonable: rarely more than €10. However, if you're thinking of taking in a few, the Museumkaart

SHORTLIST

Classic art
- Rijksmuseum (p129)

Cutting edge art
- Jordaan (p121)
- Stedelijk Museum (p129)

Entering the past
- Amsterdams Historisch Museum (p75)
- Concertgebouw (p134)
- Hermitage aan de Amstel (p100)
- Museum Amstelkring (p56)
- Verzetsmuseum (p104)

Back to the future
- Eastern docklands (p110)
- Nemo (p113)

For a religious experience
- Joods Historisch Museum (p102)
- Nieuwe Kerk (p57)
- Oude Kerk (p57)
- Portugese Synagogue (p103)

Cheerful Dutch clichés
- Bloemenmarkt (p95)
- Brouwerij 't IJ (next to a windmill; p105)

Sex & drugs
- Erotic Museum (p56)
- Red Light District (p52)

Longest queues in town
- Anne Frankhuis (p84)
- Van Gogh Museum (p130)

Most scenic canals
- Brouwersgracht (p82)
- Leliegracht (p82)
- Prinsengracht (p84)

Getaways
- Artis (p100)
- Hortus Botanicus (p102)
- Vondelpark (p126)

Power houses
- Koninklijk Paleis (p56)
- Huis Marseille (p85)

Artis Butterfly House p100

(Museum Card) is a steal: €30 for adults and €15 for under-25s (plus a €4.95 administration fee for first-timers). The card offers users free or discounted admission to over 400 attractions in the Netherlands, and is valid for a year from date of purchase; discounted or free entry offered to holders of the card is denoted in the listings of this guide by the letters 'MK'. You can buy the card at participating museums.

The Amsterdam Tourist Board (p185) also sells a savings pass, the I amsterdam Card, which gives you free entry to major museums, free public transport and a free canal trip, along with a hefty 25 per cent discount at participating tourist attractions and restaurants. It costs €33 for 24 hours, €43 for 48 hours and €53 for 72 hours. Log on to www.amsterdammuseums.nl for a list of all major museums across the city and their programmes.

Sights unseen

Much of Amsterdam's charm comes from what remains hidden from the untutored eye. For instance, there is an awful lot more to absorb than just sex and drugs in the Red Light District. A mix of prostitutes, clerics, schoolkids, junkies, carpenters and cops all interact with a strange brand of social cosiness, with the tourists as mere voyeurs. It's all pretty harmless, just so long as you remember that window girls do not like having their pictures taken and that drug dealers react to unwanted eye contact like dogs to bones.

Then there are the local *hofjes* or almshouses, many of which are pretty and deliciously peaceful, the most famous being the Begijnhof. Most are concentrated in the Jordaan. The best known are the Venetiae (Elandsstraat 106-36), the Sint Andrieshofje (Egelantiersgracht 107-14), the Karthuizerhof (Karthuizerstraat 21-31), the Suyckerhofje (Lindengracht 149-63), the Claes Claesz Hofje (1e Egelantiersdwarsstraat 3), the Raepenhofje (Palmgracht 28-38), and oldest by far, the Lindenhofje (Lindengracht 94-112). The art of *hofje*-hopping is a gamble, as entrances are sometimes locked in deference to the residents. But take a chance and you may get lucky.

Meanwhile, the major canals and their radial streets are where the real Amsterdam exists. What they lack in sights, they make up for as a place for scenic coffee slurping, quirky shopping, aimless walks and meditative gable gazing.

Neighbourhood hopping

Of course, Amsterdam's infamous ground zero of consumerism, vice, entertainment and history is the Old Centre, which is bounded by Prins Hendrikkade to the north, Oudeschans and Zwanenburgwal to the east, the Amstel to the south and Singel to the west.

Within these borders, the Old Centre is split into the New Side (west of Damrak and Rokin) and the Old Side (east of Damrak and Rokin). Within the famous Old Side – roughly in the triangle formed by Central Station, the Nieuwmarkt and the Dam – is the famed Red Light District. But the area is also home to the epic Oude Kerk (p57) and the menacing De Waag (p53). The New Side, on the other hand, acts as the Old Side's kinder, gentler twin with its history tied in with the city's intelligentsia, thanks to its many book shops, brown cafes and the various buildings of the University of Amsterdam.

The *grachtengordel* ('girdle of canals') that guards the Old Centre is pleasant, idyllic and uniquely Amsterdam. And now it boasts the two most interesting new arrivals to the local sighseeing scene: the Tassenmuseum (see box p94) and the City Archives (p93). It is also home to the Anne Frank House (p84), the Westerkerk (p85) and two rather intriguing photography museums: Foam (p90) and Huis Marseille (p85). For ease of use, we've split the canals in half: Western Canal Belt denotes the stretch of canals to the west and north of Leidsegracht, while Southern Canal Belt covers the area east of here, thus taking

in Leidseplein and Rembrandtplein. This split is historically justified by the fact that the western girdle was completely finished before work on the eastern half began.

The area around Waterlooplein, just east of the Old Centre, was settled by Jews four centuries ago, and so took its name – Jodenbuurt – from them. The Plantage, lying east and south-east of Waterlooplein, holds many delights, among them the Hortus Botanicus and Artis. Further east – or Oost – lies the Tropenmuseum, before the city opens up and stretches out.

Once the gateway to prosperity, Amsterdam's Waterfront is now the setting for one of Europe's most inspired architectural developments. Traditional sights may be few, but the eastern stretch in particular is home to thousands of new residents and is developing as a strong arts and nightlife boulevard.

Over in the other direction, the Westelijke Eilanden link up nicely with the Jordaan, bordered by Brouwersgracht, Prinsengracht, Leidsegracht and Lijnbaansgracht, which is arguably Amsterdam's most charming neighbourhood. Working-class stalwarts here rub shoulders with affluent newcomers in an area that, while lacking the grandiose architecture of the canals, wants for nothing in terms of character.

Highlighted by its world-class museums and some stupendously posh emporia of high-class fashion, Amsterdam's Museum Quarter is a mix of culture (Museumplein) and couture (PC Hooftstraat). However, its two new museums – covering diamonds (p132) and booze (p128) – aren't exactly inspiring.

Against all odds, the Pijp has managed to remain a wonderful cultural melting pot, even though gentrification has been in full effect for several years now.

DON'T MISS: 2008

LOS PILONES
CANTINA MEXICO

ENJOY OUR

AUTHENTIC "MEX-MEX" FOOD

AND A GREAT TEQUILA COLLECTION

we are open monday through sunday from 16.00 to 1.00
Kerkstraat 63   1017GC   Amsterdam   Tel.: 020 - 320 4651
www.LosPilones.com

Dauphine

Eating, Drinking & Smoking

While many restaurants continue to drop like flies into pea soup, there has been an almost endless stream of new – and often daring – ventures to replace them. Gossip seems most fevered around places that combine culinary delight with eccentric locations: De Kas (p106) is set in an old greenhouse, Hotel de Goudfazant (p113) inside a vast warehouse, Dauphine (p105) in a former car showroom and Pont 13 (p114) in a retired ferry. And be sure to grab at least a coffee and a view at 11 (p116), located atop the former post office building, now serving as a temporary home to the famous Stedelijk Museum (p129).

All this action makes one forget that the term 'Dutch cuisine' used to inspire only peals of laughter. But well-travelled chefs have returned home to apply their lessons to fresh local and often organic ingredients (you can even source your own at Noordermarkt's Saturday organic market; p123). Transcending its setting on a land best suited to spuds, cabbages, carrots and cows, the nation is now employing its greenhouses to grow a startling array of great ingredients.

Fish, gruel and beer formed the trinity of the medieval diet. (Yes, Homer: beer! Would *you* be happy to drink the canal water?) During the Golden Age, the rich indulged in hogs and pheasants, although apparently only after having these table-groaning meals painted for posterity – as various pictures in the Rijksmuseum collection clearly attest. But it was with Napoleonic rule at the dawn of the 19th century that the middle classes were seduced by innovations like herbs, spices and the then radical concept that overcooking is bad. Sadly, a century later it all went terribly wrong (see box p135). But still, there's nothing quite like a hotchpotch of potato, hot, crispy bacon and still-crunchy greens, all rather diligently dammed to hold a pool of gravy. Traditional Dutch food can still hit the mark, and frequently does.

Rich, spicy food from Indonesia re-eroticised the Dutch palate after World War II, when the colony was granted its independence and the Netherlands took in Indonesian immigrants. Take your pick from the various cheap Surinamese-Indonesian-Chinese snack bars or visit the purveyors of the *rijsttafel*

('rice table'), where every known fish, meat and vegetable is worked into a filling extravaganza. Along with the fondue – a 'national' dish shamelessly stolen from the Swiss because its shared pot appealed to the Dutch sense of the democratic – Indo is the food of choice for any celebratory meals. Other waves of immigrants helped create today's vortex of culinary diversity.

If you prefer to stroll, here are a few tips. Go to the Pijp if you crave econo-ethnic. Cruise the eateries of Haarlemmerstraat, Utrechtsestraat, Nieuwmarkt, the 'Nine Streets' area and Reguliersdwarsstraat if you want something posher; and only surrender to Leidseplein if you don't mind being gravely overcharged for a cardboard steak and day-old sushi (although we do note some worthy exceptions). Also, check out the web: local foodies weigh in at www.iens.nl and www.specialbite.nl, with the latter being a real winner that can reliably offer you the scoop on all the latest – not to mention the most trendy – restaurant openings.

Prik p19

Sure, check out the posh places, but quality and economic snack opportunities can be found in the form of fish – raw herring, smoked eel – available from the ubiquitous fishstalls, with rolled 'pizzas' from Turkish bakeries, Dutch *broodjes* (sandwiches) from local bakers and butchers, and more spicy Surinamese *broodjes* from 'Suri-Indo-Chin' snack bars. And you really should visit an Albert Heijn supermarket to get an insight into Dutch eating habits. After all, sometimes you can find yourself eating some of your best meals from the comfort of a peaceful canal-side bench.

Drinking

The café (or bar – the line between the two is quite blurred) is central to Dutch social life, variously serving as a home-from-home, community centre and nightlife hub at all hours of both the day and night (most cafés open in the morning and don't shut until 1am, or until 3am to 4am during weekends). As a result, the drinking scene in Amsterdam offers oodles of choice. One thing it definitively isn't is dynamic – few people here will be lured into the grim trap of Toblerone mojitos – but that still doesn't mean that Amsterdam drinking isn't a wildly intoxicating experience. Quite the contrary: it's one of the most highly satisfying places in Europe to get smashed, and one with a real sense of continuity. If many bars in town look as if they've been around forever, that's because they have; Café Chris (p120) and Wynand Fockink (p66) both vie for the title of Amsterdam's longest-serving bar.

But old doesn't have to mean fusty. For the last couple of years, Korte Leidsedwarsstraat is where glammed-up drinkers head to sip appletinis. A more dressed-down (but just as cool), music-loving

S H O R T L I S T

Best newcomers
- Hotel de Goudfazant (p113)
- Vyne (p88)

Sybaritic sipping
- Bubbles and Wines (p60)
- Harry's Bar (p76)
- Caffe Oslo (p131)
- Onassis (p114)

Outdoor drinking
- Amstelhaven (p104)
- 't Blauwe Theehuis (p130)
- 't Smalle (p122)

Made for music lovers
- Kamer 401 (p92)
- Bitterzoet (p81)
- Vaaghuyzen (p77)

A taste of the old school
- Twee Zwaantjes (p86)
- Wynand Fockink (p66)

Beers of distinction
- 't Arendsnest (p86)
- Gollem (p142)

Lush lunches
- De Bakkerswinkel (p58)
- Latei (p63)
- Small World Catering (p122)

Vegetarian delights
- Green Planet (p76)
- De Peper (p131)

Traditional eating for cheap
- Hap Hmm (p92)

Posh and proud
- De Kas (p106)
- La Rive (p92)

Dining on a ship's deck
- Pont 13 (p114)

Spice of life
- Tempo Doeloe (p93)

Best for beach bums
- Blijburg (p113)

Views to die for
- 11 (p116)

bunch concentrate in and around Kamer 401 (p92), nearby. A short hop in the other direction brings you to Reguliersdwarsstraat, the preened centre of the gay scene. Amsterdam's newest and best gay bar, Prik (p77) – everyone's new favourite bubbly, prosecco, is on tap – is just outside the gay village, over on Spuistraat.

Away from the neon, the Jordaan is awash with *bruin cafés*, so called because they've been stained brown through decades of smoking and chewing the fat. Befitting the area's gentrified status, many, like Café Thijssen (Brouwersgracht 107, 623 8994), are teeming with wealthy nouveau residents; nearby bars, though, will be filled with the last vestiges of the local working-class population. A similar scene is to be found in the equally poshed-up Pijp, a great place to wander around between trendy drinking spots and more homely salt-of-the-earth watering holes.

Apart from the basic international brands, spirits drinkers can opt for the gin-like *jenever*, drunk neat from a tiny glass. *Jong* is lighter and more refreshing, *oud* darker and mellower. It comes in a wide range of fruit-infused varieties.

Wine buffs will be underwhelmed, so if you are aghast at the prospect of a beaker of unspecified red or white, head to Bubbles and Wines (p60) or Vyne (p88), both part of a new breed of bar specialising in pairing posh nosh with fine wine.

Beer, though, is the local drink of choice: in most places the *pils* is Heineken or Amstel, but every bar will offer a good-to-brilliant range of potent Belgian brews and there are several specialist Belgian bars, like Gollem (p142). For a proper taste of all NL has to offer, 't Arendsnest (p86) has a huge range of tasty native brews – around 500 to be precise.

blowverbod
wegens overlast in de buurt
boete €50,- art. 2.8 lid 4 APV

Smoking

Love it or loathe it, Amsterdam's unique selling point is the fact that you can walk into a café and buy drugs. You can also get a coffee and munchies-abating snacks, but you won't be able to have a beer with your spliff: on 1st April 2007, booze was banned from the city's coffeeshops, part of the creeping resistance movement against lax marijuana laws. The power of the antis means that there have been no new coffeeshops for years, but trends still develop: you won't get very far without stumbling across organic (bio) highs, which don't pack quite the same serious punch as genetically modified (and often terrifyingly potent) hydroponic skunk. That said, Dutch weed is still known the world over for its unprecedented quality and supreme strength, so if you're a beginner or used to less powerful dope (Brits, take note), go easy – and be sure to brush up on your coffeeshop etiquette (see box p68).

Shopping

Shopping inside the Netherlands presents what at first appears to be an oxymoronic conundrum. On the one hand, you have a nation spiritually shaped by Calvinism, which makes for parsimony and an unwillingness to abandon oneself to excess, consumer or otherwise. On the other, you've got a wealthy country (seventh in the EU's rich list) that was first founded on the practice of buying and selling.

What this basically translates into for the visitor – who doesn't need to feel a guilty twinge each time cash is parted with – is a rather satisfying shopping experience. Lack of excess means no horrible hypermarkets or megamalls: consumerism is still very much a localised, town-centre activity. Apart from one or two rare exceptions like IKEA and the huge Villa ArenA furniture 'village' over in Duivendrecht, the out-of-town shop experience hasn't impacted here and probably never will – not least because the enormous swathes of land necessary for constructing the monster arcades aren't available in this small, overpopulated, watery country. Add to this the fact that the natives love to wander between different vendors while sniffing out a special offer, and the very act of hopping between bakers, cheese- and fishmongers seems here to stay.

Market forces

The place where you can really see people in their natural shopping state is, of course, the market. For a small city, Amsterdam is rather

DON'T MISS: 2008

well served by them, with markets among the few places where the multi-ethnic make-up of the town actually meets and mingles. The most famous is Albert Cuypmarkt (Europe's longest one, apparently; p143), snaking all the way through the heart of the Pijp; all of Dutch life is here, from smoked eel to Surinamese sherbets to plain old buckets and mops. Neighbourhoods tend to have their own version: the Dappermarkt in Oost and the Lindenmarkt in Jordaan are the most authentically untouristy. Also located in the Jordaan, Saturday's Noordermarkt (p118) is the place to buy organic farmers' produce among more well-heeled shoppers; the same crowd is back on Monday morning to pick through bric-a-brac and antiques, at a much smaller (yet infinitely superior) variation on Waterlooplein's tourist trap (p109).

A passion for fashion

Take a glance at the average *burger*, and you'll notice that more sartorial matters aren't always top priority. Nevertheless, a fair few designers have struggled against the odds, and the country can certainly hold its head high in the catwalk stakes – after all, it produced avant darlings Viktor & Rolf, whose clothes are the centrepiece at Van Ravenstein (p89), alongside the most recent creations of the Antwerp bunch.

A couple of Dutch brands have also made maximum impact on street style: Gsus and G-Star Raw. The former, which works alongside the Fair Wear Foundation to protest against sweatshop production, is available at De Bijenkorf (p78).

The fashion map of Amsterdam is divided along clear lines: head to PC Hooftstraat for top-whack designer duds; head to the Kalverstraat area for high street stalwarts like HEMA (p49) – with countless branches in Amsterdam – and Zara (p81),

SHORTLIST

Best newcomers
- Crumpler (p123)
- For Our Friends (p133)
- Vlaamsch Broodhuis (p125)

Fancy pants
- Marlies Dekkers (p134)
- Paars (p80)

Desirable duds
- Bits and Pieces (p133)
- Van Ravenstein (p89)

Kiddy winkels
- Joe's Vliegerwinkel (p69)
- 't Klompenhuisje (p69)

Grown-up pleasures
- Absolute Danny (p66)
- De Bierkoning (p78)
- Dampkring (p78)

Gifts for granny
- Delftshop (p95)
- Geels & Co (p67)

Prettiest interiors
- Jacob Hooy & Co (p67)
- Lairesse Apotheek (p134)

Unmissable markets
- Albert Cuypmarkt (p143)
- Bloemenmarkt (p93)

Blocks of chocs
- Puccini Bomboni (p69)
- Unlimited Delicious (p124)

Cheesy pleasers
- Boerenmarkt (p123)
- De Kaaskamer (p88)

Pre-owned treasures
- Brilmuseum/Brillenwinkel (p88)
- Nic Nic (p89)
- Ree-member (p89)

Best for bibliophiles
- American Book Center (p77)
- Waterstone's (p81)

Teenage kicks
- Reprezent (p124)
- Seventy Five (p69)
- Tom's Skate Shop (p70)

which continues to offer catwalk fashions at cut down prices. One thing Amsterdam does lack, alas, is an abundance of good boutiques – wander around the Jordaan and Damstraat areas to find outlets offering quirkier and home-grown labels, or try Blue Blood Jeans' new outlet For Our Friends (p133), located near the museums.

Design driven

Although fashion sense can slip by the populace, in terms of design the Dutch lead the world: think of Tord Boontje's Garland shade and the infamous Droog Design collective's innovations – shown at their outlet gallery in the Old Centre (see p50). To assault your eyes with design of all kinds, from seriously high-end homewear to swanky jewellery, sniff out Utrechtsestraat; Overtoom and Rozengracht are also much-coveted furnishing destinations.

Culture vultures

Dutch people are truly mad about reading. Bookworms should head straight to Spui, bounded at one end by a mighty Waterstone's store (p81) and with the American Book Center (p77) at the other, both of them multi-storey giants of English language lit. Smaller scale reading pleasures can be found upon the shelves of multilingual Atheneum (p77), a veritable treasure trove of magazines in all languages, and in Friday's second-hand book market.

Incredible edibles

While the Dutch tend not to be so famed for culinary finesse (though that is changing), they are renowned for hearty appetites, which means that food is available pretty much every step you take. If you're hoping to pick up edible souvenirs, you're truly spoiled for choice; head to De Kaaskamer (p88) and you'll also be

American Book Center

spoiled for cheese – there are more than 200 types, including plenty of local specialities. For fishy dishes, pick up smoked eel, herring or tiny North Sea shrimps from any number of fish stalls dotted around town. Head to Holtkamp (see box p135) for an array of cakes displayed in a beautiful interior, and to see how the shop has made the humble *kroket* gourmet by adding the likes of fine truffles and foie gras.

Talking shop

In general, local shops are open from 1pm to 6pm on Monday (if they do open at all), 10am to 6pm Tuesday to Friday (with many open until 9pm on Thursday), and 9am to 5pm on Saturday. Amsterdam is the only city in the Netherlands that boasts regular Sunday shopping (other places rotate on a monthly basis, if at all), with stores usually open between noon and 5pm. Still smaller shops are more erratic.

Credit card payment is not quite universally accepted, so as a rule of thumb, be sure to take enough cash.

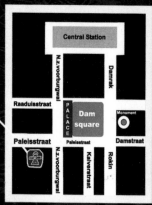

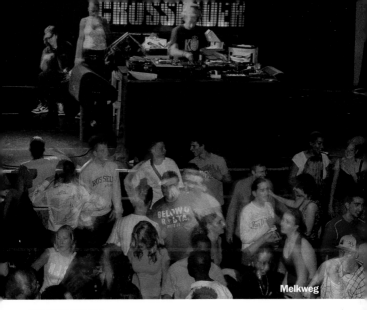
Melkweg

Nightlife

A city with sound at its fingertips, you'll never have to wander far in Amsterdam to soothe your soul with melodic noise – or dissonance, if that's your bag. Even if a list of Dutch musical icons fails to trip off your tongue, the musical prowess of this city may be understated but it should never be underestimated.

Ever cruised down the road while humming the now classic bassline to Golden Earring's rock standard 'Radar Love'? Or danced an entire night away to Tiësto or Junkie XL? Ever settled down for a relaxing evening in with soothing Mahler symphonies performed by the Royal Concertgebouw Orchestra? Or been awe-struck by the classy jazz moves of talents like Misha Mengelberg or Han Bennink?

Throw in more eclectic and less mainstream musical genres like drum 'n' bass, heavy metal, art rock, hip hop and Frisian fado, and the list of Dutch musical innovators flows ever on and on.

On top of all that there are also international acts aplenty. With Amsterdam firmly established as one of the world's most important ports of call for visiting musicians thanks to such iconic venues as Paradiso (p96) and Melkweg (p95), it's apparent that whatever you're seeking, it'll be readily available within close proximity of the canal ring. And that's just the tip of the iceberg – keep your eyes and ears peeled and you may also discover a performance by your favourite band or DJ is but a train ride away.

Clubland Amsterdam

Since it first arrived two years ago, Nachttheater Sugar Factory (p95) has set itself up as one of the most happening clubs in town by offering a genuine alternative to the more regular city dance scene. It also hosts frequent live shows, along with theatre acts, dance, leftfield performance art and plain, old-fashioned craziness, and is perfect if you want jazz grooves for crazy dancing rather than chin stroking – WickedJazzSounds every Sunday provides a raw mix of old vinyl juggling matched by expressive live band sets. With other relative newcomers such as Studio 80 (p96), 11 (p116), Bitterzoet (p81) and most recently Flexbar (p125), it's safe to say that local clubs have slowly become more homely, less pretentious and even attractive to barflies who would normally prefer their ceilings low and who like the option of having their social raving uninterrupted in a quiet corner. And don't forget the city's decent clutch of smaller, DJ-friendly bars along Nieuwezijds Voorburgwal, between the Dam and Spui square.

In general, clubbing in the capital is really no different from clubbing in any large city in the world. All venues have bouncers; few – if any – are susceptible to bribery (you're much better off showing up on time and with a mixed boy/girl group). Storing your coat in a cloakroom sets you back €1, but tipping is far from mandatory; toilets are between €0.50 and €1, but in many clubs set outside the city centre they're free. Dutch people as a rule are far from being great tippers at the bar, so don't feel too bad for cheapskating; if you are feeling generous, however, a 15 per cent tip is usually considered huge – really huge. Almost no one will actually be inside a club before midnight:

people are either at home or in a bar somewhere else, and besides, few venues offer discount prices if you show up before a certain time.

Once inside the club, don't be afraid to strike up conversations with fellow clubbers – practically all the natives speak English fluently. One subject has been swept under the rug by a recent oppressive wave, though: drugs. While weed and hash are still fine, it is unwise to solicit for anything stronger, as undercover cops have now started appearing at the larger techno parties.

Another word of warning goes to groups of men: if you must have your stag night here, don't expect to welcomed by the hipper venues without a smattering of girls in tow.

Gay capital

After a couple of years of serious hand-wringing about whether or not Amsterdam still deserved the title of Gay Capital – the confusion largely inspired by a sad spate of homophobic incidents – the city seems to be getting back on track. Local political parties have made a real effort to make Amsterdam gay-friendly for residents and visitors alike. Even the council promotes the pinkness of the city on a special website (www.amsterdam4gays.nl). Amsterdam Pride (see box p87) has gone the way of many others by embracing corporate sponsorship – some major companies and banks even have their own floats to make sure the spectators get the message (although the main message they're pumping is employee diversity).

Despite both enjoying a range of venues, the respective scenes for gay men and lesbians are still quite separate. Each group tends to keep to its own favourite places and the two only get together rarely on special occasions like Queen's Day and Pride, or during one-off parties like the mighty Love Dance.

Also on the upside, clubland has been reinvigorated with a wealth of young talent and plenty of fresh faces: bars such as Prik (p77) have opened and several new one-off parties are going strong. A word of warning, though: free condoms aren't universal on the scene, and a range of STDs – including HIV – are on the up, with barebacking as popular and controversial here as in any other big city.

Finger on the pulse

Both the GWK and larger post offices (look for the Postkantoor sign) sell tickets for concerts, plays and other events. The city's main ticket retailer is the Amsterdam Uitburo (AUB), which operates an elaborate online database and sales point for events at www.aub.nl, as well as a personal service at the AUB Ticketshop in Leidseplein – open from 10am to 7.30pm daily, except Sundays when it opens at noon. You can also buy their tickets by phone, although commission is even higher and you'll be paying premium phone rates at 0900 0191 (+31 20 621 1288 from abroad); lines are open 9am to 8pm daily.

Before you buy, it helps to know what's on when. Pick up the English-language listings mag *Amsterdam Weekly* (www.amsterdamweekly.nl) or the AUB's free monthly magazine *Uitkrant* (pronounced 'out-krant'), both available in theatres, bars, bookshops and the AUB Ticketshop, which is also a great place to browse the different flyers and other listings magazines. They are also home to the Last Minute Ticket Shop (www.lastminuteticketshop.nl), which shifts tickets at half their face value for musical and theatrical events happening that night from noon every day of the week.

Above all, know that timing is everything: Amsterdam is city that sleeps, but when it's awake, it's alive.

SHORTLIST

Best newcomer
- Flexbar (p125)

Full-on cultural experiences
- Nachttheater Sugar Factory (p95)

Superclubs to the rescue
- Paradiso (p96)
- Melkweg (p95)
- 11 (p116)
- Jimmy Woo's (p95)
- Panama (p117)

Cosier clubbing
- Bitterzoet (p81)
- Studio 80 (p96)

Live music on tap
- Paradiso (p96)
- Melkweg (p95)

Big bands on a budget
- Club 3voor12 (p109)

Weird and wild venues
- Winston (p70)
- OCCII (p134)
- Skek (p65)

Jazz hands clapping
- Bimhuis (p116)
- Badcuyp (p143)

Bustling neighbourhoods
- Nieuwezijds Voorburgwal (p73)
- Leidseplein (p89)
- Rembrandtplein (p89)

Best one-off parties
- NDSM (p117)
- Westergasfabriek (p125)
- Post CS (p110)

Where life's a beach party
- Blijburg (p113)
- Strand West (p125)

Gays of glory
- Getto (p61)
- Prik (p77)

Cocktails of the unexpected
- Mansion (p134)

DON'T MISS: 2008

Chiellerie p30

Arts & Leisure

The Dutch are a cultured lot, and the capital bristles with world-class venues for every form of self-expression. Add to all this an active underground scene of free-thinking old hippies and ex-squatters, and you have lively arts events at every level. The breadth and quality of the Amsterdam arts experience is also due, partly at least, to enlightened funding from government and city alike, resulting in many festivals and new buildings such as the Muziekgebouw (p117); such forward thinking also helps integrate the work of diverse groups and venues. In the case of Leidseplein, this integration will be literal – work is being done to link the Melkweg (p95) to the Stadsschouwburg (p97), due for completion in March 2008.

The art scene

This town has more than its share of squat nostalgists weeping for those '80s and '90s salad days when cultural squats provided the coolest, edgiest and most fiercely frolicsome happenings in town. While some may cast these past-dwellers as whiners, it is true that the powers-that-be decided at the turn of the century to close many of these epic cultural beehives in the name of building condos and office spaces to help make Amsterdam a better 'business gateway to Europe', thus resulting in a lot of expensive empty spaces. But since Amsterdam has always been largely defined by its artistic traditions, the loss of such affordable studio spaces was soon seen as a monumental blunder.

Happily, though rather belatedly, the powers-that-be have admitted that they screwed up big time and set aside millions for places called *broedplaatsen* ('breeding grounds'), where artists can do their thing for cheap. Most such places – many former squats – are hugely vibrant, like the former shipping yards-turned-arts complex NDSM (p117). And while not an official breeding ground as such, the sprawling Westergasfabriek (p125) certainly retains an equitable street cred. Also worthy of note is the gallery W139 (p73) – more than 20 years old but still alive with an atittude largely derived from its historical links with squatters – and the ever-innovative Chiellerie (p72).

The silver screen

The biggest event of 2007 was the homecoming of Paul Verhoeven, who returned from his Hollywood hideout with *Black Book*, the most expensive film ever to be shot in the Netherlands and filled to the brim with huge explosions, ravishing beauties, noble Nazis and traitorous resistance fighters. One more recent cinematic style that continues to flourish is the multicultural comedy genre, the biggest exponent of which is Martin Koolhoven. His films, like *'N Beetje Verliefd*, tend to draw large, young crowds attracted to the irreverent humour and playful stereotypes, though critics argue that they view the integration issue through rose-coloured glasses.

That's something that can't really be said about Eddy Terstall, perhaps the most relevant Dutch director working today. Terstall's films usually take place in his own home neighbourhood of the Jordaan – *Simon*, for example, his acclaimed story of the friendship between a gruff pot dealer with a big heart and a gay dentist – and promote the best of tolerant Dutch values.

W139

Theatre & dance

Amsterdam plays home to countless choreographers and companies, a relatively recent phenomenon again thanks to enlightened funding. The Muziektheater (p73) is home to the internationally renowned company De Nederlandse Ballet. Still smaller companies who've made a name on the world stage (and who perform regularly inside the capital) include Dansgroep Krisztina de Châtel and Het Internationaal Danstheater.

The city is also well served with a truly outstanding theatre scene – Ivo van der Hove's Toneelgroep Amsterdam at Stadsschouwburg is just one of many – but if language is a barrier, then the multipurpose, multimedia De Balie (p96) is worth checking in on, as it often stages performances in many tongues. Alternatively, NDSM also mounts regular site-specific pieces that transcend linguistic limitations. The Over het IJ and De Parade fests (both p36) are worthy of attention, or – if you prefer the outdoors – pack up a picnic basket and head for the Vondelpark's Openluchttheater (p137). Alternatively, if apocalyptic grandeur is your thing, try the Robodock festival (p32). One recent addition is the Amsterdam Fringe Festival (p37), with underground companies performing on the main stages of more established theatres and rewriting rules as they go.

Classical music

Many of the greatest orchestras from across the world perform here and there is access for all – typically for little more than the price of the biggest rock or pop concerts, and frequently considerably less. And thanks to enlightened funding, you'll not only hear the classics played in the grand halls, but alongside canals, in parks or even on the streets.

Of course, Amsterdam is also the home of some of the most renowned orchestras and soloists around. Led by chief conductor Mariss Jansons, the Royal Concertgebouw Orchestra is one of the world's most famous. They play at home during most weeks in the cultural season – if you get the chance, even just for a lunch concert, don't pass it up.

The sporting life

Football remains the game most special to many, with fans still pining for the '70s and '80s glory days of Cruijff and Van Basten. While plenty of young starlets like Arjen Robben and Robin van Persie have made their names and riches internationally, the magic spark stays missing from the national team, and the country's heart is left battered and bruised after every big failure. Yet that desire to be the best often pays off elsewhere, and in field hockey, ice skating, swimming, darts and cycling, Dutch stars still manage to bag medals on a regular basis, achieving the coveted status of national heroes as they do so.

SHORTLIST

Total sporting experience
- Ajax (p109)

Interdisciplinary agendas
- De Balie (p96)
- Frascati (p73)

Golden age film screenings
- Nederlands Filmmuseum (p136)
- Pathé Tuschinski (p97)

World class jazz acts
- Bimhuis (p116)

Best classical
- Concertgebouw (p134)

Best modern classical
- Muziekgebouw (p117)

Most intimate clubbing
- Bitterzoet (p81)
- Nachttheater Sugar Factory (p95)
- Studio 80 (p96)

Cutting-edge contemporary
- Gasthuis Werkplaats & Theater (p136)
- Kinetic Noord at NDSM (box p115)

Underground vibes
- W139 (p73)
- Westergasfabriek (p125)

Regular gallery openings
- Chiellerie (p72)

Big bands on a small scale
- Melkweg (p95)
- Paradiso (p96)

International belly laughs
- Boom Chicago (p97)
- Comedy Theatre (p72)
- Toomler (p137)

Non-Western theatre
- KIT Tropentheater (p109)

Best creative festivals
- Over het IJ (p36)
- De Parade (p36)

Calendar

Queen's Day p35

Dates in **bold** are public holidays.

September 2007

2-9 **Gaudeamus Music Week**
Muziekgebouw (p117)
www.gaudeamus.nl
Contemporary classical music.

6-15 **Africa in the Picture**
Various locations
www.africainthepicture.nl
Features, docs and shorts from Africa.

8-9 **Open Monumentendag**
Various locations
www.openmonumentendag.nl
Free or cheap entry to historic buildings.

21 Sept-Jan 2008 **Barcelona 1900**
Van Gogh Museum (p130)
Celebrates turn-of-the-century Barcelona.

22-29 **Picnic '07**
Westergasfabriek (p125)
www.crossmediaweek.org
Gathering for world creative industries.

23 **Dam tot Damloop**
Amsterdam to Zaandam
www.damloop.nl
Long-running mini-marathon.

Late Sept **Robodock**
NDSM (p117)
www.robodock.org
Spectacular theatre festival featuring
robots, pyrotechnics and performances.

October 2007

Ongoing Barcelona 1900 (see Sept)

12 Oct-17 Feb 2008 **Andy Warhol:
Other Voices, Other Rooms**
Stedelijk Museum
at Post CS Building (p130)
Multimedia celebration of pop art icon.

13 Oct-5 May 2008 **Art Nouveau**
Hermitage on the Amstel (p100)
www.hermitage.nl
Riches from the St Petersburg collection.

14-21 **Sweelinck Festival**
Oude Kerk (p57)
Popular organ music festival for fans
of more rousing classical favourites.

14-28 **Cinekid Festival**
Various locations
www.cinekid.nl
Child-centred film and media festival.

Mid Oct **Rocket Cinema Festival**
Various locations
www.rocketcinema.nl
Old movies re-scored with specially commissioned dance music.

18-20 **Amsterdam Dance Event**
Various locations
www.amsterdam-dance-event.nl
Dance music festival and conference.

21 **ING Amsterdam Marathon**
Various locations
www.amsterdammarathon.nl
Running around town.

26-28 **Bock Beer Festival**
Beurs van Berlage (p53)
www.pint.nl
Festival of seasonal beer.

Late Oct **International Buddhist Film Festival Europe**
Nederlands Filmmuseum (p137)
www.ibff-europe.eu
Movies inspired by or about the faith.

November 2007

Ongoing Barcelona 1900 (see Sept); Art Nouveau (see Oct); Andy Warhol: Other Voices, Other Rooms (see Oct)

Early Nov **Jewish Film Festival**
Various locations
www.joodsfilmfestival.nl
Three days of Jewish movies.

2-3 **London Calling**
Paradiso (p96)
www.londoncalling.nl.
New rock and pop from the UK.

3 **Museum Night**
Various locations
www.n8.nl
Late night opening and special events.

Mid Nov **Crossing Border**
The Hague
www.crossingborder.nl
International literature and music fest.

18 **Sinterklaas Intocht**
Prins Hendrikkade, Dam to Leidseplein
Children's Christmas parade.

19-23 **High Times Cannabis Cup**
Various locations
www.cannabiscup.com
Contest promoting morally questionable levels of cannabis consumption.

20-29 **Shadow Festival**
Various locations
www.shadowfestival.nl
Documentary fringe festival.

22 Nov-2 Dec **International Documentary Film Festival (IDFA)**
Various locations
www.idfa.nl
The mother of all documentary fests.

December 2007

Ongoing Barcelona 1900 (see Sept); Art Nouveau (see Oct); Andy Warhol: Other Voices, Other Rooms (see Oct)

1 **Lovedance**
Paradiso (p96)
www.lovedance.nl
World AIDS day charity gala.

Early Dec **Resfest**
Various locations
www.dnerve.com
Travelling digital media festival.

5-6 **Sinterklaas**
Various locations
Traditional gift-giving parties.

Late Dec **Roze Film Dagen**
Various locations
www.rozefilmdagen.nl
International queer film festival.

25 Eerste Kerstdag (Christmas)

26 Tweede Kerstdag (Boxing Day)

31 **Oudejaarsavond**
All over Amsterdam, including Dam and Nieuwmarkt
New Year's celebrations with plenty of excitement and lots of fireworks.

January 2008

Ongoing Barcelona 1900 (see Sept 2007); Art Nouveau (see Oct); Andy Warhol: Other Voices, Other Rooms (see Oct 2007)

1 Nieuwjaarsdag (New Year's Day)

Late Jan **Amsterdam International Fashion Week**
Westergasfabriek (p125)
www.aifw.nl
Putting the city on the fashion map.

Over het IJ p36

Late Jan/early Feb
Chinese New Year
Nieuwmarkt (p69)
www.zeedijk.nl
New Year's celebrations with plenty of
dramatic fireworks displays.

February 2008

Ongoing Art Nouveau (see Oct);
Andy Warhol: Other Voices, Other
Rooms (see Oct 2007)

March 2008

Ongoing Art Nouveau (see Oct)

Early Mar **Amsterdam
Restaurant Week**
Various locations
www.restaurantweek.nl
Special deals on dining out in selected
restaurants across the capital.

15 **Stille Omgang**
Spui, Red Light District
www.stille-omgang.nl
Silent procession commemorating the
14th-century Miracle of Amsterdam.

Mid Mar **Amnesty
International Film Festival**
www.amnestyfilmfestival.nl
Screenings of various films concerned
with the subject of human rights.

Mid Mar **Boekenweek**
www.boekenweek.nl
Week of events promoting literature
and reading throughout the city.

23 **Eerste Paasdag
(Easter Sunday)**

24 **Tweede Paasdag
(Easter Monday)**

28-29 **London Calling**
See November 2007.

Late Mar **CinemAsia**
Various locations
www.cinemasia.nl
Screenings of pan-Asian features and
cutting-edge documentaries.

April 2008

Ongoing Art Nouveau (see Oct)

5-6 **National Museum Weekend**
Various locations
www.museumweekend.nl
Free or cheap entry to the city's many
museums, plus special events; bear in
mind that venues are packed as a result.

Mid Apr **Motel Mozaïque**
Rotterdam
www.motelmozaique.nl
Three-day music, theatre and art fest
in the real culture capital.

23 Apr-31 Dec UNESCO World Book Capital 2008
Various locations
www.amsterdamwereldboekenstad.nl
Amsterdam's bookish side celebrated with numerous readings and events.

28-29 Roze Wester Festival
Homomonument (p85)
www.stichting-gala.nl
Lesbian and gay open-air party.

29 Queen's Night
All over Amsterdam
The Fall of Rome in orange.

30 Queen's Day
All over Amsterdam
Open air disco-cum-flea market and one of the biggest parties of the year.

Late Apr Amsterdam Fantastic Film Festival
Various locations
www.afff.nl
Eights days of silver screen schlock, horror, splatter and trash.

Late Apr-mid June World Press Photo
Oude Kerk (p57)
www.worldpressphoto.com
Global photojournalism exhibition.

May 2008

Ongoing Art Nouveau (see Oct); UNESCO World Book Capital 2008 (see April); World Press Photo (see April)

1 Hemelvaartsdag (Ascension Day)

4 Memorial Day
Dam Square
7.30pm ceremony remembering those who lost their lives in World War II.

5 Liberation Day
Various locations
www.amsterdamsbevrijdingsfestival.nl; www.oosterparkfestival.nl
Marking national liberation from Nazi occupation. Music and speeches at the Museumplein's own Bevrijdingsfestival and celebrations in the Oosterpark.

10 National Windmill Day
Around the Netherlands
www.visitamsterdam.nl
Windmills spin sails and open to the public in this quaintest of celebrations.

11 Eerste Pinksterdag (Pentecost)

12 Tweede Pinksterdag (Pentecost)

Mid May Art Amsterdam
Amsterdam RAI Theater (p136)
www.artamsterdam.nl
Huge, commercial, five-day exhibition of national and international galleries.

Mid May Kunstvlaai
Westergasfabriek (p125)
Edgy art for the discerning masses.

Late May Open Studios
Westelijke Eilanden
www.oawe.nl
Artists open their doors to the public.

June 2008

Ongoing UNESCO World Book Capital 2008 (see April); World Press Photo (see April)

Early June Arab Film Festival
Various locations
www.arabfilmfestival.nl
Three days of shorts, documentaries and features by Arabic filmmakers.

Early June-mid Aug Openluchttheater
Vondelpark
www.vondelpark.nl
Open-air stage featuring performances from classical to urban to kids' stuff.

Early June Beeld voor Beeld
Tropenmuseum (p103)
www.beeldvoorbeeld.nl
Anthropological documentary festival.

Early June Hindustaans Film
Nederlands Filmmuseum (p137)
Public screenings of the best of the previous year's Bollywood offerings.

Mid Jun Amsterdam Roots
www.amsterdamroots.nl
See box p107.

Mid June Holland Festival
Various locations
www.holndfstvl.nl
Huge, popular and varied arts festival.

Mid June Oerol
Terschelling
www.oerol.nl
For a fortnight, the Frisian island of Terschelling stages 200 theatre acts.

Mid June **Gardens in Bloom**
Various locations
www.amsterdamsegrachtentuin.nl
Hidden gardens open up to the public.

Late Jun-mid Aug **Kwakoe**
Bijlmerpark
www.kwakoe.nl
Free festival staged in Amsterdam's
more multicultural suburbs.

July 2008

Ongoing UNESCO World Book
Capital 2008 (see April); Kwakoe
(see June); Openluchttheater
(see June)

1-31 **Julidans**
Various locations
www.julidans.nl
Month-long international dance festival
drawing big names and bigger crowds.

Early July **Cinedans International
Dance Film Festival**
Nederlands Filmmuseum (p137)
www.cinedans.nl
Eclectic dance and choreography film
screenings for stage enthusiasts.

Early July **5 Days Off**
Various locations
www.5daysoff.nl
Techno, drum 'n' bass, house and mad
electro mash up for serious beat freaks.

5-15 **Over het IJ**
NDSM (p117)
www.overhetij.nl
International festival of large-scale,
avant-garde theatrical projects.

11-13 **North Sea Jazz**
Rotterdam
www.northseajazz.nl
Internationally renowned jazz festival.

Mid July **Amsterdam
International Fashion Week**
See January.

Late July **Amsterdam Tournament**
ArenA (p109)
www.lgamsterdamtournament.com
Pre-season international footie friendlies.

August 2008

Ongoing UNESCO World Book
Capital 2008 (see April); Kwakoe
(see June); Openluchttheather
(see June)

FILM FOR THOUGHT

IDFA

Documentary Film Festival p33

1-3 **Amsterdam Gay Pride**
Various locations
www.amsterdamgaypride.nl
See box p87.

Early Aug **De Parade**
Martin Luther Kingpark
www.deparade.nl
Travelling circus-style theatre festival
popular with families.

Mid Aug **Grachtenfestival**
Various locations
www.grachtenfestival.nl
Canalside classical music concerts with
performances in truly tranquil settings.

Mid Aug **Appelsap**
Oosterpark
www.appelsap.net
Free outdoor hip hop festival.

Mid Aug **Hartjesdag**
Zeedijk
www.hartjesdagen.nl
An ancient Amsterdam celebration
re-invented by local businesses and
transvestites: plenty of drinking, cross-
dressing, jazz and fireworks.

Mid Aug **Open Haven Podium**
Java-eiland
www.openhavenpodium.nl
Harbour-themed art, music, theatre
and children's activities.

22-24 Lowlands
Walibi World
www.lowlands.nl
The Dutch answer to Glastonbury; a three-day beano featuring the latest bands, comedy, global food and fashion.

29-31 Uitmarkt
Various locations
www.uitmarkt.nl
Open-air preview of the coming cultural season: theatre, opera, dance and music.

Late Aug Het Theaterfestival
All over Amsterdam
www.tf-1.nl
Showcase for Dutch and Belgian theatre, also shadowed by the Edinburgh-style Amsterdam Fringe Festival.

September 2008

Ongoing UNESCO World Book Capital 2008 (see April)

Early Sept Open Monumentendag
See September 2007.

Early Sept Africa in the Picture
See September 2007.

Late Sept Robodock
See September 2007.

October 2008

Ongoing UNESCO World Book Capital 2008 (see April)

Mid Oct Rocket Cinema Festival
See October 2007.

Mid Oct Cinekid
See October 2007.

Late Oct International Buddhist Film Festival Europe
See October 2007.

November 2008

Ongoing UNESCO World Book Capital 2008 (see April)

Early Nov Jewish Film Festival
See November 2007.

Mid Nov London Calling
See November 2007.

Mid Nov International Documentary Film Festival
See November 2007.

Mid Nov Crossing Border
See November 2007.

Late Nov Shadow Festival
See November 2007.

December 2008

Ongoing UNESCO World Book Capital 2008 (see April)

1 Lovedance
See December 2007.

Early Dec Resfest
See December 2007.

5-6 Sinterklaas
See December 2007.

Late Dec Roze Film Dagen
See December 2007.

25 Eerste Kerstdag (Christmas)

26 Tweede Kerstdag (Boxing Day)

31 Oudejaarsavond
See December 2007.

De Parade

Itineraries

Canal Dreams

On a sojourn through the city of Amsterdam, Hans Christian Andersen wrote: 'The view from my window, through the elms, onto the canal outside, is like a fairy tale.' The canals are still what everyone imagines when they think about Amsterdam, and they continue to engender enchantment today. Like any city built on water, it's best seen from a boat. There are over 47 miles (76 kilometres) of waterways in the city, spread across 165 canals and spanned by 1,400 bridges (more than Venice): look at the bottom right corner of a bridge to find out its individual number.

The tourist boats between them provide a doughty service, but they can't get into the smaller waterways. Self-piloted hire boats were sadly banned years ago, so you may need to befriend a boat-bearing local or even charter a tour (see p180). If you can't get a boat, you can still always do it by bike or foot – but it won't be as much fun as bobbing cheerily along the waterways.

The tour begins on the Amstel, in front of the **Stopera**. Head up the Singel, the watery channel built to engirdle city in 1450. Go through the tunnel under the Munt; during the summer particularly, note the hundreds of empty bottles and cans – this here is the boating community's partying HQ-turned-recycling depot – and watch out for spiders. Pass along the back of the **Bloemenmarkt** (p95), minding that you avoid getting squirted by the hideous fire-gnomes' hoses just before the first bridge. A couple of hundred yards before the third bridge, hover mid-canal to try and espy high-profile visitors entering **Yab Yum** (Singel 295, 624 9503, www.yabyum.nl), an upmarket knocking shop notable for its large green lantern on your right.

Sail on for another two bridges; as you start coming closer to the second, the Torensluis – the widest in the city at 42 metres (138 feet) – note the steps on both sides leading down to barred windows and doors. These were once used as prison cells for vagabonds and drunkards, and date from the 1800s – pull up and press your face to the railings for the full, grim story. If you need to, quickly duck into **Villa Zeezicht** (Torensteeg 7, 626 7433, www. villazeezicht.com) for a drink or a toilet break, or continue on to the end of Singel for an alternative stopping point: there's a very handy platform outside the 17th-century architect Adriaan Dortsman's lovely yet ill-fated **Koepelkerk** (it caught fire in 1822 and 1993). Good food (and a loo) can be found inside **Village Bagels** (Stromarkt 2, 528 9152, ww.villagebagels.nl).

Take a left into Brouwersgracht (beware the big tour boats). During the 17th and 18th centuries, this still gorgeous canal was lined with breweries. There are no proper sights these days, just a glimpse at the now converted warehouses in one of Amsterdam's most des res addresses. Tourist boats only go a short distance here, so persist to the end – you'll get a proper look and have it all to yourself as a result. Next, veer into Prinsengracht while copping a glance up and right at cheerful café **Papeneiland** (No. 2, 624 1989). Below the water you're sailing on, there's a tunnel running to the opposite bank; during the period of religious persecution in the 17th century, this was used to deliver Catholics over to a secret church on the far side.

Continue towards the scaffolded Westerkerk. Just before the second bridge, on the right, you'll see the Egelantiersgracht, where **'t Smalle** (p122) has by far the boat-friendliest terrace in town, perfect for a quick

break and a beer. Alternatively, duck into Bloemgracht to see the Jordaan at its residential best.

Pass beneath the bridge by the Westerkerk and just after you'll see the **Hotel Pulitzer** (p167). This is the place to be in mid August, when the hotel hosts the finale of the Grachtenfestival (www.grachtenfestival.nl), which sees hundreds of boats bob along to classical music blaring out from a floating pontoon.

Hang a left into Leidsegracht, then right into Keizersgracht. Two bridges down, you can't miss the modernist masterpiece **De Bazel** (see box p93); as you pass under Vijzelstraat, glance back over your shoulder to get a real idea of its scale, dwarfing the dainty houses you've seen so far.

Next, hang a sharp right into Reguliersgracht, going as far as the sign declaring *doodlopende vaart* ('dead end'). Turn and look back: these are the famous seven bridges, best viewed illuminated at night.

Sail back and take the third left into Herengracht. You are now entering the Gouden Bocht or 'Golden Bend', the 17th century's most desirable address. It is here you'll find the great mansions that refute all those famous claims about the Dutch disinclination to flaunt wealth. No. 508-10 is one of the most exuberantly decorated: note the frolicking sea gods rising from the sculpted foam of the gables. Cut your boat's engine outside the house with the columns a couple of doors down; you may see Job Cohen in his pyjamas, as this is the official mayoral residence. Don't even think about trying to land on its stage, though: the signs reading *streng verboden* translate into 'strongly forbidden', and sadly they aren't joking either, especially after the late filmmaker Theo van Gogh's murderer threatened to exact

a similar fate upon Cohen in the note that he left pinned by a knife to his victim's body.

After passing under two more bridges (and a couple of hundred metres before the third) look right into Beulingsluis. This is the only Venetian-style canal in town, with houses directly on the water. In the unlikely event that you've managed to procure a gondola or rowing boat, float down and puzzle as to how exactly people get into their homes.

Four bridges on, turn left into Leliegracht, where there's pull-up potential at the café **Spanjer & van Twist** (No. 60, 639 0109). Before turning left into Keizersgracht, look up at the beautiful Emaux de Briare mosaic of an angel and child on the Jugendstil building on the corner, an old insurance office – you can still see its initials, EHLB, in the wrought iron of the tower. Continue past the Homomonument (don't be tempted to moor here either: it's a memorial), and carry on heading back down the Keizersgracht for a leisurely stretch of nine scenic bridges.

You've been along this one before (sailing in the opposite direction) but the ever-changing cityscape never gets boring or repetitive. Peer up at gable details, or enviously across at other people's pleasure-craft. At the tenth bridge, under Utrechtsestraat, exercise caution: only low boats can get under. This short stretch before the river is a great place to ogle other people's houseboats. On the Amstel, turn right, then another right again into Prinsengracht. Again, watching for low bridges, head back under Utrechtsestraat and moor at the final point of the canal tour, **Café Marcella** (Amstelveld 21, 623 1900) After all that hard work, you're well in line for a few cold beers, and this is a great place to enjoy them as the ancient water rolls on endlessly beside you.

On the Waterfront

Amsterdam's eastern dockland area is the city's up-and-coming eating and entertainment hotspot. But, perhaps more interestingly, it's also a fantastic showcase for the Netherlands' rather more out-there experiments in residential living. If you want to explore the future of Amsterdam, hop on a bike, grab a map and get moving.

First, head north-west of Centraal Station to the **Westelijke Eilanden** (Western Islands), near the Jordaan, to get a taste of how things were when Amsterdam was the richest port in the world. These artificial islands were originally created in the 17th century for shipping-related activities. Although there are now trendy warehouse flats and a yacht basin on Realeneiland, Prinseneiland and Bickerseiland – where one-time shipyards, tar distillers, and salters and smokers of fish were located –

the area still remains the city's best setting for a scenic stroll that harks back to seafaring times, a fact aided in no small measure by the sizeable community of local artists.

Since 1876, ocean access has been via the North Sea Canal. Because the working docks are also to the west, there is very little activity on the IJ behind Centraal Station other than a handful of passenger ships and the free ferries that run across to Amsterdam Noord – one of which will take you to the vibrant cultural breeding ground of **Kinetic Noord**, which is found located in former shipping yard **NDSM** (p117 and box p115). Here, vivid apocalyptic splendour, artistic endeavours and old-school squat aesthetics can be found alongside student container housing and the brand new **MTV headquarters** – an epitome of old-meets-new if ever there was one.

NDSM

If you stay on the south side, hug the water eastward from Centraal Station before hooking up with and following Oostelijke Handelskade and its parallel boardwalk. First, you pass the **Muziekgebouw** (p117). This new epicentre of new music, also home to the **Bimhuis** (p116), comes appended with studios, rehearsal spaces, exhibition galleries and a grand café and restaurant complete with a terrace overlooking the scenic wateriness of the IJ. Its close neighbour is the visually spectacular glass wave-shaped **passenger terminal** for luxury cruise-ships (www.pta.nl lists all docking times should you want to admire them in situ).

Before heading further on to hot club **Panama** (p117), restaurant **Odessa** (p114) and the erstwhile-youth-prison-turned-designer-accommodation block **Lloyd Hotel** (p162), take the spacey street Jan Schaeferbrug to the left that begins by going through the **Pakhuis de Zwijger** (www.dezwijger.nl), an old warehouse that has recently been re-invented as a new media centre – the more culturally curious may also want to pop in for a drink at its charming in-house café.

The bridge will take you to the tip of **Java-eiland**, although the less energetic can travel on the free ferry, which departs every 20 minutes from directly behind Centraal Station. At first glance, Java-eiland may look like a dense designer prison, but it's not hard to be charmed while on the island's bisecting walking street, which will have you crossing canals on funkily designed bridges and passing beside a startling variety of architecture. At Azartplein, the island suddenly changes its name to **KNSM-eiland**, named after the Royal Dutch Steam Company that was once located here.

From here, veer north following Surinamekade, with its houseboats on one side and the visible interiors of artist studios on the other. Pass 'Black Widow' tower – you'll know it when you see it – then loop around the island's tip and head back along KNSM-laan, hanging a left into Barcelonaplein and then a right when you pass through the abstract but strangely suggestive sculpted steel archway. You may also want to make some time for refreshment at one of the waterside bars and restaurants or invest in an art coffin at the alternative burial store **De Ode**, but definitely linger and check out the imposing residential **Piraeus building** from German architect Hans Kollhoff, if only for its eye-twisting inner court.

The two peninsulas to the south are **Borneo-Sporenburg**, the work by urban planners and landscape architects West 8. The plots are all sized differently in a direct attempt to inspire the many participating architects – a veritable who's who of the internationally acclaimed – to come up with creative low-rise living. Cross to Sporenburg via the Verbindingsdam to the building that has probably already caught your eye: the mighty raised silver **Whale residential complex**, designed by architect Frits van Dongen, over on Baron GA Tindalplein. For folksy contrast, a floating **Styrofoam park** produced by erstwhile Provo Robert Jasper Grootveld has been placed in front of it on Panamakade.

From here, cross over to Borneo via a swooping red bridge. Turn left up Stuurmankade – and past a yet more violently undulating pedestrian bridge – and enjoy the view at the end while imagining the even better one enjoyed by those living in the blue and green glass cubes that jut out of the buildings. Then head back west by way of Scheepstimmermanstraat, easily Amsterdam's most eccentric architectural street, where every single façade on show – from twisting steel to haphazard plywood – manages to be more bizarre and inspired than the next.

Where Panamalaan meets Piet Heinkade, you may opt to take the IJtram from CS to IJburg – the stop is right by the stack of giant tables with beehives underneath – although more energetic types might prefer to make a 20-minute bike ride over to IJburg, heading south via C van Eesterenlaan and Veelaan and then left down Zeeburgerdijk. This in turn connects up with Zuiderzeeweg, which then turns into a bridge that ends at a set of traffic lights. Here, follow the cycle path to the right, which takes you **IJburg**. When finally completed in 2012, the seven islands here will be home to 45,000 people in more than 18,000 separate residences, many of which will even float on the water. It will also be a showcase for Dutch landscape and residential architecture, with houses that combine thrilling new aesthetic forms with all the most cutting-edge and environmentally friendly modcons. That said, there's already plenty to look at, with funky beach **Blijburg** (p115) the clear highlight.

Heading back to town, be sure to explore the south end of the eastern half of **Zeeburg island**, one of the few 'free' places where squatters and artists are still allowed to make their funky homes from trailers and boats, and where they throw some of the city's more eccentric parties despite governmental efforts during recent years to clamp down on such communities. In fact, the vibe that permeates Zeeburg once defined the whole area before the yuppies came to town a few years ago, and thus inspires a fair amount of nostalgia in those still carrying a torch for the heyday of squat culture. Sure, the overall atmosphere may not be half as lively as it once was, but the architecture, as you'll have seen on your trip, is a vast improvement. For more detailed information on architectural tours of these areas, call **ARCAM** (p109).

droog

Droog Design p50

Design for Life

The history of Dutch design has always fluttered between strict orderliness (thanks to Calvinism and the early 20th-century modernist movement De Stijl) and a strong desire for more personal expression (perhaps an echo of the stubbornness required to battle the sea). Maybe as a direct result, the designs that spring from this contradiction are often both highly functional and downright witty, resulting in much of worldwide acclaim – so much, in fact, that even the tourist board has jumped on the bandwagon with www.coolcapitals.com.

A dedication to arrangement is already on display as one descends on Schiphol and sees the Mondrian-like grid pattern of the landscape. Some even see it in the ballet-like elegance of Dutch football players, who open space to score and close space to defend. And, of course, it's there in much of the art, the product

of what happens when these same ingrained compulsions are applied to paper, canvas and the computer. In fact, design is now so integrated with daily life here that it's even making inroads into the world of death, as witnessed by designer coffin outfit **De Ode** (Levantkade 51, 419 0882, www.uitvaart.nl/ode) in the eastern docklands.

Representing that part of a Dutch psyche craving order, the artists of **De Stijl** ('The Style') – founded in 1917 and involving abstractionists Theo van Doesburg, Piet Mondrian and Gerrit Rietveld – sought rules of equilibrium that are as useful in everyday design as they are in art. You only have to surf the web, leaf through *Wallpaper**, visit IKEA or pick up a White Stripes album to see their lingering influence.

Since the 1980s there has also been a strong reaction against the anti-functionalism of conceptual art,

Airline flights are one of the biggest producers of the global warming gas CO_2. But with **The CarbonNeutral Company** you can make your travel a little greener.

Go to **www.carbonneutral.com** to calculate your flight emissions then 'neutralise' them through international projects which save exactly the same amount of carbon dioxide.

Contact us at **shop@carbonneutral.com** or call into the office on **0870 199 99 88** for more details.

CarbonNeutral®flights

a trend that would have pleased adherents of De Stijl, who hoped that the future would bring a frenzy of cross-disciplinary action. Not only can photographers (Anton Corbijn, Rineke Dijkstra), cartoonists (Joost Swarte) and even architects (Rem Koolhaas) easily pass themselves off as 'artists', but the inspired work of John Körmeling and Atelier van Lieshout – equal parts artistry and extreme oddball carpentry – is itself perfect fusion of function, whimsy and good old-fashioned aesthetics. Meanwhile, many people who would have called themselves artists in the past now proudly call themselves designers. The nation's art, design and architecture colleges have helped this process by making artists and designers study together and also by welcoming a large number of foreign students, the latter resulting in the creation of a more universal visual language across the country.

To witness how design has today infiltrated every level of Dutch life, one need only walk into any branch of **HEMA**, the ubiquitous department store. A quarter of the Dutch population wakes to the ring of a HEMA alarm clock, one in three men wears HEMA underwear and one in four women wear a HEMA bra. HEMA sells 506,000 kilograms of liquorice every year, while the cashiers of their 250 national outlets annually process 14 million units of *tompouce* (a pink-glazed custard cake) and one smoked sausage per second. But while HEMA remains an economical place to shop for basics, it's also made a name for itself as a source of affordable, no-nonsense design objects – even their sales flyers are graphics classics. They've had their products designed by bigwigs like Piet Hein Eek, Gijs Bakker and Hella Jongerius, and had a big hit in their Le Lapin whistle

Frozen Fountain p50

kettle, which shifted over 250,000 units. Of course, they've had a few flops – their award-winning hairless toilet brush, for example – but that's life. Serious shoppers simply love HEMA, and not without reason.

For a stroll deep into the core of local design, it's best to begin in the heart of Amsterdam's most iconic of design wonders: the canal girdle. **Galerie Binnen** (Keizersgracht 82, 625 9603), for example, is both an industrial and interior design specialist boasting plenty of room in which to show work by unusual Dutch and international designer names (Sottsass, Kukkapuro, Studio Atika) while also hosting unusual exhibits of things like toilet brushes, Benno Premsela vases and ceramic pieces that craftily subvert Dutch cliches (www.dutch-souvenirs.org).

From here, one may wander the always charming and arty **Jordaan** (p118-25) and perhaps steal a peek into the windows of design industry wonderkind (not to mention noted inventor of the popular Knotted Chair) **Marcel Wanders'** new studio, located inside a former school building at Westerstraat 187 (www.marcelwanders.com).

Anyone with a serious interest in designer T-shirts, meanwhile, should head over to **SML.X** in Westerpark (Donker Curtiusstraat 11, 681 2837, www.sml-x.com), which itself offers an open podium for Dutch graphic designers and hip graffiti artists to silkscreen their own shirts, with the resulting products then sold exclusively at this shop and gallery.

Next, backtrack into town down Rozengracht, which has its own range of hugely colourful design and furniture stores, including the ultimately upscale but always funky **SPRMRKT** (p124). Take a sharp right down the north side of Prinsengracht to one of the city's most notorious design temples, the awesome **Frozen Fountain**

(Prinsengracht 629, 622 9375, www.frozenfountain.nl): it's a paradise for lovers of both modern furniture and design items. While staying abreast of innovative young Dutch designers such as furniture god Piet Hein Eek, the 'Froz' also shows and sells international stuff by the likes of Marc Newson, plus recent classics and photography.

The surrounding **Nine Streets** area (p84) is also a great place to wander randomly in the search for designer eye candy. If you end up near Spui square, you can drop by **Athenaeum Nieuwscentrum** (p78), categorically 'the' place for buying Amsterdam-centric design books and mags, before continuing further north-east down Lange Brugsteeg and Grimburgwal and taking a left down Oudezijds Achterburgwal. Perched on the edge of Rusland is **WonderWood** (Rusland 3, 625 3738, www.wonder wood.nl). The name says it all: truly wonderful sculpted wood in the form of shop-made originals, re-editions of global classics and rare plywood from the 1940s and '50s.

After following Rusland to take a right down Kloveniersburgwal and a left down the painfully scenic Staalstraat, one reaches the shop of the city's most internationally famed design collectives. **Droog Design** (Staalstraat 7A/B, 523 5050, www.droogdesign.nl) can rightfully lay claim to having the wittiest selection around thanks to the likes of Marcel Wanders, Hella Jongerius, Richard Hutten and Jurgen Bey.

All of which will leave even the most enthusiastic of culture vultures gasping for some light refreshment. While in the area, round of your cultural tour with a beer at nearby **De Jaren** (p63), or – rather appropriately – indulge in a gutful of design-orientated chocs from the always charming **Puccini Bomboni** (p69).

Amsterdam by Area

De Waag

The Old Centre

One side embraces shopping and pursuits of the mind; the other sex and religion. The compelling Old Centre (aka Oud Centrum) surfs on a wave of contradiction. Marked off by Centraal Station, Singel and Zwanenburgwal, the area is bisected by Damrak, which turns into Rokin south of Dam Square. Within the Old Centre, the saucier area to the east is the ancient Old Side (Oude Zijde), while the gentler area to the west – whose most notable landmark is Spui Square – is the far-from-new New Side (Nieuwe Zijde).

The Old Side

Straight up from Centraal Station, just beyond touristy Damrak and the **Beurs van Berlage**, lies **Dam Square**, the heart of the city

since the first dam was built across the Amstel here in 1270. Once a hub of social and political activities, today it's a convenient meeting point for tourists, the majority of whom convene under the mildly phallic **Nationaal Monument**, a 22-metre (70-foot) white obelisk dedicated to the Dutch servicemen who died in World War II. The west side of the Square is flanked by the **Koninklijk Paleis** (Royal Palace); next to it is the 600-year-old **Nieuwe Kerk**.

The nearby Red Light District is at the root of Amsterdam's infamy. Although sex is the main hook upon which the area hangs its reputation, it's actually secondary to window-shopping. People do buy here – it's estimated to be a €500-million-per-year trade – but mostly they wander around, gawping at the live exhibits and ducking in and out of the **Erotic Museum** or **Hash Marihuana Hemp Museum**. The **Oude Kerk**, Amsterdam's oldest building, is literally in the centre of the sleazy action. The equally pious **Museum Amstelkring** is also nearby.

At the bottom of Zeedijk is the castle-like **De Waag**, or 'Weigh House'. It stands in the centre of terrace-rich Nieuwmarkt and dates from 1488, when it was built as a gatehouse and was later home to an Anatomical Theatre (where Rembrandt painted his *Anatomy Lesson of Dr Nicolaes Tulp*). Yet more relative tranquillity exists on the Nes, home to many of the city's theatres and several charming cafés. When you reach the end of Nes, take a turn left to cross a bridge and hunt down the **Oudemanhuis Book Market**. This is where Van Gogh once bought prints to decorate his room – a high-calibre recommendation if ever there was one.

Sights & museums

Allard Pierson Museum

Oude Turfmarkt 127 (525 2556/www. allardpiersonmuseum.nl). Tram 4, 9, 14, 16, 24, 25. **Open** 10am-5pm Tue-Fri; 1-5pm Sat, Sun. **Admission** €5; €2.50 4s-15s, over-65s; free under-4s, MK. No credit cards. **Map** p55 D5 ❶

Established in Amsterdam in 1934, the Allard Pierson claims to hold one of the world's richest university collections of archaeological exhibits, gathered from ancient Egypt, Greece, Rome and the Near East. However, if you didn't spend several years at university studying stuff like this, you'll probably be bored witless. Many of the exhibits (statues, sculptures, ceramics etc) are unimaginatively presented, as if they are aimed solely at scholars. Some items are instantly accessible and interesting – the full-size sarcophagi, the model of a Greek chariot – but otherwise this is a frustrating experience.

Dam Square

Beurs van Berlage

Damrak 277, entrance at Beursplein 1 (530 4141/Artiflex tours 620 8112/ www.beursvanberlage.nl). Tram 4, 9, 14, 16, 24, 25. **Open** 10am-10pm daily for exhibitions. **Admission** varies. No credit cards. **Map** p55 D2 ❷

Designed in 1896 by Hendrik Berlage as the city's stock exchange, the palatial Beurs paved the way for the Amsterdam School. Although some jaded critics thought it 'a big block with a cigar box on top', it's now considered the country's most important piece of modern architecture. It's also a socialist statement: much of its interior artwork warns against capitalism, and each of the nine million bricks was intended by Berlage to represent the individual. The Beurs is now a concert hall, exhibition space and media centre.

Erotic Museum

Oudezijds Achterburgwal 54 (624 7303). Tram 4, 9, 16, 24, 25/Metro Nieuwmarkt. **Open** 11am-1am Mon-Thur, Sun; 11am-2am Fri, Sat. **Admission** €5. No credit cards. **Map** p55 D2 ❸

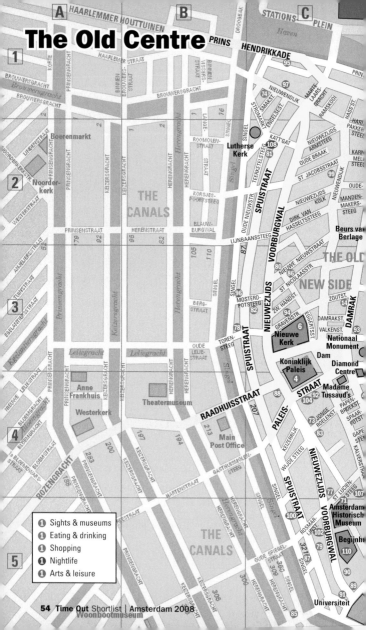

The Old Centre

STATIONS C PLEIN

A HAARLEMMER HOUTTUINEN B

PRINS HENDRIKKADE

Haven

1

KORTE PRINSENGRACHT

HAARLEMMER STRAAT

BROUWERSGRACHT

Brouwersgracht

Brouwersgracht

BINNEN WIERINGER STRAAT

BROUWERSGRACHT

HAARLEMER STRAAT

LAHGE

SINGEL

76

ROOMOLEN-STRAAT

Lutherse Kerk

NIEUWENDIJK

74

SMAKS.

LENGELSESTR.

MARE LAARS

RAMSKOOI

95

97

KATT'GAT

108

81

NIEUWEZIJDS ARMSTEEG

OUDE BRAAK

ST. JACOBSSTRAAT

NIEUWEZIJDS KOLK

OUDE-MANDEN-MAKERS-STEEG

99

HARI PAKKER STEEG

KARN MELI STEEG

NOORDERKERK STR.

LINDENGRACHT

Boerenmarkt

PRINSENGRACHT

KEIZERSGRACHT

HERENGRACHT

HERENGRACHT

2 Noorderkerk

WESTERSTRAAT

TEERKETELSTEEG

KORSJES-POORTSTEEG

BLAUW-BURGWAL

SPUISTRAAT

DIRK VAN HASSELTSSTEEG

Beurs van Berlage

THE OLD

PRINSENSTRAAT

HERENSTRAAT

96

95

82

105

110

LIJNBAANSSTEEG

87

OUDE NIEUWSTR.

NIEUWE NIEUWEZIJDS VOORBURGWAL

NIEUWE NIEUWESTRAAT

86

ST. NICLAASSTR.

94

NEW SIDE

ANJELIERSSTRAAT

TUINSTRAAT

3

ESELANTIERSSTRAAT

BERGSTRAAT

MOSTERD-POTSTEEG

52

ZW. HANDSTR.

GRAVENSTR.

ZOUTST.

14

DAMRAKSTR.

DAMRAK

VALKENST.

93

EGELANTIERSGRACHT

Prinsengracht

Keizergracht

Leliegracht

Leliegracht

SINGEL

56

78

BERGSTRAAT

OUDE LEIJE-STRAAT

TOREN-STEEG

SPUISTRAAT

Nieuwe Kerk 6

Nationaal Monument

Diamond Centre

4

Anne Frankhuis

Westerkerk

Theatermuseum

PRINSENGRACHT

KEIZERSGRACHT

HERENGRACHT

HERENGRACHT

Koninklijk Paleis 4

Dam

STRAAT

104 92

Madame Tussaud's

PAPEN-BROEKST.

SPAAR-POTST.

RAADHUISSTRAAT

207

88

NIEUWEZIJDS VOORBURGWAL

PALEIS-

DE JONGE-ROELENST.

GAPE STE

KALVERSTR.

197

194

213

Main Post Office

GASTHUISMOLEN-STEEG

KEIZERSGRACHT

WILDE STEEG

KEIZERSTRAAT

SPUISTRAAT

NIEUWEZIJDS VOORBURGWAL

83

ROZENGRACHT

BLOEMGRACHT

186

200

283

PRINSENGRACHT

PRINSENGRACHT

HARTENSTRAAT

77

ST. LUCIEN-

71

107

100

Amsterdam Historisch Museum

Begijnhof

BLOEMDWARS-STRAAT

BLOEMGRACHT

SINGEL

102

ROSMAR.

79

321

110

NIEUWE LEIJESTRAAT

THE CANALS

OUDE SPIEGELSTR.

SINGEL

HERENGRACHT

❶ Sights & museums
❶ Eating & drinking
❶ Shopping
❶ Nightlife
❶ Arts & leisure

309

360

380

THE CANALS

90

91

Universiteit

306

85

Woonbootmuseum

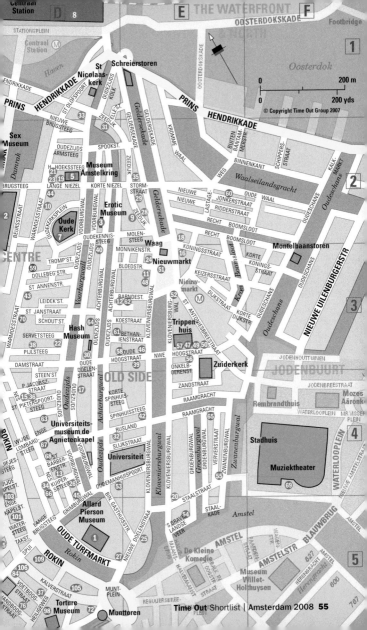

THE WATERFRONT
OOSTERDOKSKADE
NORTH

D 8

Centraal Station

STATIONSPLEIN

Centraal Station Ⓜ

Haven

E

Footbridge

F

Oosterdok

0   200 m
0   200 yds

© Copyright Time Out Group 2007

1

St Nicolaas-kerk

Schreierstoren

PRINS HENDRIKKADE

HENDRIKKADE

PRINS

Sex Museum

Damrak

Museum Amstelkring

Oude Kerk

Erotic Museum

Waag

Nieuwmarkt

Montelbaanstoren

2

CENTRE

Hash Museum

Trippenhuis

Zuiderkerk

JODENBUURT

3

Universiteits-museum de Agnietenkapel

Universiteit

Rembrandthuis

Waterlooplein

Mozes Aäronk

Stadhuis

Muziektheater

4

Allard Pierson Museum

OUDE TURFMARKT

ROKIN

Amstel

De Kleine Komedie

AMSTEL

Museum Willet-Holthuysen

BLAUWBRUG

AMSTELSTR

MUNT-PLEIN

Torture Museum

Munttoren

5

Koninklijk Paleis

than out: the Citizen's Hall, with its Baroque decoration in grand marble and bronze that depicts a miniature universe (with Amsterdam as its obvious centre), is meant to make you feel about as worthy as the rats seen carved into the stone over the door of the Bankruptcy Chamber. Gentler displays of creativity can be seen in the chimney pieces, painted by the likes of Ferdinand Bol and Govert Flinck, both pupils of Rembrandt (who had his own sketches rejected). The city hall was transformed into a royal palace in 1808, after Napoleon had made his brother, Louis, King of the Netherlands, and a fine collection of furniture from this period can be viewed inside.

Museum Amstelkring

Oudezijds Voorburgwal 40 (624 6604/ www.museumamstelkring.nl). Tram 4, 9, 14, 16, 24. **Open** 10am-5pm Mon-Sat; 1-5pm Sun. **Admission** €7; €5 students, over-65s; €1 5s-18s; free under-5s, MK. No credit cards. **Map** p55 D2 ❺

The Museum Amstelkring is one of Amsterdam's best-kept secrets. The main attraction is upstairs, and goes by the name of Ons' Lieve Heer op Solder, or 'Our Sweet Lord in the Attic'. Built in 1663, this attic church was used by Catholics during the 17th century when they were banned from worshipping after the Alteration. It's been beautifully preserved, and the altarpiece features a painting by the noted 18th-century artist Jacob de Wit.

The Erotic Museum may be appropriately located in the middle of the Red Light District, but it's none the more authentic or interesting for that. Its prize exhibits include an odd bicycle-powered dildo and a few of John Lennon's erotic drawings, while lovers of Bettie Page (and there are many) will enjoy the original photos of the S&M muse on display. In general, though, the museum's name is somewhat inaccurate: despite best efforts, it's as thoroughly unsexy as can be.

Koninklijk Paleis (Royal Palace)

Dam (information 620 4060/tours 624 8698/www.koninklijkhuis.nl). Tram 1, 2, 4, 5, 9, 13, 14, 16, 17, 24, 25. **Open** *July, Aug* 11am-5pm daily. *Sept-June* times vary. **Admission** €4.50; €3.60 5s-16s, over-65s; free under-6s. No credit cards. **Map** p54 C3/4 ❹

The Royal Palace, designed along classical lines by Jacob van Campen in the 17th century, will be closed for renovation until summer 2008 – and it's a damn shame. It's even grander inside

Nieuwe Kerk (New Church)

Dam (626 8168/recorded information 638 6909/www.nieuwekerk.nl). Tram 1, 2, 4, 5, 9, 13, 14, 16, 17, 24, 25. **Open** 10am-6pm daily. **Admission** varies. No credit cards. **Map** p54 C3 ❻

The sprightly Nieuwe Kerk dates from 1408, although the sundial on its tower was used to set all of the city's clocks until as recently as 1890. In 1645, the building was gutted by the Great Fire; the ornate oak pulpit and great organ (the latter designed by Jacob van Campen) are thought to have been constructed shortly after the blaze. Behind the black marble tomb of naval hero Admiral de Ruyter (1607-76) is a white marble relief depicting the sea battle in which he died. Poets and Amsterdam natives including PC Hooft and Joost van den Vondel are also buried here.

Oude Kerk

Oudekerksplein 1 (625 8284/www.oude kerk.nl). Tram 4, 9, 16, 24, 25, 26. **Open** 11am-5pm Mon-Sat; 1-5pm Sun. **Admission** €5; €4 over-65s, students; free under-12s, MK. No credit cards. **Map** p55 D2 ⑦

Originally built in 1306 as a simple wooden chapel, the Oude Kerk is the city's oldest and most interesting church. One can only imagine the Sunday Mass chaos during its heyday of the mid-1500s, when it had 38 altars each with its own guild-sponsored priest. Keep your eyes peeled for the Gothic and Renaissance façade above the northern portal, and the stained-glass windows, parts of which date from the 16th and 17th centuries. Rembrandt's wife Saskia, who died in 1642, is buried here. If you want to be semi-shocked, check out the carvings in the choir benches of men evacuating their bowels – apparently they tell a moralistic tale. Occasional art shows exhibit a range of fascinating subjects from contemporary Aboriginal art to photographs documenting the realities of life in modern Africa.

Eating & drinking

1e Klas

Line 2B, Centraal Station (625 0131). Tram 1, 2, 4, 5, 6, 9, 13, 16, 17, 24, 25. **Open** 8.30am-11pm daily. €€€. **Café. Map** p55 D1 ⑧

This former brasserie for first-class commuters is now open to anyone who wants to kill some time in style – with a full meal or just a snack – while waiting for their train. The delightful art nouveau interior will whisk visitors straight back to the 1890s.

A Fusion

Zeedijk 130 (330 4068). Tram 4, 9, 14, 16, 24, 25/Metro Nieuwmarkt. **Open** noon-11pm daily. €€€. **Chinese. Map** p55 E2 ⑨

This laidback, loungey affair has obviously been taking notes from the hipper, more happening side of NYC's Chinatown. The dark and inviting interior harbours big screens playing Hong Kong music videos, bubble teas (lychee!), and some of the tastiest pan-Asian dishes in town.

De Bekeerde Suster p58

Café Bern p60

De Bakkerswinkel

*Warmoesstraat 69 (489 8000/www.
bakkerswinkel.nl). Tram 1, 2, 4, 5,
9, 13, 14, 16, 17, 24, 25.* **Open** 8am-
4pm Tue-Sat; 10am-4pm Sun. No credit
cards. **Café**. **Map** p55 D2 ⑩
De Bakkerswinkel is a fantastic little
bakery and tearoom where you can
indulge lunchtime hunger pangs with
lovingly prepared sandwiches, hearty
soups and the most divine slabs of
quiche you've ever tasted.

De Bekeerde Suster

*Kloveniersburgwal 6-8 (423 0112/www.
beiaardgroep.nl). Tram 4, 9, 14, 16,
24, 25.* **Open** 4pm-1am Mon; noon-1am
Tue-Thur; 11am-2am Fri, Sat; noon-
midnight Sun. **Bar**. **Map** p55 E3 ⑪
Those shiny copper vats and elaborate
gleaming pipes aren't just for looking
pretty: the fact is that the Amsterdam
Steambrewery Company has been
making beer onsite since 2002. Home
brews include refreshing white Witte
Ros and seasonal bocks, as well as a
comprehensive list of international
beer that leans heavily toward the
Belgian end of the spectrum.

Blauw aan de Wal

*Oudezijds Achterburgwal 99 (330
2257). Tram 9, 16, 24.* **Open** 6.30-
11pm Mon-Sat. €€€€. **French**.
Map p55 D3 ⑫
Down an alley in the carnal heart of the
Red Light District lies this oasis of rev-
erence for the finer things in life. The
hallmarks of this culinary landmark
are tempting dishes (largely French in
origin) and a wine list likely to inspire
bouts of grateful contemplation.

Brasserie Harkema

*Nes 67 (428 2222/www.brasserie
harkema.nl). Tram 4, 9, 14, 16,
24, 25.* **Open** 11am-1am daily.
€€€. **French**. **Map** p55 D4 ⑬
This former tobacco factory has titil-
lated the local scene with its sense of
designer space, excellent wines and a
kitchen that stays open late pumping
out reasonably-priced French food.

Brasserie De Roode Leeuw

*Damrak 93-94 (555 666/www.restaurant
deroodeleeuw.com). Tram 4, 9, 14, 16,
24, 25.* **Open** 7am-11.30pm daily.
€€€€. **Dutch**. **Map** p54 C3 ⑭

Laws of attraction

What better way to stamp out crime than by legalising it? Granted, the story which follows isn't quite that straightforward, but here's a fact known the world over: Amsterdam does sex and drugs with fewer hang-ups than anywhere else on the planet.

Prostitution in Amsterdam has its roots in the 13th-century: as the city developed as a port it drew money, merchants and sailors. But it wasn't just randy men who influenced the sex industry's growth, but also the local women who were separated for months on end from their seafaring husbands, and left with little or no means of sustaining themselves and their children.

Amsterdam has always resisted efforts to banish sex as an industry and eventually the authorities came to accept the many advantages of a more pragmatic approach. Although working as a prostitute has been legal here since 1911,

it wasn't until 2000 that the formal ban on brothels was lifted, thus officially permitting window and brothel-based sex work. With this same legalisation inevitably came bureaucratisation. Nowawadays, all sex workers must have an EU passport, and a 200-page rule book was introduced to govern the selling of sex, covering everything from fire escapes to the proper length of a prostitute's fingernails. No stone was left unturned creating the national sex 'industry'.

There's also a prostitutes' rights organisation, De Rode Draad (Red Thread), and a sex workers' union, Vakwerk. You can find out about both – or just buy a spicy postcard – at the **Prostitution Information Centre** (Enge Kerksteeg 3, 420 7328, www.pic-amsterdam.nl, noon-7pm Tue-Sat).

The new situation, however, is by no means perfect. The legal reforms were aimed, in part, at reducing the number of illegal immigrants working in prostitution, but in actual fact only a small minority of prostitutes have no legal status, and there are still many exploitative situations that involve 'boyfriends' and a myriad of unfortunate problems related to substance abuse. But the legal changes did legitimise prostitution as a profession, which means that sex workers have access to social services and can legitimately band together to improve their working conditions. However, the stigma remains and prostitutes continue to have problems when trying to get bank accounts, mortgages and insurance, despite being liable for taxes and generating an estimated €450 million a year between them.

Oude Kerk p57

This brasserie is housed in the oldest covered terrace in Amsterdam. As you might guess, it harks back to classier times, but what's more surprising is its embrace of the digital age as a Wi-Fi point. It specialises in pricey Dutch fare, and also boasts a wide range of Dutch wines.

Bubbles and Wines

NEW *Nes 37 (422 3318/www.bubbles andwines.com). Tram 4, 9, 14, 16, 24, 25.* **Open** *3.30pm-1am Mon-Sat.* **Bar**. **Map** p55 D4 ⓯
A long, low-ceilinged room with the feel of a wine cellar – albeit one with mood lighting and banquettes. There are more than 50 wines available by the glass and 180 by the bottle with accompanying posh nosh (Osetra caviar, truffle cheese, foie gras). The final bill is unlikely to suit either the faint-hearted or the light of wallet.

Café Bern

Nieuwmarkt 9 (622 0034). Tram 4, 9, 14, 16, 24, 25/Metro Nieuwmarkt. **Open** *4pm-1am daily.* €€. No credit cards. **Dutch**. **Map** p55 E3 ⓰

Despite its Swiss origins, the Dutch adopted the cheese fondue as a noted 'national dish' long ago. Sample its culinary conviviality at this suitably cosy bar that was established – oddly enough – by a nuclear physicist.

Café Roux

The Grand, Oudezijds Voorburgwal 197 (555 3560/www.thegrand.nl). Tram 4, 9, 14, 16, 24, 25. **Open** *Breakfast 6.30-10.30am, lunch noon-3pm, tea 3-5pm, dinner 6.30-10.30pm daily.* €€€€. **French**. **Map** p55 D4 ⓱
The food here may be overseen by the great man himself, but despite Albert Roux's extraordinary status among gastronomes, meals here still represent good value for money, especially at lunchtime and during afternoon tea. The sommelier is excellent too.

Café Stevens

Geldersekade 123 (620 6970). Tram 4, 9/Metro Nieuwmarkt. **Open** *10am-1am Mon-Thur, Sun; 10am-3am Fri, Sat.* No credit cards. **Bar**. **Map** p55 E2 ⓲
With a living-room feel, plenty of seats and views over De Waag, this is simply a perfect spot to while away a day,

AMSTERDAM BY AREA

Brasserie Harkema p58

fair weather or foul. The majority of patrons are locals, with a good number of tourists and students drinking in the view and sinking a few with sandwiches and (excellent) thick chips.

Centra

Lange Niezel 29 (622 3050). Tram 4, 9, 14, 16, 24, 25. **Open** 1.30-10.30pm daily. €€. No credit cards. **Spanish**. **Map** p55 D2 ⑲

Good, wholesome, homely Spanish cooking with a suitably unpretentious atmosphere to match. The tapas, lamb and fish dishes are all great, and the place gets justifiably busy as a result.

De Doelen

Kloveniersburgwal 125 (624 9023). Tram 9, 14/Metro Waterlooplein. **Open** 9am-1am daily. No credit cards. **Bar**. **Map** p55 E4/5 ⑳

An old-fashioned drinking hole – complete with gritted floors – on one of the main tourist drags. Rough edges are smoothed by sophisticated breakfasts (fruit smoothies, muesli), international snacks (houmous, tapenade) and frosty jugs of sangria in summer.

Getto

Warmoesstraat 51 (421 5151/www. getto.nl). Tram 4, 9, 16, 24, 25. **Open** 4pm-1am Tue-Thur; 4pm-2am Fri, Sat; 4pm-midnight Sun. €€. **Global**. **Map** p55 D2 ㉑

Cheap and cheerful food in surprisingly plush surroundings catering to a mostly gay and lesbian crowd. On Wednesday nights all burger dinners cost just €10. Combined with the popular weekday two-for-the-price-of-one cocktail happy hours, this is the ideal place for an inexpensive date.

Greenhouse

Oudezijds Voorburgwal 191 (627 1739/ www.greenhouse.org). Tram 4, 9, 14, 16, 24, 25. **Open** 9am-1am Mon-Thur, Sun; 9am-3am Fri, Sat. No credit cards. **Coffeeshop**. **Map** p55 D3 ㉒

This legendary coffeeshop tenders highly potent weed with prices to match. They've won the Cannabis Cup over 30 times and, with the Grand Hotel next door, occasional celebrities stop by to get caned. The vibe inside has grown a bit commercial, but it's still worth a peek, if only to see the

Night and the city

For years, small bands of locals and tourists alike have been led through the town on night-time tours beneath the light of a silvery full moon. And they're always being led by the same enigmatic Amsterdammer: none other than Miss Moon herself. Born with the name Josephine Moons, it seemed fated that she would soon combine her passion for that bright orb of the evening sky with her knowledge of all things Amsterdam, and so she began organising **Full Moon Walks** in a style that differs wildly from more usual see-everything-in-a-day tours of the city.

For one, Miss Moon's presence – and of course that of the full moon above – are the only two elements of the tour that remain constant; the meeting point, route and setting are always changing. One night she'll lead you through the Jordaan on the trail of noted Amsterdam photographer Frits Weeda; another night may include a boat ride along the IJ, or a walk through the streets of Chinatown to celebrate the first full moon of

the Chinese New Year. A warmer evening could mean riding bikes through the polders, those large flat fields reclaimed from the sea to the north of Amsterdam, with plenty of cows and sheep to gander at. At the end of winter, when a few stubborn snowflakes still linger in the cold air, she might take you on a brisk walk through the Pijp, ending up at a snug café for warming drinks.

Miss Moon has run diamond tours through the old Jewish area, beer walks (stumbles?) through the old brewers' district and, in December, a stroll with Sinterklaas, sharing the history and legends surrounding the Dutch holiday while ambling through the harbour where he arrives on his steamboat. Every walk comes with a story and usually photos of what that particular piece of Amsterdam looked like in the past. Depending on plans for the evening, prices range from €15 to €35. And bear in mind that spots fill up fast, so it's best to reserve early. See www.fullmoonwalk.nl for more info.

beautifully handmade interior with sunken floors, ornate mosaic stones and elaborate blown-glass lamps.

Greenhouse Effect

Warmoesstraat 53 (624 4974/www. greenhouse-effect.nl). Tram 4, 9, 16, 24, 25. **Open** 9am-1am Mon-Thur, Sun; 9am-3am Fri, Sat. No credit cards. **Coffeeshop**. Map p55 D2 ㉓

This snug shop is shaped like a long, sleek train carriage with a polished interior and reliably high-quality ganja. It tends to fill up fast, but they have a separate space of the same name next door where you will find a full bar and regular DJs. If the drink and dope combination renders you immobile, head for one of the hotel rooms upstairs. Also next door is Getto, arguably the best gay/straight friendly bar/restaurant in town, where the atmosphere is always jumping and toking is also allowed.

Hill Street Blues

Nieuwmarkt 14 (no phone/www. hillstreet-blues.nl). Tram 4, 9, 14, 16, 24, 25/Metro Nieuwmarkt. **Open** 9am-1am daily. No credit cards. **Coffeeshop**. Map p55 E3 ㉔

With comfy couches and natural lighting via well-placed windows, this cosy corner on the Nieuwmarkt is ideal for a mellow high. Delectable milkshakes, smoothies, space cookies and space truffles are also worth an indulgence. The basement has pool tables and arcade games, a back window overlooks the Damrak canal and, with a police station next door, you can savour a legal toke near the law. How's that for ironic, Alanis? Hill Street Blues is also a favourite of Irvine Welsh.

De Jaren

Nieuwe Doelenstraat 20-22 (625 5771/ www.cafe-de-jaren.nl). Tram 4, 9, 14, 16, 24, 25. **Open** 10am-1am Mon-Thur, Sun; 10am-2am Fri, Sat. **Bar**. Map p55 E5 ㉕

An entire cross-section of Amsterdam – students, tourists, lesbigays, cinema-goers and the fashion pack – come here for lunch, coffee or something stronger all day long, making it sometimes difficult to bag a seat. Be prepared to fight for a spot on the popular Amstel-side outdoor terrace in summer.

Kapitein Zeppos

Gebed Zonder End 5 (624 2057/www. zeppos.nl). Tram 4, 9, 14, 16, 24, 25. **Open** 11am-1am Mon-Thur, Sun; 11am-3am Fri, Sat. **Bar**. Map p55 D4 ㉖

A hidey-hole down the poetically named 'Prayer Without End' alley – a reference to the Santa Clara convent that stood here in the 17th century. Now it's a light-drenched, multi-roomed café and restaurant with an understated Belgian theme: it's named after a 1960s Flemish TV detective, there's Belgian beer on tap and the soundtrack of choice is *chanson*.

Katoen

Oude Turfmarkt 153 (626 2635/www. goodfoodgroup.nl). Tram 4, 9, 14, 16, 24, 25. **Open** 10am-1am Mon-Thur, Sun; 11am-3am Fri, Sat. No credit cards. **Café**. Map p55 D5 ㉗

If shopping on Kalverstraat gets too much, run screaming across Rokin to this oasis of calm on the edge of the Old Centre. It has the stripped-down good looks of the 1950s (formica tables, polished wood) and an inventive lunch menu of salads, rolls and wraps.

Latei

Zeedijk 143 (625 7485/www.latei.net). Tram 4, 9, 14, 16, 24, 25/Metro Nieuwmarkt. **Open** 8am-6pm Mon-Wed; 8am-10pm Thur, Fri; 9am-10pm Sat; 11am-6pm Sun. No credit cards. **Café**. Map p55 E2 ㉘

Packed with kitsch bric-a-brac and funky Finnish wallpaper – all of which, including the wallpaper, is for sale – this little café serves up healthy juices and snacks all day, plus vegetarian dinners based around its immaculately prepared speciality couscous.

Nam Kee

Zeedijk 111-113 (624 3470/www.nam kee.nl). Tram 4, 9, 14, 16, 24, 25/ Metro Nieuwmarkt. **Open** noon-11pm Mon-Sat; noon-10pm Sun. **€€**. No credit cards. **Chinese**. Map p55 E2 ㉙

Night Mayor on Fun Street

For years, people complained that Amsterdam's nightlife was dead. Local law forced clubs and pubs to close early; underground parties were stopped. It was generally agreed that if you wanted a night out, you went to Rotterdam. Not everyone, though, was ready to give up and leave.

In 2003, a big group of DJs and party organisers collectively donned the title of **Nachtburgemeester** or 'Night Mayor' (www.nachtburge meesteramsterdam.nl). Though not an official post, the group nevertheless began examining problems in the capital's nightlife, working out solutions and building bridges between nocturnal souls and daytime politicians. Three years later, current incumbent Chiel Van Zelst (pictured) was elected to the position.

This self-titled 'Dutch Art Jockey' and native Amsterdammer has spent much of his life in the underground art scene. Chiel founded legendary squat Vrieshuis Amerika and helped to arrange openings for countless young indie artists, while the **Chiellerie** (p72), his own current gallery, boasts new openings every Friday night, serving as an ideal hangout for him and other hipsters from the scene (and you too, if you're around). Many of Amsterdam's emerging nightlife movements have their source at the Chiellerie, where new ideas are concocted while drinking beer and taking in and talking about the latest art.

Dedication is key to the job. Van Zelst goes out every night, talks to everybody, and finds out what they really want. The answer tends to be a late-night, low-key, laidback city scene. And, naturally, longer opening hours. 'The most common thing I hear is: "Get us later hours for nightlife!"' he says.

To further spur on nocturnal activities, Van Zelst arranges special parties and awards, like the Prix de Nuit for the best new nighttime initiative. He was also essential in ensuring that the freight ship turned floating art haven MS Stubnitz was given an annual home in the harbour. For an unofficial position with no real pay, it's quite a busy life. So when does the night mayor manage to sleep amidst such a punishingly nocturnal regime? 'Well, I do try to get at least five hours of sleep each day. Last night I went to bed at 4am and was back up again at 9am. Still,' he adds in a whisper, 'I do go to sleep early sometimes.'

Don't worry Chiel, your secret's safe with us.

Cheap and terrific food has earned this Chinese joint a devoted following – the oysters in black bean sauce have achieved cult status. If it's busy, try sister operation and dim sum maestros Nam Tin nearby (Jodenbreestraat 11-13, 428 8508), or neighbour New King (Zeedijk 115-117, 625 2180).

Oriental City

Oudezijds Voorburgwal 177-179 (626 8352/www.oriental-city.nl). Tram 4, 9, 14, 16, 24, 25. **Open** 11.30am-11pm daily. **€€€. Chinese. Map** p55 D3 ❸⓿
The views from Oriental City are truly awesome, overlooking Damstraat, the Royal Palace and the canals, plus the dim sum is some of the best you'll find in all of Amsterdam.

Queen's Head

Zeedijk 20 (420 2475/www.queens head.nl). Tram 4, 9, 16, 24, 25/Metro Centraal Station. **Open** 4pm-1am Mon-Thur; 4pm-3am Fri, Sat; noon-1am Sun. No credit cards. **Bar. Map** p55 D2 ❸❶
The Queen's is a fun and attitude-free gay bar with a similarly minded clientele, plus a great view over a canal at the back. Tuesdays bring show night with drag acts and Thursday is the ArtLaunch café. It also hosts special parties on – not surprisingly – Queen's Day, plus skin nights, football nights (during the cup season), *Eurovision Song Contest* nights and so on.

Rusland

Rusland 16 (627 9468). Tram 4, 9, 14, 16, 24, 25/Metro Nieuwmarkt/ Waterlooplein. **Open** 10am-midnight Mon-Thur, Sun; 10am-1am Fri, Sat. No credit cards. **Coffeeshop**. **Map** p55 D4 ❸❷
Well known as the longest-running coffeeshop in the city, this 'Russian' den has hardwood floors and colourful cushions that complement an efficient multi-level design. The top floor has a bar with 40 different loose teas, down below is a decent pipe display and up front is a dealer's booth providing the main attraction. It's off the tourist path, meaning cheaper prices and fewer crowds for the punter.

Skek

NEW *Zeedijk 4-8 (427 0551/www. skek.nl). Tram 4, 9, 16, 24, 25.* **Open** noon-1am Mon-Thur, Sun; noon-3am Fri, Sat. **Cafe. Map** p55 D1 ❸❸
This cheap little café-cum-music joint is new to the scene but is already living up to its potential. Run by the same student organisation heading up the Filmtheater Kriterion, its main focus is on value and quality. While students lap up the discounts, music lovers will get more out of the regular singer/songwriter and jazz shows, both entertaining and great for those working with smaller budgets.

Tara

Rokin 85-89 (421 2654/www.thetara. com). Tram 4, 9, 14, 16, 24, 25. **Open** 10am-1am Mon-Thur, Sun; 10am-3am Fri, Sat. **Bar. Map** p55 D4 ❸❹
Never overdoing the Irish theme, this multi-roomed bar has many faces: the Nes side is loungey, the Rokin side full of rowdy, football-watching Brits, while the middle is a snug conversation pit with sofas and a roaring fire. There's the black stuff, plus Caffrey's, Murphys and cider. Food is always reliable and – hallelujah! – bar snacks include Walkers crisps.

Thaise Snackbar Bird

Zeedijk 72 (snack bar 420 6289/ restaurant 620 1442/www.thai-bird.nl). Tram 1, 2, 4, 5, 9, 13, 14, 16, 17, 24, 25. **Open** *Snack bar* 5-11pm daily. *Restaurant* 4-10pm daily. **€€€. Thai**. **Map** p55 E2 ❸❺
Easily the most authentic Thai place in town. No doubt because of this, it's also the most crowded, but it's worth waiting for all the same, whether you drop by to pick up a pot of tom yam soup or go for a full-blown meal. If you plan to linger, settle down in the restaurant across the street rather than the snack bar itself.

Van Kerkwijk

Nes 41 (620 3316). Tram 4, 9, 14, 16, 24, 25. **Open** 11am-1am Mon-Thur, Sun; 11am-3am Fri, Sat. No credit cards. **Bar. Map** p55 D4 ❸❻

Far from the bustle of Dam Square, though really just a few strides away, on one of Amsterdam's most charming streets. Airy by day, more romantic and candlelit by night, it's equally good for group chats or tête-à-têtes. Lunch brings sandwiches and the evening more substantial food, though the emphasis is as much on genteel drinking. Be careful of the almost vertical stairs leading down to the toilets if you have over-indulged.

Vleminckx

Voetboogsteeg 31 (no phone). Tram 1, 2, 5. **Open** 11am-6pm Mon-Sat; noon-5.30pm Sun. **€.** No credit cards. **Chips**. **Map** p55 D5 **37**

Chunky Belgian chips served with your choice of toppings. Go for the *oorlog* (war) variety: chips with mayo, spicy peanut sauce and onions.

Wynand Fockink

Pijlsteeg 31 (639 2695/www.wynand-fockink.nl). Tram 4, 9, 14, 16, 24, 25. **Open** 3-9pm daily. No credit cards. **Bar**. **Map** p55 D3 **38**

Carefully tucked away behind the Krasnapolsky and largely unchanged since 1679, this tasting house has been a meeting place for Freemasons since the year dot, with a prestigious list of past visitors including such luminaries as Churchill and Chagall. The menu of liqueurs and jenevers (many available in take-out bottles) reads like a list of yet-to-be-written experimental novels: Parrot Soup; The Longer the Better; Rose Without Thorns.

Shopping

2πR

Oude Hoogstraat 10-12 (421 6329). Tram 4, 9, 14, 16, 24, 25. **Open** noon-7pm Mon; 10am-7pm Tue, Wed, Fri, Sat; 10am-9pm Thur; noon-6pm Sun. **Map** p55 E3 **39**

This funky little number is just for the boys. Two shops side by side on Oude Hoogstraat between themselves offer urban street wear and killer threads from the likes of Helmut Lang, Psycho Cowboy and D-Squared.

Absolute Danny

Oudezijds Achterburgwal 78 (421 0915/www.absolutedanny.com). Tram 4, 9, 16, 24. **Open** 11am-9pm Mon-Thur, Sun; 11am-10pm Fri, Sat. **Map** p55 D3 **40**

A fetish shop stocking everything from rubber clothing to erotic toothbrushes.

Betsy Palmer

Rokin 9-15 (422 1040/www.betsy palmer.com). Tram 4, 9, 14, 16, 24, 25. **Open** 10.30am-6.30pm Mon-Fri; 10am-6pm Sat; 1-6pm Sun. **Map** p54 C4 **41**

Tired of seeing the same shoes in every store, Dutch fashion buyer Gertie Gerards put her money where her mouth was and set up shop. Betsy Palmer is her in-house label, which sits alongside a huge variety of other labels that change regularly as they sell out.

Book Exchange

Kloveniersburgwal 58 (626 6266). Tram 4, 9, 14/Metro Nieuwmarkt. **Open** 10am-6pm Mon-Fri, Sat; 11.30am-4pm Sun. No credit cards. **Map** p55 E4 **42**

The owner of this bibliophiles' treasure trove is a shrewd buyer who's willing to do trade deals. Choose from a range of second-hand English and American titles (mainly paperbacks).

Condomerie het Gulden Vlies

Warmoesstraat 141 (627 4174/www. condomerie.com). Tram 4, 9, 14, 16, 25. **Open** 11am-6pm Mon-Sat. **Map** p55 D3 **43**

An astounding variety of innovative and imaginative rubbers of the non-erasing kind, designed to wrap up trouser snakes of all shapes and sizes.

Geels & Co

Warmoesstraat 67 (624 0683/www. geels.nl). Tram 4, 9, 14, 16, 24, 25. **Open** *Shop* 9.30am-6pm Mon-Sat. **Map** p55 D2 **44**

Coffee beans and loose teas, plus a large range of coffee-making contraptions and decorative serving utensils. Upstairs you'll find a small museum of brewing equipment, which is open only on Saturday afternoons.

Getto p61

Grimm Sieraden

Grimburgwal 9 (622 0501/www.grimm sieraden.nl). Tram 16, 24, 25. **Open** 11am-6pm Tue-Fri; 11am-5pm Sat. **Map** p55 D4 ⓸⓹
While Elize Lutz's shop features the most avant-garde of Dutch jewellery designers, she has the decency and sound commercial sense to concentrate her stock on the most wearable and affordable pieces from their ranges.

Head Shop

Kloveniersburgwal 39 (624 9061/www. headshop.nl). Tram 4, 9, 14, 16, 24, 25/Metro Nieuwmarkt. **Open** 11am-6pm Mon-Sat. **Map** p55 E3 ⓸⓺
Land at the Head Shop and you'll think Jimi, Janis and Jim are all still alive. There is a wide selection of pipes, bongs, jewellery, incense and books, plus mushrooms and spores.

De Hoed van Tijn

Nieuwe Hoogstraat 15 (623 2759/ www.dehoedvantijn.nl). Tram 4, 9, 14, 16, 24, 25. **Open** noon-6pm Mon; 11am-6pm Tue-Fri; 11am-5.30pm Sat; *Oct-Dec* noon-5pm Sun. **Map** p55 E3 ⓸⓻

Mad hatters of all ages will delight in this vast array of bonnets, Homburgs, bowlers, sombreros and caps, plus a range of second-hand and handmade items. A genuine Amsterdam original.

Jacob Hooy & Co

Kloveniersburgwal 12 (624 3041/www. jacobhooy.nl). Tram 4, 9, 14, 16, 24, 25/Metro Nieuwmarkt. **Open** 1-6pm Mon; 10am-6pm Tue-Fri; 10am-5pm Sat. **Map** p55 E3 ⓸⓼
Established in 1743, this chemist sells a huge variety of medicinal herbs, teas, homeopathic remedies and cosmetics, many under their own brand. The untouched 18th-century shop interior is worth a visit in itself.

Joe's Vliegerwinkel

Nieuwe Hoogstraat 19 (625 0139/www. joesvliegerwinkel.nl). Tram 4, 9, 16, 24, 25/Metro Nieuwmarkt. **Open** noon-6pm Mon; 11am-6pm Tue-Fri; 11am-5pm Sat. **Map** p55 E3 ⓸⓽
Kites, kites and yet more kites – well, you've got to make the most of all the Dutch wind. Also a quirky array of boomerangs, yo-yos and kaleidoscopes at this wonderfully colourful shop.

Toke is cheap

For many, stepping into their first coffeeshop is a moment of lost virginity: the initial encounter might be awkward, but it feels great to finally get inside. Whether you're new to the smoke or an old pro, arriving well versed in coffeeshop etiquette can smooth things out.

When you walk in, ask to see a menu first – it will list the available drugs and their prices, and staff can explain the effects of each. You're welcome to see and smell everything before you buy. Prices vary: expect to pay around €5 to €6 for a gram of decent bud or a chunk of hash. For better quality, bring more currency.

Hash is typically named after its country of origin (Morrocan, Afghan, Lebanese), whereas weed usually bears invented names very loosely referring to a single element of the strain (White Widow, Super Skunk, Silver Haze). These are mostly genetic hybrids developed over a number of years for the gravity of their psychoactive effects, and should be approached with caution by the uninitiated.

Previously, the big rage was for extremely potent skunk weed reared hydroponically under indoor lights. Such gear is still available, but many people now prefer the less powerful organic herb: various coffeeshops across the city carry a good bio selection; some now stock nothing but.

To save your lungs, opt for eating spacecake – just make sure you're free for the next five hours. Many establishments also offer bongs, pipes and even vaporisers for use, but if you want to blend in with the locals, roll a joint. If you lack the skills, pre-rolled joints are always available, but usually contain low-grade ingredients (though a few city shops do pride themselves on excellent pre-rolls). If you've already got grass and need a place to smoke, no shop will deny you having a seat, but you should at least buy a drink.

Every coffeeshop boasts its own unique atmosphere, but with roughly 300 venues in town, you're almost sure to find one well suited to you. Happy smoking!

't Klompenhuisje

*Nieuwe Hoogstraat 9A (622 8100/
www.klompenhuisje.nl). Tram 4, 9,
14/Metro Nieuwmarkt.* **Open** 10am-
6pm Mon-Sat. **Map** p55 E3 ⑩
Delightfully crafted and reasonably
priced shoes, traditional clogs and
handmade leather and woollen slippers
from baby ranges up to size 35.

Nieuwmarkt Antique Market

*Nieuwmarkt (no phone). Tram 9,
14/Metro Nieuwmarkt.* **Open** Apr-
Aug 9am-5pm Sun. **Map** p55 E3 ⑪
A few streets away from the ladies in
the windows, this antiques and bric-a-
brac market attracts browsers looking
for other kinds of pleasures. And
there's plenty to be found, including
old books, furniture and objets d'art.

Oriental Commodities

*Nieuwmarkt 27 (626 2797/www.oriental
group.nl). Tram 4, 9, 14, 16, 24, 25/
Metro Nieuwmarkt.* **Open** 9am-6pm
Mon-Sat; 10.30am-5pm Sun. No credit
cards. **Map** p55 E3 ⑫
Visit Amsterdam's largest Chinese
food emporium for the full spectrum of
Asian foods and ingredients, from
shrimp- and scallop-flavoured egg noo-
dles to fried tofu balls and fresh veg.
There's also a fine range of traditional
Chinese cooking appliances and utensils.

Oudemanhuis Book Market

*Oudemanhuispoort (no phone).
Tram 4, 9, 14, 16, 24, 25.* **Open**
11am-4pm Mon-Fri. No credit cards.
Map p55 D4 ⑬
People have been buying and selling
books, prints and sheet music from this
shop since the 18th century.

Palm Guitars

*'s Gravelandseveer 5 (422 0445/
www.palmguitars.nl). Tram 4, 9,
16, 24, 25.* **Open** noon-6pm Wed-
Sat. **Map** p55 E5 ⑭
Palm Guitars stocks new, antique, used
and rare musical instruments (and
their parts). The excellent website features a calendar of upcoming local
gigs, all of a worldly and rootsy nature.

Puccini Bomboni

*Staalstraat 17 (626 5474/www.puccini
bomboni.com). Tram 9, 14/Metro
Waterlooplein.* **Open** noon-6pm Mon;
9am-6pm Tue-Sat; noon-6pm Sun.
Map p55 E4 ⑮
Tamarind, thyme, lemongrass, pepper
and gin are just some of the flavours
of these delicious and imaginative
hand-made chocolates, all completely
lacking in artificial ingredients.

Seventy Five

*Nieuwe Hoogstraat 24 (626 4611/www.
seventyfive.com). Tram 4, 9, 14/Metro
Nieuwmarkt.* **Open** noon-6pm Mon;
10am-6pm Tue-Sat; noon-5pm Sun.
Map p55 E3 ⑯
Trainers for folk who have no intention
of ever having to insert a pair of Odor
Eaters: high fashion styles from Nike,
Puma, Converse and Diesel.

Stoffen & Fourituren Winkel a Boeken

*Nieuwe Hoogstraat 31 (626 7205).
Tram 4, 9, 16, 24, 25.* **Open** noon-
6pm Mon; 1pm-6pm Tue, Wed, Fri;
10am-8pm Thur; 10am-5pm Sat.
Map p55 E3 ⑰
The Boeken family has been in the rag
trade hawking fabrics since 1920. Just
try to find somewhere else with the
kind of variety on offer here: latex,
Lycra, fake fur and sequins abound.

Tom's Skate Shop

*Oude Hoogstraat 35-37 (625 4922/
www.tomsskateshop.nl). Tram 4, 9,
14/Metro Nieuwmarkt.* **Open** noon-
6pm Mon; 10am-6pm Tue-Sat; noon-
6pm Sun. **Map** p55 D3 ⑱
Dual-gender gear from the likes of Nike
SB, Zoo York, local label Rockwell and
London label Addict. Also in stock are
limited edition trainers, sunnies by
Electric and plenty of skateboards.

Nightlife

Winston International

*Warmoesstraat 125-129 (623 1380/
www.winston.nl). Tram 1, 2, 5, 13, 14,
16, 17, 24, 25.* **Open** 9pm-3am Mon-
Thur, Sun; 9pm-4am Fri, Sat. No credit
cards. **Map** p55 D3 ⑲

Betsy Palmer p66

An intimate venue that attracts a mixed crowd with its alternative rock and indietronica. Winston's yearly Popprijs gives hope to many student rock bands; Cheeky Mondays brings relief to yet another working week with jungle and drum 'n' bass; and other nights see live music from garage to folk to funky ska.

Arts & leisure

Amsterdam Marionetten Theater

Nieuwe Jonkerstraat 8 (620 8027/www. marionettentheater.nl). Tram 5, 9, 13, 14, 16, 17, 24, 25. Map p55 E2 ⑩

Opera performed as you've never seen it before: put together puppets in rich velvet costumes, puppeteers and classic operas by Mozart or Offenbach, and you've got a show from the Amsterdam Marionetten Theater. One of the last outposts of an old European tradition, the theatre also offers private lunches, dinners or high teas, consumed while the puppets perform.

Amsterdams Centrum voor Fotographie

Bethaniënstraat 9-13 (622 4899/www. acf-web.nl). Tram 16, 24, 25. No credit cards. Map p55 D3 ⑪

Photo hounds love this sprawling space within flashing distance of the Red Light District. Besides exhibitions (also at No.39), the centre has a range of workshops and a black-and-white darkroom for hire.

Bethaniënklooster

Barndesteeg 6B (625 0078/www. bethaniënklooster.nl). Tram 4, 9, 16, 24, 25/Metro Nieuwmarkt. No credit cards. Map p55 E3 ⑫

Hidden down a small alley between Damstraat and the Nieuwmarkt, this former monastery is a wonderful stage for new talent to cut its musical teeth. In between free public performances by Amsterdam's top music students, you'll also find reputable ensembles and quartets.

De Brakke Grond

Nes 45 (622 9014/www.brakkegrond.nl). Tram 4, 9, 14, 16, 24, 25. No credit cards. Map p55 D4 ⑬

Belgian culture does stretch beyond beer, and De Brakke Grond is here to prove it. Mind you, some good Belgian beer will go down a treat after a fix of progressive Flemish theatre, and if you're really lucky you might find an actor or two joining you at the bar of the adjoining café/restaurant.

Cannabis College

Oudezijds Achterburgwal 124 (423 4420/www.cannabiscollege.com). Tram 4, 9, 14, 16, 24, 25/Metro Nieuwmarkt. Map p55 D3 ⑭

The college, occupying two floors in a 17th-century listed monument in the Red Light District, provides the public with an impressive array of information about the cannabis plant (including its medicinal uses). The place is run by volunteers and admission is free; however, staff request a €2.50 donation if you want to take a wander around the indoor garden (no prizes for guessing what's growing).

Read 'em and weep

It's official: Amsterdam adores books. There's a dedicated book week each March and UNESCO has deemed the city World Book Capital 2008; locals also speak English with élan, so it's no surprise to find the shelves are awash with English tomes. And while buying brand new literature in the language is usually an eye-wateringly pricey affair, savvy second-hand shoppers will, with a little rooting around, find the best for their bookshelves at some seriously pleasing prices.

The big events to look out for are the **Boeken Op De...** fairs, which occur monthly from spring to autumn in Dam Square, Marie Heinekenplein or along the Amstel in front of the Stopera: look out for posters around town for dates. These enormous affairs are most usually organised around a theme – travel books, for example, or photography – and always have a good range of works in English, cheapo soft-covers and plenty of genuine rarities for sale.

Little sister to these bonanzas is weekly **book market on the Spui** (www.deboekenmarktophetspui.nl). Chock-full of specialist dealers who come from around the country, it's a rummager's delight, and some

real bargains can be found here, including ancient Penguin Classics and an abundance of art volumes. And if you can't resist sniffing freshly printed paper, then Spui is also book-ended by two real behemoths of new English lit: the **American Book Center** (p77; pictured) and **Waterstone's** (p81).

Elsewhere, the Old Centre, filled as it is with official University of Amsterdam faculty buildings, is understandably studded with used book opportunities. Most charismatic are the stalls dotted along the **Oudemanhuispoort**, an old covered alley between Kloveniersburgwal and Oudezijds Voorburgwal. This Monday to Saturday book market has been providing bibliophiles with their fix since 1787. Subjects tend to lean towards the academic end and conditions are generally very high. Close by, the **Book Exchange** (Kloveniersburgwal 58, 626 6266) is the destination to while away a rainy day among the dusty stacks. British and American volumes are the house speciality on the shelves of this truly sprawling shop, where titles are bought, sold and – as its name implies – traded between eager readers.

Geels & Co p66

Chiellerie

*Raamgracht 58 (320 9448/www.
chiellerie.nl). Metro Nieuwmarkt.*
No credit cards. **Map** p55 E4
Home to 'Night Mayor' Chiel van Zelst
(see box p64), and with a new exhibition
every week or two culled from members
of the local arts scene, this gallery is
more hang-out than mere art hanger.

Comedy Theatre

*Nes 110 (422 2777/www.comedy
theater.nl). Tram 4, 9, 14, 16,
24, 25.* **Map** p55 D4
This old tobacco hall was reopened in
April 2007 to house a new comedy
theatre on the city's oldest theatre
street. Hyping itself as the 'club house'
for comedians, the programming com-
bines ascerbic, politically hard-hitting
performers with those who do stand
up. Expect local legends like Javier
Guzman and international ones like
Tom Rhodes or Lewis Black. To make
sure that at least some of the acts are
English-speaking on the night you're
visiting, it's best to phone in advance.

De Engelenbak

*Nes 71 (626 3644/ www.engelenbak.nl).
Tram 4, 9, 14, 16, 24, 25.* No credit
cards. **Map** p55 D4

Theatre productions by amateurs is
what you get at De Engelenbak. The
main draw is Open Bak, an open-stage
event (10.30pm Tuesdays) where anything goes: it's the longest-running theatre programme in the country, where
everybody gets their 15 minutes.
Arrive half an hour early to get a ticket
(€7.50), and bear in mind that the best
groups tend to stage performances
between Thursday and Saturday.

Frascati

*Nes 63 (751 6400/tickets 626 6866/
www.indenes.nl). Tram 4, 9, 14, 16,
24, 25.* No credit cards. **Map** p55 D4
A cornerstone of progressive Dutch
theatre since the 1960s, Frascati gives
promising artists the chance to stage
their productions on one of its three
stages. Their mission? To challenge the
bounds of traditional theatre by team-
ing up artists with trained back-
grounds with those from the street,
resulting in a varied selection of theatre
and dance shows featuring MCs, DJs
and VJs, like the youthful Breakin'
Walls festival. If you want to meet a
thespian rather than just see one on
stage, the adjoining café, Blincker, has
plenty of actors in permanent, loqua-
cious residence at its bar.

Muziektheater

Amstel 3 (625 5455/www.muziek theater.nl). Tram 9, 14/Metro Waterlooplein. **Map** p55 F4 ⑥⑨

The Muziektheater is Amsterdam at its most ambitious. This plush, crescent-shaped building, which opened in 1986, has room for 1,596 people and is home to both Dutch National Ballet and De Nederlandse Opera, though the stage is also used by visiting companies such as Nederlands Dans Theater, Bill T. Jones/Arnie Zane Dance Company and Batsheva. On top of that, the lobby's panoramic glass walls offer impressive views out over the River Amstel.

W139

Warmoesstraat 139 (622 9434/www. w139.nl). Tram 4, 9, 14, 16, 24, 25. No credit cards. **Map** p55 D3 ⑦⓪

In its two decades of existence, W139 has never lost its squat aesthetics or sometimes overly conceptual edge, while a recent renovation has brought even more light and fresh inspiration.

The New Side

The Spui is the square that caps the three main arteries that start down near the west end of Centraal Station: middle-of-the-road walking and shopping street Kalverstraat (called Nieuwendijk before it crosses the Dam), Nieuwezijds Voorburgwal and the Spuistraat.

The nearby **Begijnhof** is a group of houses built around a secluded courtyard and garden. Established in the 14th century, it originally provided modest homes for the Beguines, a religious sisterhood. Nowadays, its residents are still female and it's the best known of the city's many *hofjes* (almshouses). In the centre is the **Engelsekerk** (English Reformed Church), built around 1400 and given over to Scottish (no, really) Presbyterians living in the city in 1607. Also in the courtyard is a Catholic church, secretly converted from two houses

in 1665 following the banning of open Catholic worship after the Reformation. Also close by is one of several entrances to the Amsterdams Historisch Museum.

The Spui square itself plays host to many markets – the most notable being the busy book market held on Fridays. You can leave Spui by going up Kalverstraat, Amsterdam's main shopping street, or Singel past Leidsestraat: both routes lead directly to the **Munttoren** (Mint Tower) at Muntplein. Right across from the floating flower market, this medieval tower was once the western corner of Regulierspoort, a gate in the city wall in the 1480s. The Munttoren is prettiest when it's floodlit at night, but daytime visitors may enjoy hearing its carillon ringing out at noon.

From here, walk down Nieuwe Doelenstraat past the **Hôtel de l'Europe** (a mock-up of which featured in Hitchcock's *Foreign Correspondent*). This street also connects with scenic Staalstraat, which is the city's most popular film location, having appeared in everything from *The Diary of Anne Frank* to *Amsterdamned*. Walk up here to end up in **Waterlooplein**.

Sights & museums

Amsterdams Historisch Museum

Kalverstraat 92 (523 1822/www.ahm.nl). Tram 1, 2, 4, 5, 9, 14, 16, 24, 25. **Open** 10am-5pm Mon-Fri; 11am-5pm Sat, Sun. **Admission** €7; €3.50 6s-16s; free under-6s; €5.25 over-65s, MK. No credit cards. **Map** p54 C5 ⑦①

Amsterdam's Historical Museum is a gem: illuminating, interesting and entertaining. It starts with the build-ings in which it's housed – a lovely col-lection of 17th-century constructions built on the site of a 1414 convent – and continues with the museum's first exhibit, a computer-generated map of the area showing how Amsterdam has

Think global, snack local

You must, yes, you simply *must* try raw herring. We don't want any excuses. The best time is between May and July when the *nieuw* (new) catch hits the stands, as they don't need any extra fripperies like onions or pickles because the flesh is at its sweetest – thanks to the high fat content the herring was planning to burn off in the arduous business of breeding. There are quality fish stalls or stores on most street corners, which also offer smoked eel and other – perhaps less controversial – fish for filling sandwiches. On top of that they're as cheap as chips (or, at the very least, a heck of a lot cheaper than sushi).

Speaking of chips, the best of these are the chunky Belgian ones (*Vlaamse*) that are double-fried to insure a crispy exterior and creamy interior. Enjoy them served along with your pick of toppings, such as *oorlog* (war): a mix of mayo, spicy peanut sauce and onions.

The correct local terminology for a greasy snack – *vette hap* – can be translated literally as 'fat bite', which says a lot for the honesty of the Dutch when it comes to the less healthy spectrum of belly-ballast. The most iconic grease purveyor is the ubiquitous **Febo** (pronounced 'Fay-bo'), where you can put your change into a glowing *automaat* and, in return, get a dollop of grease in the form of a hot(ish) hamburger, *bamibal* (a deep-fried noodley ball of vaguely Indonesian descent), or a *kaas soufflé* (a cheese treat that, despite being unrelated to any established form of soufflé, is still surprisingly tasty if eaten when still hot). The most popular choice is the *kroket*, a native version of the croquette: a mélange of meat and potato with a crusty, deep-fried skin best served on a bun with lots of hot mustard. The single best place to try these is **Van Dobben** (Korte Reguliersdwarsstraat 5-9, 624 4200), just off Rembrandtplein. And while this 1945-vintage late-night venue is the uncontested champion when it comes to the *kroket*, you can also find a more refined shrimp variation at nearby bakery **Holtkamp** (Vijzelgracht 15, 624 8757). Either way, it's proof that this is a great city to fill your belly without emptying your wallet.

changed over the last 800 years or so. It then takes a chronological trip through Amsterdam's past, using archaeological finds (love those 700-year-old shoes), works of art (by the likes of Ferdinand Bol and Jacob Corneliszoon) and plenty of quirkier displays: tone-deaf masochists may care to play the carillon in room 10A, while lesbian barflies will want to pay homage to Bet van Beeren, late owner of the infamous Het Mandje.

Orange Football Museum

Kalverstraat 236 (589 8989/www. supportersclub-oranje.nl). Tram 4, 9, 16, 24, 25. **Admission** €7; €5 children. No credit cards. **Map** p55 D5 ⑫

This enthusiastic museum has four floors of photos, art, songs and videos relating to the national football team.

Eating & drinking

Abraxas

Jonge Roelensteeg 12-14 (625 5763/ www.abraxas.tv). Tram 4, 9, 16, 24, 25. **Open** 10am-1am daily. No credit cards. **Coffeeshop. Map** p54 C4 ⑬

Tucked away down a narrow alley, this lively shop is a tourist hot spot. The staff are friendly, internet is free and chess boards are plentiful – as are the separate rooms connected by spiral staircases. They also have a healthy-sized drug menu, including half a dozen bio weeds and space cakes.

Al's Plaice

Nieuwendijk 10 (427 4192). Tram 1, 2, 4, 5, 9, 14, 16, 17, 24, 25. **Open** noon-10pm daily. €. No credit cards. **Fish & chips. Map** p54 C1 ⑭

Visiting Brits will spot the pun from 50 paces: yep, it's an English fish 'n' chip shop with all the trimmings. Besides fish, there's a selection of pies, pasties, peas and downmarket tabloids.

Café de Dokter

Rozenboomsteeg 4 (626 4427/www. cafe-de-dokter.nl). Tram 1, 2, 4, 5, 9, 13, 14, 16, 17, 24, 25. **Open** 4pm-1am Tue-Sat. No credit cards. **Bar. Map** p55 D5 ⑮

Officially the smallest bar in all of Amsterdam, Café de Dokter is also one of the oldest, dishing out the cure for whatever ails you since 1798. Centuries of character and all kinds of charming gewgaws are packed into the compact space, giving it a unique old-world ambience. Whisky figures large (there's a monthly special) and the range of old-school bar snacks includes smoked osseworst with gherkins.

Dampkring

Handboogstraat 29 (638 0705/www. dedampkring.nl). Tram 1, 2, 5. **Open** 10am-1am Mon-Thur; 10am-2am Fri, Sat; 11am-1am Sun. No credit cards. **Coffeeshop. Map** p55 D5 ⑯

Known for it's unforgettable (even by stoner standards) interior, the visual experience acquired from Dampkring's decor could make a mushroom trip look grey. Moulded walls and sculpted ceilings are covered in deep auburns laced with caramel-coloured wooden panelling, making a perfect location for the movie *Ocean's Twelve*. In case you missed it, they've set up monitors in the shop logging the same George Clooney and Brad Pitt scene all day long.

Delores

Nieuwezijds Voorburgwal, opposite No.289 (626 5649). Tram 1, 2, 5. **Open** noon-6pm Mon-Wed, Fri-Sun; noon-9pm Thur. **Café. Map** p54 C4 ⑰

Conveniently located in the hipster bar zone, this former police post is now a decent café. The greasy fries of yester-year have been replaced with healthy snacks and well-prepared meals; harsh colours and neon forsaken for a more welcoming air of funky warmth.

Green Planet

Spuistraat 122 (625 8280/www.green planet.nl). Tram 1, 2, 5, 13, 17. **Open** 5.30pm-midnight Mon-Sat; 5.30-10.30pm Sun. €€€. No credit cards. **Vegetarian. Map** p54 B3 ⑱

The best vegetarian restaurant in the city tips wholly organic ingredients into soups, lasagnes and stir fries. Finish with the house cognac and a slice of chocolate heaven.

AMSTERDAM BY AREA

Abraxas p75

Harry's Bar

Spuistraat 285 (624 4384). Tram 1, 2, 13, 14, 17. **Open** 5pm-1am Mon-Thur, Sun; 3pm-3am Fri, Sat. **Bar**. **Map** p54 C5 ⓭

Small, dark and intimate, Harry's Bar is the perfect place to while away an afternoon lounging on a leather sofa. There's everything here to suit all manner of movers and shakers, from Cristal champagne to Montecristo cigars.

Homegrown Fantasy

Nieuwezijds Voorburgwal 87A (627 5683/www.homegrownfantasy.com). Tram 1, 2, 5, 13, 17. **Open** 10am-midnight Mon-Thur, Sun; 10am-1am Fri, Sat. No credit cards. **Coffeeshop**. **Map** p54 C3 ⓰

One of the most popular coffee shops with visitors, this brightly-lit establishment bears an ever-changing line-up of artwork, tables with chess boards and a UV light in the toilet that makes your pee a trippy colour. The ganja is all organic and Dutch-grown, including their famous cheese weed, and the (non-alcoholic) drink selection is vast. Those hoping to get mashed before joining a cult (it helps, apparently) will find the Scientology HQ conveniently located right across the street.

Keuken van 1870

Spuistraat 4 (620 4018/www.keuken van1870.nl). Tram 1, 2, 5. **Open** 4-10pm Mon-Sat. €€. No credit cards. **Dutch**. **Map** p54 C2 ⓱

This former soup kitchen has been renovated and reinvented but retains a menu of authentic Dutch standards and, in a homage to its roots, a set three-course menu for €7.50. Diners often end up sharing tables, so hopefully you'll enjoy rubbing shoulders with a cross-section of Dutch society.

Prik

NEW *Spuistraat 109 (320 0002/www. prikamsterdam.nl). Tram 1, 2, 5, 13, 17.* **Open** 4pm-1am Tue-Thur, Sun; 4pm-3am Fri, Sat. No credit cards. **Bar**. **Map** p54 C3 ⓲

Queer or not, Prik is hot. True to the bar's slogan, this recent addition to the gay scene succeeds in getting a diverse crowd that enjoys its movie nights, delicious snacks and groovy sounds.

Supperclub

Jonge Roelensteeg 21 (344 6400/www. supperclub.nl). Tram 1, 2, 5, 13, 17. **Open** 7.30pm-1am Mon-Thur, Sun; 7.30pm-3am Fri, Sat. €€€€. **Global**. **Map** p54 C4 ⓳

With its white decor, beds for seating, irreverent food combos and wacky acts, this arty joint is casual to the point of being narcoleptic. At the very least, we can promise that you'll remember your visit. The owners also have their own cruise ship that trawls the local waters offering dinners with a more dramatic backdrop.

Tokyo Café

Spui 15 (489 7918/www.tokyocafe.nl). Tram 1, 2, 4, 5, 9, 14, 16, 24, 25. **Open** 11am-11pm daily. €€€.
Japanese. Map p55 D5 ③④
Thought to be haunted, this Jugendstil monument now hosts its umpteenth eatery in the form of an authentic Japanese café complete with a lovely terrace, *teppanyaki* pyrotechnics and a sushi and sashimi bar. High quality dishes that may offer little protection against local ghosts, but will certainly keep hunger at bay.

Tweede Kamer

Heisteeg 6 (422 2236). Tram 1, 2, 5. **Open** 10am-1am Mon-Thur, Sun; 10am-2am Fri, Sat. No credit cards.
Coffeeshop. Map p54 C5 ③⑤
Small and intimate, this shop embodies the refined look and feel of vintage jazz sophistication – which makes it an extremely pleasant place to get stoned. Aided by a bakery just around the corner, their spacecakes are delicious and hugely effective. The house hash is highly regarded, but seating inside is limited; if there's no room, walk over to nearby Dutch Flowers (Singel 387).

Vaaghuyzen

Nieuwe Nieuwstraat 17 (420 1751/www. vaaghuyzen.net). Tram 1, 2, 5, 13, 14, 17. **Open** 5pm-1am Mon-Thur, Sun; 5pm-3am Fri, Sat. No credit cards. **Bar**. Map p54 C3 ③⑥
This dinky DJ bar is a great place to pick up flyers and find out what's happening in clubs all over the city centre. That said, there are also plenty of reasons to stay, including top-notch turntablists and interactive evenings like Singles Night, where punters bring and play the tunes.

Blue Note from Ear & Eye p78

D'Vijff Vlieghen

Spuistraat 294-302 (530 4060/www. d-vijffvlieghen.com). Tram 1, 2, 5, 13, 17. **Open** 6pm-10pm daily. €€€€.
Dutch. Map p54 C5 ③⑦
The Five Flies achieves a rich Golden Age vibe – it even has a Rembrandt room, with etchings – but also works as a purveyor of over-the-top kitsch. The food is best described as posh Dutch. Unique, and appropriately pricey.

Shopping

Albert Heijn

Nieuwezijds Voorburgwal 226 (421 8344/www.ah.nl). Tram 1, 2, 4, 5, 9, 13, 14, 16, 17, 24, 25. **Open** 8am-10pm daily. No credit cards. **Map** p54 C4 ③⑧
This massive shop, just behind Dam Square, is one of over 40 branches of Albert Heijn in Amsterdam. It contains virtually all the household goods you could ever need, though some of the range is unnecessarily expensive.

American Book Center

Spui 12 (625 5537/www.abc.nl). Tram 1, 2, 4, 5, 9, 14, 16, 24, 25. **Open** 10am-8pm Mon-Wed, Fri, Sat; 10am-9pm Thur; 11am-6.30pm Sun. **Map** p54 C5 ③⑨

Now located at a fancier establishment a mere two blocks from the old shop and an Amsterdam institution since 1972, the American Book Center stocks a truly enormous selection of English-language books and magazines from the US and UK to a loyal core of comfortably bilingual Dutch customers.

Artplein Spui

Spui (www.artplein-spui.nl). Tram 1, 2, 4, 5, 9, 14, 16, 24, 25. **Open** *Mar-Dec* 10am-6pm Sun. No credit cards. **Map** p54 C5 ⑨⓪

Oil paintings, acrylics, watercolours, graphic arts, sculpture, ceramics and jewellery are found at this small open-air (and therefore weather-dependent) Sunday arts and crafts market. There's a rotating system for the 60 or so artists, and buskers are usually on hand to lend a little atmosphere while the crowds browse wares. The perfect place to take a chilled Sunday stroll.

Athenaeum Nieuwscentrum

Spui 14-16 (bookshop 514 1460/news centre 514 1470/www.athenaeum.nl). Tram 1, 2, 5. **Open** *Bookshop* 11am-6pm Mon; 9.30am-6pm Tue, Wed, Fri, Sat; 9.30am-9pm Thur; noon-5.30pm Sun. *News centre* 8am-8pm Mon-Wed, Fri, Sat; 8am-9pm Thur; 10am-6pm Sun. **Map** p54 C5 ⑨①

This is where Amsterdam's highbrow literary browsers usually choose to hang out and chew the cultural fat. The Athenaeum Nieuwscentrum, as its name might suggest, also stocks newspapers from across the world, as well as a wide choice of magazines and periodicals in many languages.

De Bierkoning

Paleisstraat 125 (625 2336/www. bierkoning.nl). Tram 1, 2, 5, 13, 14, 16, 17, 24, 25. **Open** 1-7pm Mon; 11am-7pm Tue, Wed, Fri; 11am-9pm Thur; 11am-6pm Sat; 1-6pm Sun. **Map** p54 C4 ⑨②

Named in honour of its location behind the Royal Palace, the Beer King stocks a head-spinning 850 brands of quality beer from around the world.

De Bijenkorf

Dam 1 (552 1700/www.bijenkorf.nl). Tram 1, 2, 4, 5, 9, 13, 14, 16, 17, 24, 25. **Open** 11am-7pm Mon; 9.30am-7pm Tue, Wed; 9.30am-9pm Thur, Fri; 9.30am-6pm Sat; noon-6pm Sun. **Map** p54 C3 ⑨③

Amsterdam's most notable department store has a great household goods section and a decent mix of clothing (designer and own-label), kids' wear, jewellery, cosmetics, shoes and accessories. The top floor Chill Out department caters to funky youngsters in need of streetwear, clubwear, wacky foodstuffs and kitsch accessories.

Blue Note from Ear & Eye

Gravenstraat 12 (428 1029). Tram 1, 2, 4, 5, 9, 13, 16, 24, 25. **Open** 11am-6pm Tue-Sat; noon-5pm Sun. **Map** p54 C3 ⑨④

This conveniently central shop stocks a full spectrum of jazz, from '30s stompers to mainstream dinner jazz, avant-garde and eclectic Afro grooves.

Dampkring

Prins Hendrikkade 10-11 (422 2137/ www.dampkringshop.com). Tram 1, 2, 4, 5, 9, 16, 17, 24, 25/Metro Centraal Station. **Open** 9am-6pm Mon-Fri; 9am-5pm Sat. **Map** p54 C1 ⑨⑤

A new member of the green-fingered Dampkring family, this delightful emporium has everything needed to set up a cannabis grow centre at home: from hydroponics and organic equipment to bio-growth books and videos.

Female & Partners

Spuistraat 100 (620 9152/www.female andpartners.nl). Tram 1, 2, 5, 13, 17. **Open** 1-6pm Mon, Sun; 11am-6pm Tue, Wed, Fri, Sat; 11am-9pm Thur. **Map** p54 B3 ⑨⑥

The opposite of most enterprises here, Female & Partners welcomes women (and, yes, their partners) with an array of erotic clothes, videos and toys.

Hemp Works

Niewendijk 13 (421 1762/www.hemp works.nl). Tram 1, 2, 5, 13, 17. **Open** 11am-7pm Mon-Wed, Sun; 11am-9pm Thur-Sat. **Map** p54 C1 ⑨⑦

Free for all

Albert Heijn

Cheapskates take note: there's a wealth of, well, wealth on display throughout this fair city, but don't think for a second that you have to spend a fortune to have a fantastic time in Amsterdam. Quite the opposite, in fact. The following list of activities shows just how easily budget visitors can have fun for free across the capital.

■ The view from **Nemo**'s roof (p113).
■ Complimentary coffee at various branches of **Albert Heijn** (p77).
■ The seaworthy and scenic **ferry trips** from behind Centraal Station to the north (p52).
■ The **Rijksmuseum**'s garden on its west side (p129).
■ Open-air concerts and the great outdoors of **Vondelpark** (126).
■ The **Civic Guard Gallery** at the Amsterdams Historisch Museum (p73), best if combined with the atmospheric buildings of the **Begijnhof** (p12).
■ The **Noordermarkt** fleamarket on Monday mornings (p118).
■ Tuesday lunchtime concerts at the **Muziektheater** (p73).
■ Wednesday lunchtime concerts at the **Concertgebouw** (p134).
■ Exploring the **hofjes** – courtyard almshouses – of the Jordaan.
■ Watching horseriding in AL van Gendt's beautiful **Hollandsche Manege** bridal circuit (Vondelstraat 140, 618 0942).
■ Tasting free samples of organic foodstuffs at the Saturday **farmers' market** on Noordermarkt (p118).
■ Peering in Hendrick de Keyser's atmospheric **Zuiderkerk** (p98).
■ Smelling the flowers on sale at the floating **Bloemenmarkt** (p93).
■ Checking the biggest barometer in the Netherlands. The neon light on the **Hotel Okura Amsterdam** (p175) tells you what tomorrow's weather will be like: blue for good; green for bad; white for changeable.
■ Taking a lift to the top of **Post CS** (p110) for unsurpassed city views.
■ Picking up and having a browse through **Amsterdam Weekly**, the English-language cultural paper.
■ Lounging on a deckchair at one of the city's many **urban beaches**.
■ Attending the opening of a new exhibition, Fridays at happening art hangout **Chiellerie** (p72)
■ Going alternative queer clubbing on every first Saturday of the month at **Hot Peper**, in the fabulous De Peper café (p131).
■ Reading through countless international papers and glossy magazines at the brand new **public library** (Prinsengracht 587).
■ Seeing top-notch bands being recorded for TV at **3voor12** (p109).

Winston International p69

One of the first shops in Amsterdam to sell hemp clothes and products, and now one of the last, Hemp Works has had to diversify into seed sales and fresh mushrooms to keep its trade ticking over, and it's also been a notable Cannabis Cup winner for its homegrown strain of the stinky weed.

Lucky Brand Jeans

Heiligeweg 34-36 (422 0502/www.lucky brand.com). Tram 1, 2, 4, 5, 9, 14, 16, 24, 25. **Open** noon-6pm Mon; 10am-6pm Tue-Fri; 10am-5.30pm Sat; 10am-9pm Thur; noon-5pm Sun. **Map** p55 D5 ❾❽

A recent addition to the Amsterdam high street, Lucky sits kitty corner from Diesel off the Kalverstraat, making the surrounding area denim central for style-conscious shoppers.

Midtown

Nieuwendijk 104 (638 4252/www.mid-town.nl). Tram 1, 2, 5, 13, 17, 24, 25. **Open** noon-6pm Mon; 10am-6pm Tue, Wed, Fri, Sat; 10am-9pm Thur; noon-5pm Sun. **Map** p54 C2 ❾❾

Dance music galore: gabber (the store was one of the original pioneers of the hardcore hybrid), trance, mellow house and garage are among the styles on the shelves. Midtown is also a good source of info and tickets for hardcore parties.

Paars

Spuistraat 242 (618 2828/www.paars lingerie.nl). Tram 1, 2, 5, 13, 17. **Open** 1-7pm Mon; 11am-7pm Tue-Fri; 11am-9pm Thur; 10am-6pm Sat; 1-6pm Sun. **Map** p54 C5 ❿❿

Easily the most sophisticated lingerie shop in Amsterdam right now, Paars' collections are high end and vary regularly, making it interesting for true lingerie lovers. Galliano, Argentovivo, Ravage, Lise Charmel, Marlies Dekkers, Miss Bikini, Pin Up, D&G, Malizia, Pain de Sucre and Roberto Cavalli, among others, are all on sale.

PGC Hajenius

Rokin 92-96 (623 7494/www.hajenius. com). Tram 4, 9, 14, 16, 24, 25. **Open** noon-6pm Mon; 9.30am-6pm Tue, Wed, Fri; 9.30am-9pm Thur; noon-5pm Sat, Sun. **Map** p55 D5 ❿❶

A smoker's paradise (tobacco, not dope) for over 250 years, Hajenius offers cigarabilia from traditional Dutch pipes to own-brand cigars. Even non-smokers should enjoy gazing at its quaint art deco interior.

Postzegelmarkt

Nieuwezijds Voorburgwal, by No.276 (no phone). Tram 1, 2, 5, 13, 17. **Open** 11am-4pm Wed, Sun. No credit cards. **Map** p54 C5 ❿❷

A specialist market for more avid collectors of stamps, coins, postcards and medals, with plenty of rarities.

Rituals

Kalverstraat 73 (344 9220/www.rituals. com). Tram 4, 9, 14, 16, 24, 25. **Open** noon-6pm Mon; 10am-6pm Tue, Wed, Fri; 10am-9pm Thur; 10am-5pm Sat; noon-5pm Sun. **Map** p55 D4 ❿❸

A shop cleverly integrating products for both body and home. We all have to brush our teeth and do the dishes, and this store is full of gizmos to help ritualise daily grinds.

Vrolijk

Paleisstraat 135 (623 5142/www.
vrolijk.nu). Tram 1, 2, 5, 13, 14, 17.
Open 11am-6pm Mon; 10am-6pm
Tue-Thur; 10am-5pm Sat; 1-5pm Sun.
Map p54 C4 **104**
The best selection of rose-tinted international reading – whether fiction or
fact – you'll find in all of Amsterdam,
plus a wide variety of CDs, DVDs and
guides. It has a second-hand section
upstairs, and also offers a range of nov-
elty T-shirts, condoms and gifts that
are always popular with tourists.

Vroom & Dreesmann

Kalverstraat 203 (0900 235 8363/
www.vroomendreesmann.nl). Tram 4,
9, 14, 16, 24, 25. **Open** 11am-6.30pm
Mon; 10am-6.30pm Tue, Wed, Fri;
10am-9pm Thur; 10am-6.30pm Sat;
noon-6pm Sun. **Map** p55 D5 **105**
V&D means good quality products at
prices that are just a small step up from
those on offer at the more ubiquitous
HEMA. There's a staggering array of
toiletries, cosmetics, leather goods and
watches, clothing and underwear for
the whole family, kitchen items, suit-
cases, CDs and videos. The bakery, Le
Marché, sells delicious bread, quiches,
shakes and sandwiches, while self-
service restaurant La Place is a great
spot for a healthy lunch.

Waterstone's

Kalverstraat 152 (638 3821/www.
waterstones.co.uk). Tram 1, 2, 4, 5, 9,
14, 16, 24, 25. **Open** 10am-6pm Mon;
9.30am-7pm Tue, Wed, Fri; 9.30am-9pm
Thur; 10am-6.30pm Sat; 11am-6pm
Sun. **Map** p55 D5 **106**
A mighty temple to literature in an area
already bursting with bookshops.
Thousands of books, magazines and
videos, all of them in English, are on sale
in this reputable store, and the children's
section is especially delightful.

Zara

Kalverstraat 72 (530 4050/www.zara.
com). Tram 1, 2, 4, 5, 9, 14, 16, 24,
25. **Open** noon-6pm Mon, Sun; 10am-
6pm Tue, Wed, Fri, Sat; 10am-9pm
Thur. **Map** p54 C4 **107**

Imagine that you have a lean, mean
fashion machine that can almost
instantaneously churn out decent
approximations of the latest catwalk
creations at a fraction of the price you'd
pay at the outlet shops of the designers. Now imagine how much money
you'd make doing it. Oops! Too late,
Zara beat you to it.

Nightlife

Bitterzoet

Spuistraat 2 (521 3001/www.bitterzoet.
com). Tram 1, 2, 5. **Open** 8pm-3am
Mon-Thur, Sun; 8pm-4am Fri, Sat.
No credit cards. **Map** p54 C2 **108**
This busy, comfy and casual bar doubles as a venue for theatrical and musical performances. Both bands and DJs
tend to embrace the jazzy, world and
urban sides of sound, as demonstrated
by once-a-monther Crime Jazz: words,
poetry and beyond for hipper literates.

Arts & leisure

Arti et Amicitiae

Rokin 112 (623 3508/www.arti.nl).
Tram 4, 9, 14, 16, 24, 25. **Open**
1-6pm Tue-Sun. No credit cards.
Map p55 D5 **109**
This marvellous old building houses a
private artists' society, whose initiates
regularly gather in the first-floor bar.
Members of the public can climb a
Berlage-designed staircase to a large
exhibition space, home to some great
temporary shows.

Engelse Kerk

Begijnhof 48 (624 9665/www.erc
adam.nl). Tram 1, 2, 4, 5, 14, 16, 24,
25. No credit cards. **Map** p54 C5 **110**
Nestled tightly within the idyllic
courtyard of Begijnhof, the English
Reformed Church has been hosting
weekly concerts of baroque and classical music here since the early 1970s,
and has remained a popular venue
throughout. Combined with a particular
emphasis on the use of authentic period
instruments, the church's acoustics
are genuinely haunting. Its healthy
evening schedule also raises funds to
help secure the building's future.

The Canals

Singel was the original medieval moat of the city; the other canals – Herengracht, Keizersgracht and Prinsengracht – that follow its line outward were part of a Golden Age urban renewal scheme for the rich. The connecting canals and streets, originally built for workers and artisans, have the most cafés and shops, while smaller canals worth seeking out include Leliegracht, Bloemgracht, Egelantiersgracht, Spiegelgracht and the historical and charming Brouwersgracht.

In this guide, for ease of use, we've split venues on the canals into two: the Western Canal Belt (between Singel and Prinsengracht, south of Brouwersgracht, north and west of Leidsegracht); and the Southern Canal Belt (between Singel and Prinsengracht, running from Leidsegracht south-eastward towards the Amstel.

Western Canal Belt

Cross Singel at Wijde Heisteeg, and opposite you on Herengracht is the **Bijbels Museum** (Bible Museum). A stroll south, and the Netherlands Institute of War Documentation (Herengracht 380, 523 3800, www. niod.nl) is home to Anne Frank's diary, donated by her father Otto. Head north and you'll reach an architectural gem now housing the **Theater Instituut**. For a look not only inside a 17th-century interior, but also at the history of purses, try the **Tassenmuseum** (see box p94). Hopping over to Keizersgracht, there is the equally epic home of the photography foundation, **Huis Marseille**.

Prinsengracht is easily the most charming of the canals. Pompous façades have been mellowed with shady trees, cosy cafés and some

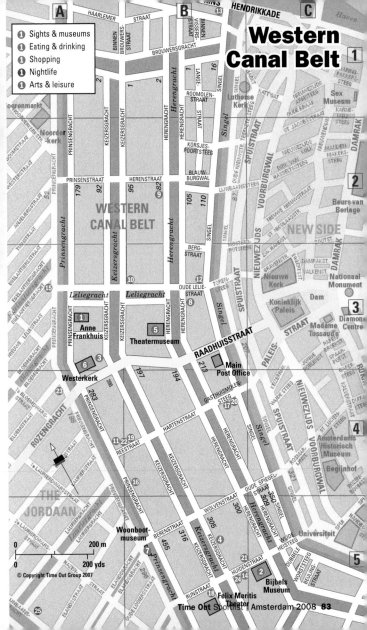

Western Canal Belt

Map legend:
- Sights & museums
- Eating & drinking
- Shopping
- Nightlife
- Arts & leisure

WESTERN CANAL BELT

NEW SIDE

THE JORDAAN

Anne Frankhuis

Theatermuseum

Westerkerk

Main Post Office

Woonboot-museum

Felix Meritis Theater

Bijbels Museum

Noorder-kerk

Lutherse Kerk

Roomolen-straat

Korsjes-poortsteeg

Blauw-burgwal

Berg-straat

Oude Lelie-straat

Nieuwe Kerk

Koninklijk Paleis

Dam

Madame Tussaud's

Diamond Centre

Nationaal Monument

Beurs van Berlage

Sex Museum

Amsterdams Historisch Museum

Begijnhof

Universiteit

0   200 m
0   200 yds

© Copyright Time Out Group 2007

Huis Marseille

of Amsterdam's more funkadelic houseboats. There's also some good shopping to be had; further north, the smart 'Nine Streets' linking Prinsengracht, Keizersgracht and Herengracht all offer a diverse pick of speciality shops for browsing.

On your way up Prinsengracht, the tall spire of the 375-year-old **Westerkerk** should rear into view. Its tower is the tallest structure in this part of town, and if you choose to climb it you'll be able to look down upon the **Anne Frank Huis**. Meanwhile, serious fans of René Descartes – and if you think, you therefore probably are – can pay tribute at his former house around the corner at Westermarkt 6.

Sights & museums

Anne Frank Huis

Prinsengracht 267 (556 7105/www.anne frank.nl). Tram 13, 17. **Open** *Jan-Mar, Sept-Dec* 9am-7pm daily. *Apr-Aug* 9am-9pm daily. **Admission** €7.50; €3.50 10s-17s; free under-10s. **Map** p83 A3 ❶

It was in this 17th-century canal-side house that the young Jewish diarist Anne Frank and her family hid for two years during World War II, sustained by friends who risked everything to help them. On 4 August 1944, the occupants were arrested and transported to concentration camps, where Anne died with sister Margot and their mother. Her father, Otto, survived, and decided that Anne's diary should be published to reveal the tragic story at its heart. The rest, as they say, is history: tens of millions of copies have since been printed in 55 languages, and Anne's story has been written into legend.

Bijbels Museum

Herengracht 366-368 (624 2436/www. bijbelsmuseum.nl). Tram 1, 2, 5. **Open** 10am-5pm Mon-Sat; 11am-5pm Sun, public holidays. **Admission** €7.50; €3.75 13s-17s; free under-13s, MK. No credit cards. **Map** p83 C5 ❷

Housed in two handsome Vingboons canal houses, Amsterdam's own Bible Museum aims to illustrate life and worship in biblical times with archaeological finds from Egypt and the Middle East (including the remarkable mummy of an Israeli woman), models of ancient temples and a slideshow. There's also a splendid collection of Bibles from several centuries (including a rhyming Bible from 1271). A little dry in places, the museum also attracts folk merely looking to admire the restored houses, splendid Jacob de Wit paintings and the sprawling gardens.

Homomonument

Westermarkt. Tram 13, 14, 17. **Map** p83 A3 ❸

Unveiled some 20 years ago, Karin Daan's three-sectioned pink triangular monument to the memory of persecuted gays and lesbians was a world first. Flowers are often left on it for personal remembrance, especially during large gatherings such as World AIDS Day. More information on gay and lesbian life in the city is available from COC Amsterdam (p182).

Westerkerk

Huis Marseille

Keizersgracht 401 (531 8989/www. huismarseille.nl). Tram 1, 2, 5. **Open** 11am-5pm Tue-Sun. **Admission** €5; €3 over-65s, students; free under-17s, MK. No credit cards. **Map** p83 B5 **❹**

Located in a monumental 17th-century house, the walls of this photography foundation might host the latest from such hotshot snappers as Hellen van Meene, David Goldblatt or Naoya Hatakeyama, or new work from one of modern photography's most influential duos, Bernd and Hilla Becher.

Theater Instituut

Herengracht 168 (551 3300/www. tin.nl). Tram 1, 2, 5, 13, 17. **Open** 11am-5pm Mon-Fri; 1-5pm Sat, Sun. **Admission** €4.50; €2.25 students, 6s-16s, over-65s; free under-6s, MK. **Map** p83 B3 **❺**

The ever-changing displays here are largely drawn from the institute's collection of costumes, props, posters, memorabilia and ephemera, much of which is digitally catalogued. Upstairs there is a massive library; call ahead for information on hours and prices.

Westerkerk

Prinsengracht 277-279 (624 7766/tower 689 2565/www.westerkerk.nl). Tram 13, 14, 17. **Open** *Apr-Sept* 11am-3pm Mon-Fri. **Admission** *Tower* €5. No credit cards. **Map** p83 A3 **❻**

The 186-stair Westerkerk tower is a good place from which to view the surrounding city, provided you don't suffer from vertigo: the 85m (278ft) tower sways by 3cm (1.2in) in a good wind. It's thought that Rembrandt is buried in the church itself, though no one is sure where: Rembrandt died a pauper, and as a direct result is commemorated inside with a simple plaque. Though his burial on 8 October 1669 was recorded in the church register, the actual spot was not, but there's a pretty good chance that he shares a grave here with his son, Titus.

Woonbootmuseum

Prinsengracht, opposite No.296 (427 0750/www.houseboatmuseum.nl). Tram 13, 14, 17. **Open** *Jan, Feb, Nov, Dec* 11am-5pm Fri-Sun. *Mar-Oct* 11am-5pm Tue-Sun. Closed last 2wks Jan. **Admission** €3.25; €2.50 children under 152cm (5ft). No credit cards. **Map** p83 B5 **❼**

The Houseboat Museum is not just a museum about houseboats: it's actually on one. Aside from a few explanatory panels, the Hendrika Maria is laid out exactly as a houseboat would be to help visitors imagine what it's like to live on the water. It's more spacious than you might expect and does a good job of selling the lifestyle afforded by its unique comforts. Until, that is, you notice the pungent scent of urine emanating from the public toilet or 'curlie' (as they are called), right by the boat.

Eating & drinking

Amnesia

Herengracht 133 (no phone). Tram 13, 14, 17. **Open** 9.30am-1am daily. No credit cards. **Coffeeshop**. **Map** p83 B3 **❽**

A shop with swank decor, comfortable cushions and deep red walls. Located off the main tourist routes, it's often cool and quiet – though it occasionally fills up with locals. Their pre-rolled joints are strong and very smokeable. Summertime brings tranquil outdoor seating on their quiet canal street.

't Arendsnest

Herengracht 90 (421 2057/www.arends nest.nl). Tram 1, 2, 5, 13, 14, 17. **Open** 4pm-midnight Mon-Thur, Sun; 4pm-2am Fri, Sat. **Bar. Map** p83 B2 ❾

A temple to the humble hop, the 'Eagle's Nest', in a lovely old canal house, sells only Dutch beer. Many of the customers are real ale types, but even amateurs will have a ball sampling the wares: 350 standard brews and 250 seasonal, from house ale Herengracht 90 to the well-named Texelse Skuumkoppe. The affable owner is happy to offer suggestions.

Brandon

NEW *Keizersgracht 157 (626 4191). Tram 1, 2, 5, 13, 14, 17.* **Open** 11am-1am Mon-Thur, Sun; 11am-3am Fri, Sat. No credit cards. **Bar. Map** p83 B3 ❿

When the previous owners hung up their pinnies in the 1980s after 40 years behind the bar, they sealed up their café, retired upstairs and eventually passed away. Twenty years later, the new owners reopened this ghost bar just as they found it: furniture, photos, billiard room and all. A decidedly old-fashioned ambience lingers, enhanced by tasteful jazz music tinkling for added effect in the background.

Envy

NEW *Prinsengracht 381 (344 6407/ www.envy.nl). Tram 13, 14, 17.* **Open** varies. €€€. **Italian. Map** p83 A4 ⓫

A poshed-up designer deli and restaurant serving an arsenal of delicacies both from the streamlined cool cabinets that line the walls and from the fancy kitchen in the back. Perfect for when you want to try a little of everything.

Grey Area

Oude Leliestraat 2 (420 4301/www. greyarea.nl). Tram 1, 2, 5, 13, 14, 17. **Open** noon-8pm daily. No credit cards. **Coffeeshop. Map** p83 B3 ⓬

Run by two blokes living the modern American dream: get the f*@k out of America. They did so by opening this stellar coffeeshop, which offers some of the best weed and hash on the planet (try the Bubble Gum or Grey Mist Crystals). Also on offer are large glass bongs, a vaporiser and free refills of organic coffee. The owners are highly affable and often more baked than the patrons: sometimes they stay in bed and miss the noon opening time.

Kobalt

Singel 2 (320 1559/www.cafekobalt.nl). Tram 1, 2, 5, 9, 13, 17, 24, 25. **Open** 8am-1am Mon-Thur, Sun; 8am-3am Fri, Sat. No credit cards. **Bar. Map** p83 B1 ⓭

This rather sophisticated bar near Centraal Station is a great way of beating train delay blues. There's free Wi-Fi, round-the-clock food from breakfast to tapas to dinner, and any drink you could name, from ristretto to champagne. DJs spin Friday nights, while Sunday afternoons are dedicated to slinky live jazz shows.

De Pels

Huidenstraat 25 (622 9037). Tram 1, 2, 5. **Open** 10am-1am Mon-Thur, Sun; 10am-3am Fri, Sat. No credit cards. **Bar. Map** p83 B5 ⓮

The Nine Streets are littered with characterful bars, and this one is a lovely old-style, tobacco-stained example with an intellectual bent. In fact, De Pels can rightly claim a prime spot in Amsterdam's literary and political legacy: writers, journalists and social activists regularly meet at this erstwhile Provo hangout to chew the fat, although it's a nice spot to chill even if you aren't feeling in a cerebral mood.

Twee Zwaantjes

Prinsengracht 114 (625 2729/www.de tweezwaantjes.nl). Tram 1, 2, 5, 13, 14, 17. **Open** 10am-1am Mon, Thur, Sun; 7pm-11pm Tue; 11am-3am Fri, Sat. No credit cards. **Bar. Map** p83 A3 ⓯

Oom-pah-pah, oom-pah-pah – that's how it goes at this salt-of-the-earth bar when the locals are out in force and

As gays go by

Amsterdam Pride may be one of the lesbian and gay community's most anticipated events, but the extended weekend of crowded street parties, parades, vibrant recreational drinking and noise draws thousands of spectators – straight and gay alike – all eager to join in the procession.

The festival offers thousands of distractions running the A to Z of camp: androgyny, barely-clad boys, flirtation, loads of leather, lesbians, Muscle Marys, PVC poseurs, and, of course, theatrics. Whether you're a boy who loves boys or love girls who love girls – and all points between – it's a genuinely non-stop playground.

Then there's the dizzying array of affiliated events: street parties, more street parties, sing-alongs, performances, and Pride's apex, the awesome Saturday afternoon Canal Parade – the world's only floating pride, which winds along the Prinsengracht and Amstel River between 2pm and 6pm.

If you haven't seen the romantic canals spilling over with topless mermaids, half-naked fire fighters, Marilyn Monroe look-alikes, pole dancers, Spartans, beauty queens, angels and wrestlers all waving from a hundred different boats mere metres away, then you don't know a real photo opportunity when you see one. The Canal Parade draws thousands of onlookers – estimates put them at 350,000, and no one's clocking who's gay and who ain't – which increases levels of craziness.

The later the day gets, the less restraint is evident, as everyone is putting in overtime cultivating the following day's hangover – although they've probably drunk their way through the first one, as the partying technically starts on Friday. Or Thursday, depending on who you ask. Either way, the traditional closing party takes place during late Sunday afternoon on Rembrandtplein, with a huge number of Dutch artists, DJs and those with enough energy left to sign off the celebration.

Like Queen's Day, when the city's population doubles and crams into the centre for the event, Pride is terribly Amsterdam. It's relaxed, tolerant, positive, outrageous and definitely worth celebrating.

Brilmuseum/Brillenwinkel

the air is filled with song. It's relatively quiet during the week, but weekends are real singalong, swingalong affairs, with revellers booming out tear-jerkering tunes on such subjects as love, sweat and the Westerkerk.

Vyne

NEW *Prinsengracht 411 (344 6408/ www.vyne.nl). Tram 1, 2, 5, 7, 10, 13, 14, 17.* **Open** 5pm-1am Mon-Thur, Sat; 4pm-1am Fri; 3pm-midnight Sun. **Bar**. **Map** p83 B4 ⑯

A tasteful – in every sense of the word – addition to the city's drinking scene. The gorgeous slimline interior is dominated by an amazing wall of wine and emphasis is on pairing drink with food, such as Weissburgunder with sausage, or smoked eel and Sancerre. Also check out sister restaurant Envy (see p86).

Shopping

Brilmuseum/Brillenwinkel

Gasthuismolensteeg 7 (421 2414/www. brilmuseumamsterdam.nl). Tram 1, 2, 5. **Open** noon-5.30pm Wed-Fri; noon-5pm Sat. No credit cards. **Map** p83 B4 ⑰

Officially this 'shop' is an opticians' museum, but don't let that put you off. The fascinating exhibits are of glasses throughout the ages, and if you like what you see then most of the pairs on display are also for sale.

De Kaaskamer

Runstraat 7 (623 3483). Tram 1, 2, 5. **Open** noon-6pm Mon; 9am-6pm Tue-Fri; 9am-5pm Sat; noon-5pm Sun. No credit cards. **Map** p83 B5 ⑱

De Kaaskamer offers over 200 varieties of domestic and imported cheeses, plus pâtés, olives, pastas and wines. Have fun quizzing shop staff on the different cheese varieties and random related trivia: they seriously know their stuff.

Kramer/Pontifex

Reestraat 18-20 (626 5274/www. pontifex.fiberworld.nl). Tram 13, 14, 17. **Open** 10am-6pm Mon-Fri; 10am-5pm Sat. **Map** p83 B4 ⑲

Broken Barbies and battered bears are restored to health by Mr Kramer, a doctor for old-fashioned dolls and teddies who has been here for 25 years. In the same shop, Pontifex is a candle seller.

Nic Nic

*Gasthuismolensteeg 5 (622 8523/www.
nicnicdesign.com). Tram 1, 2, 5, 13, 17.*
Open noon-6pm Mon-Fri; 10am-5pm Sat.
Map p83 B4 ⓴
We consider this the best shop of its
kind in Amsterdam, selling 1950s and
'60s furniture, lamps, ashtrays and
kitchenware, mostly in mint condition.

Pâtisserie Pompadour

*Huidenstraat 12 (623 9554/www.
patisseriepompadour.com). Tram
1, 2, 5, 7.* **Open** 10am-6pm Mon-Fri;
10am-5pm Sat. **Map** p83 B5 ㉑
This fabulously charming bonbonnerie
and tearoom – with a delightful 18th-
century interior imported all the way
from Antwerp – is likely to bring out
the sweet-toothed little old lady in
diners of all ages. Designer chocolates,
pastries and cakes are all on hand for
more discerning indulgers.

Ree-member

Reestraat 26 (622 1329). Tram 1, 2, 5.
Open 1-6pm Mon; 11am-6pm Tue-Sat;
1-6pm Sun. **Map** p83 A3/B3 ㉒
Ree-member stocks a terrific collection of vintage clothes and 1960s standards. The shoes are the best in town
and boast prices to match, but if
you're strapped for cash, then you'll
be pleased to learn that they also sell
less-than-perfect numbers over on
Noordermarkt by the kilo.

Simon Levelt

*Prinsengracht 180 (624 0823/www.
simonlevelt.com). Tram 13, 14, 17.*
Open 10am-6pm Mon-Fri; 10am-5pm
Sat. **Map** p83 A3 ㉓
Anything and everything to do with
brewing and drinking can be found
stocked in this remarkable old shop,
actually part of a chain with locations
all across the city. The premises dates
from 1839 and the place retains much
of its original tiled decor.

Van Ravenstein

*Keizersgracht 359 (639 0067). Tram
13, 14, 17.* **Open** 1-6pm Mon; 11am-
6pm Tue-Fri; 11am-7pm Thur; 10.30am-
5.30pm Sat. **Map** p83 B5 ㉔

A superb boutique with the most eye-
catching pieces from a range of noted
Belgian designers: Martin Margiela,
Dirk Bikkembergs, AF Vandervorst
and Bernhard Willhelm, amongst
others. Victor & Rolf form the Dutch
contingent. Those who find the prices
restrictive should head to the bargain
basement for cheaper thrills.

Nightlife

Maloe Melo

*Lijnbaansgracht 163 (420 4592/www.
maloemelo.com). Tram 7, 10, 13, 14, 17.*
Open 9pm-3am Mon-Thur, Sun; 9pm-
4am Fri, Sat. **Map** p83 A5 ㉕
Well I woke up this morning, feeling
Maloe Melowed. Yes, you guessed it,
this small, pleasantly pokey little juke
joint is Amsterdam's native house of
the blues. Quality rockabilly and roots
acts play here on a regular basis, so
shed your gloom and enjoy the boogie.

Southern Canal Belt

The Southern Canal Belt boasts
two main squares: Rembrandtplein
and Leidseplein. Rembrandtplein
is unashamedly tacky and home
to tasteless establishments from
traditional striptease parlours
to seedy modern peepshow joints
and nondescript cafés. There are
a few exceptions to the prevailing
tawdriness – places like the grand
café De Kroon (No.17), the art deco
Schiller (No.26) and HL de Jong's
eclectic masterpiece, the **Pathé
Tuschinski** on Reguliersbreestraat.
Also nearby is the floating flower
market at the southern tip of Singel
(the **Bloemenmarkt**). From the
square, walk south along shopping
and eating street Utrechtsestraat,
or explore the painfully scenic
Reguliersgracht and Amstelveld.
Whichever you choose, you'll cross
Herengracht as you wander.
   As the first canal to be dug in the
glory days, Herengracht attracted
the richest of merchants and remains

home to the most overblown houses on any of Amsterdam's canals. But it's on the stretch built between Leidsestraat and Vijzelstraat, known as the **Golden Bend**, that things really get out of hand. Around the corner on Vijzelstraat is the highly imposing **Gebouw de Bazel building**, since 2007 the new home of the city archives (see box p93). Nearby on Keizersgracht is the photography museum **Foam**.

Leidseplein, reached via the always chaotic pedestrian- and tram-packed Leidsestraat or the gallery-heavy strip of Nieuwe Spiegelstraat, is the tourist centre of Amsterdam. It's packed with merrymakers drinking at pavement cafés and is visually dominated by the **Stadsschouwburg** and many cinemas, theatres and restaurants. Max Euweplein offers a route to the greener pastures of Vondelpark.

Sights & museums

Foam (Photography Museum Amsterdam)
Keizersgracht 609 (551 6500/www. foam.nl). Tram 16, 24, 25. **Open** 10am-5pm Mon-Wed, Sat, Sun; 10am-9pm Thur, Fri. **Admission** €7; €5 students, over-65s; free under-12s, MK. No credit cards. **Map** p91 C2 ㉖
This excellent photography museum, located in a renovated canal house, holds exhibitions of works by shutter-button maestros like August Sander and advertising from Amsterdam-based agency KesselsKramer. Shows cover everything from local crime scene photos to portraits of Kate Moss.

Museum Willet-Holthuysen
Herengracht 605 (523 1870/www. museumwilletholthuysen.nl). Tram 4, 9, 14. **Open** 10am-5pm Mon-Fri; 11am-5pm Sat, Sun. **Admission** €5; €3.75 over-65s; €2.50 6s-18s; free under-6s, MK. **Map** p91 D1 ㉗
Upon the death in 1889 of Abraham Willet-Holthuysen, remembered as 'the Oscar Wilde of Amsterdam', his wife

Sandrina Louisa, a hermaphrodite (that's right, a chick with a dick), left this 17th-century house and its contents to the city on the condition that it was preserved and opened as a museum. The family had followed the fashion of the time and decorated it in neo-Louis XVI style: it's densely furnished, with the over-embellishment extending to the collection of rare objets d'art, glassware, silver, china and paintings – including one of a rather shocked looking Abraham (taken on his honeymoon perhaps?).

Eating & drinking

ARC
Reguliersdwarsstraat 44 (689 7070/ www.bararc.com). Tram 1, 2, 4, 5, 9, 16, 24, 25. **Open** 4pm-1am Mon-Thur, Sun; 4pm-3am Fri, Sat. **Bar**. **Map** p91 C1 ㉘
Still looking sleek and space age, gay bar ARC is well and truly established these days and continues to attract a stylish, moneyed, polysexual crowd. The cocktails and finger food are tasty, but service can be rather slow.

Bojo
Lange Leidsedwarsstraat 51 (622 7434/www.bojo.nl). Tram 1, 2, 5. **Open** 4pm-2am Mon-Thur; 4pm-4am Fri; noon-4am Sat; noon-2am Sun. €€.
Indonesian. **Map** p91 B2 ㉙
Bojo is a fine Indo-eaterie, and one of very few places that stays open into the small hours. The price is right and the portions are large enough to glue your insides together before or after an evening of excess. Its sister operation at No.49 compensates for its earlier closing time by serving alcohol.

Café Krom
Utrechtsestraat 76 (624 5343). Tram 4, 6, 7, 10. **Open** 9am-1am Mon-Thur; 10am-2am Fri, Sat; 10am-1am Sun. No credit cards. **Bar**. **Map** p91 D2 ㉚
A glass cabinet of trophies and trinkets and a jukebox give this bar a laidback 1950s feel. It's an Amsterdam classic, by night full of barfly philosophers and locals mixed with younger night-owls staggering towards Rembrandtplein.

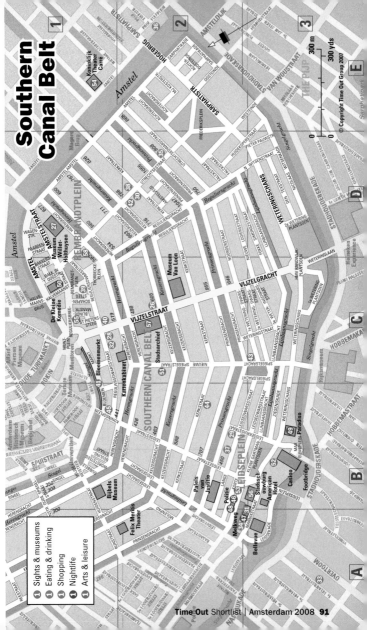

Southern Canal Belt

Koninklijk Theater Carré 54

Museum Willet-Holthuysen 27

Museum Van Loon

De Kleine Komedie 50

Stadsarchief 57

Bloemenmarkt

Kattenkabinet

SOUTHERN CANAL BELT

Bijbels Museum

Felix Meritis Theater

Palais van Justitie

Politie

Melkweg

Stadsschouwburg

American Hotel

Casino

Paradiso 49

Bellevue

THE PIJP

Heineken Experience

Legend

1 Sights & museums
1 Eating & drinking
1 Shopping
1 Nightlife
1 Arts & leisure

300 m
300 yds

Golden Bend p90

Hungry but hard up? You need some of the Dutch grandma cooking served in this canteen with a living-room feel, which packs famished punters with meat and potatoes for around €6.

Kamer 401

Marnixstraat 401 (620 0614/www. kamer401.nl). Tram 1, 2, 5, 6, 7. **Open** 6pm-1am Wed, Thur; 6pm-3am Fri, Sat. No credit cards. **Bar**. **Map** p91 A2 **34**

Art students and the terminally hip gather at this red-lacquered temple to pleasure, where there is no food or frippery, just booze, DJ-spun music and a party vibe. Nearby establishment Lux (Marnixstraat 403, 422 1412) offers a similar formula.

Onder de Ooievaar

Utrechtsestraat 119 (624 6836/www. onderdeooievaar.nl). Tram 4. **Open** 10am-1am Mon-Thur; 10am-3am Fri, Sat; 10.30am-1am Sun. No credit cards. **Bar**. **Map** p91 D2 **35**

Here you have a highly uncomplicated venue for an evening's carousing among a mixed bunch of trendies, locals and the odd visitor. Highlights include 't IJ beer on tap, the downstairs pool table and the rather lovely Prinsengracht-side terrace.

La Rive

InterContinental, Prof Tulpplein 1 (520 3264/www.restaurantlarive.com). Tram 6, 7, 10/Metro Weesperplein. **Open** noon-2pm, 6.30-10.30pm Mon-Fri; 6.30-10.30pm Sat. Closed first two weeks of Aug. **€€€€**. **French**. **Map** p91 E2 **36**

While Hôtel de l'Europe (p165) has Excelsior, it's really La Rive at the InterContinental (p170) that overshadows the rest of the high-end competition, and it does so by serving chef Edwin Kats' superb regional French cuisine without excessive formality. Perfect when money is no object.

De Rokerij

Lange Leidsedwarsstraat 41 (622 9442/www.rokerij.net). Tram 1, 2, 5, 6, 7, 10. **Open** 10am-1am Mon-Thur, Sun; 10am-3am Fri, Sat. No credit cards. **Coffeeshop**. **Map** p91 B2 **37**

Eat at Jo's

Marnixstraat 409 (638 3336). Tram 1, 2, 5, 6, 7, 10. **Open** noon-9pm Wed-Sun. **€€**. No credit cards. **Global**. **Map** p91 A2/B2 **31**

Each day brings a different menu to this cheap and eminently cheerful international kitchen, where fish, meat and vegetarian dishes are all lovingly prepared. Star spotters take note: whichever act is booked to play at the Melkweg (p95) may well be eating here beforehand.

Gala

NEW *Reguliersdwarsstraat 38 (623 6303). Tram 16, 24, 25.* **Open** 6-11pm Wed-Sun. **€€**. **Catalan**. **Map** p91 C1 **32**

A peaceful and already popular new tapas hot-spot that is in direct contrast to the more bustling Mexican noise fest Rose's Cantina, to which it is attached. Food is affordable and well prepared.

Hap Hmm

1e Helmerstraat 33 (618 1884/www. hap-hmm.nl). Tram 1, 6, 7, 10. **Open** 4.30-8pm Mon-Fri. **€**. No credit cards. **Dutch**. **Map** p91 A3 **33**

AMSTERDAM BY AREA

A marvellous discovery on an otherwise hideous touristy street by Leidseplein, De Rokerij is a real Aladdin's cave: lit by wall-mounted candles and beautiful metal lanterns, it's decorated with colourful Indian art and a variety of seating (ranging from mats thrown onto the floor to more formal decorative 'thrones').

Tempo Doeloe

Utrechtsestraat 75 (625 6718/www. tempodoeloerestaurant.nl). Tram 4, 6, 7, 10. **Open** 6-11.30pm daily. €€€€. **Indonesian**. Map p91 D2 ❸❽
This cosy and rather classy Indonesian restaurant is widely thought of as one of the city's best and spiciest purveyors of rice table, and not without reason.

Van Dobben

Korte Reguliersdwarsstraat 5-9 (624 4200/www.vandobben.com). Tram 4, 9, 16, 24, 25. **Open** 9.30am-1am Mon-Thur; 9.30am-2am Fri, Sat; 11.30am-8pm Sun. €. No credit cards. **Dutch**. Map p91 C1 ❸❾
A *kroket* is the national version of a croquette: a mélange of meat and potato with a crusty, deep-fried skin best served on a bun with lots of hot mustard – and this 1945-vintage latenighter is the uncontested champion.

Shopping

8cht

NEW *Vijzelstraat 105 (320 7007/ www.8-sneakers.nl). Tram 16, 24, 25.* **Open** 12.30-6pm Mon; 10.30am-6pm Tue-Fri; 1.30-9pm Thurs; 10.30am-5pm Sat; noon-5pm Sun. Map p91 C1 ❹⓿
Pronounced 'acht' (it's the Dutch word for eight), this is the city's latest streetwear haunt with maximum cred thanks to the super-exclusive kicks, toys and tees sourced by owner Philip.

Bloemenmarkt (Flower Market)

Singel, between Muntplein and Koningsplein (no phone). Tram 1, 2, 4, 5, 9, 14, 16, 24, 25. **Open** 9am-6pm Mon-Sat; 11am-5.30pm Sun. No credit cards. Map p91 B1/C1 ❹❶

Building atmosphere

The spanking new City Archives in the **De Bazel building** on Vijzelstraat (www.gemeentear chief.amsterdam.nl), located between Keizersgracht and Herengracht, has a history shrouded in esoteric mists. Completed in 1926, it was originally the HQ for global trade association Nederlandsche Handel-Maatschappij.

It looks a muscular, highly logical monument to modernism, yet its architect, KPC De Bazel (after whom the building is now known), was a strict follower of the religion-cum-philosophy-cum-science Theosophy, invented by chain-smoking Russian Madame Blavatsky. Followers were guided by the writings of millennia-old Tibetan masters and made to study Eastern literature, natural laws and the straight line.

After the architect embraced the new religion, he set up a bureau to put mysticism into practice, and this building is its greatest work. The pink and yellow façade represents masculinity and femininity; the grid is the *kundalini* or 'serpent power' most prevalent within Egyptian and Indian symbolism, and representing the 'total environment' or cosmic whole.

It's all at its most gloriously evident in the Schatkamer where every surface is decorated with a spiralling square pattern. It was painstakingly restored from original photographs, and should be opened to the public from August 2007 for exhibitions and guided tours.

Objects of reticule

Once an antique-collecting couple's hobby, the huge **Tassenmuseum Hendrikje Museum of Bags and Purses** spent ten long years in a private home in Amstelveen, but grew to become the world's largest collection of its kinds (total to date: 3,500 and still counting), thus necessitating a move to more accommodating premises.

As a result, Hendrikje and Heinz Ivo literally packed their bags and moved to a more central location in a grand house on the city's most prestigious canal, a confection of murals and marble floors. But despite such a fabulous display case, the collection is still the real star of the show, and includes everything from the Versace bag Madonna carried to the *Evita* premiere to a Lieber rhinestone bag made for none other than Hillary Clinton's cat.

This 3D history of handbags begins back in the 1500s with the 'body necklaces' for dangling anything from spoons to Bibles, human hair purses and tortoise-shell reticules. But it's the 20th century that's the most fascinating, when – thanks to Coco Chanel – handbags become popular fashion statements. Following fads from 1920s fake ivory up to 1950s plastic, there are also covetable classics including the Hermés Kelly alongside technology-trend hybrids like a telephone bag that can be jacked for a quick dial-up. Bringing the collection bang up to date are bags showing that 'eco' doesn't just mean organic cotton – witness the bag made from Nile perch, the all-consuming pest these days believed to have been responsible for the extinction of over 200 species of animal.

The ground floor of the mansion is dedicated to various exhibitions showcasing up-and-coming young designers from the Netherlands and abroad, and the museum shop sells a variety of related souvenirs, pictures and plenty of tote-themed coffee table tomes. And – surprise surprise – you can even purchase a bag to take them all home in.

Tassenmuseum Hendrikje

Herengracht 573 (524 6452/ www.tassenmuseum.nl). Tram 4, 9. **Open** 10am-5pm daily.

This fascinating collage of colour is the world's only floating flower market, with 15 florists and garden shops (although many also hawk rather cheesy souvenirs these days), all permanently ensconced on barges along the southern side of Singel. The plants and flowers usually last well.

Concerto
Utrechtsestraat 52-60 (623 5228/www. concerto.nu). Tram 4. **Open** 10am-6pm Mon-Wed, Fri, Sat; 10am-9pm Thur; noon-6pm Sun. **Map** p91 D2 ⓬
Head here for classic Bach recordings, obscure Beatles items or that fave Diana Ross album that got nicked from your party. There are also second-hand 45s and new releases at decent prices.

Delftshop
Spiegelgracht 13 (421 8360/www.delft shop.com). Tram 4, 9, 16, 24, 25. **Open** 9.30am-6pm Mon-Sat; 11am-6pm Sun. **Map** p91 C3 ⓭
Souvenirs with provenance. Delftshop are the official dealers of Royal Delft and Makkum pottery, the bread and butter of the Dutch antiques trade. The stock here includes pieces dating from as far back as the 17th century – for an appropriately high price, of course.

Lambiek
Kerkstraat 132 (626 7543/www. lambiek.nl). Tram 1, 2, 5. **Open** 11am-6pm Mon-Fri; 11am-5pm Sat; 1-5pm Sun. **Map** p91 B2 ⓮
Lambiek, founded in 1968, claims to be the world's oldest comic shop and has thousands of books from around the world; its on-site cartoonists' gallery hosts exhibitions every two months.

Shoe Baloo
Koningsplein 7 (626 7993/www.shoe baloo.nl). Tram 2, 3, 5, 12. **Open** noon-6pm Mon; 10am-6pm Tue, Wed, Fri, Sat; 10am-9pm Thur; 1-6pm Sun. **Map** p91 B1 ⓯
A space age men's and women's shoe shop with a glowing Barbarella-pod interior. Über cool, but well worth taking the time to cruise for Miu Miu, Costume Nationale and Patrick Cox.

Nightlife

Jimmy Woo's
Korte Leidsedwarsstraat 18 (626 3150/ www.jimmywoo.com). Tram 1, 2, 5, 6, 7, 10. **Open** 11pm-3am Wed, Thur, Sun; 11pm-4am Fri, Sat. **Map** p91 B2 ⓰
Amsterdam has never seen anything quite so luxuriously cosmopolitan as club Jimmy Woo's. Now you too can marvel at the lounge area filled with a mixture of modern and antique furniture, and then confirm for yourself the merits of its bootylicious light design and sound system. If you have problems getting inside thanks to crowds, cool off across the street at its sister bar, the swanky Suzy Wong (Korte Leidsedwarsstraat 45, 626 6769).

Melkweg
Lijnbaansgracht 234A (531 8181/ www.melkweg.nl). Tram 1, 2, 5, 6, 7, 10, 20. **Open** 8.30pm-4am daily. **Membership** €3/mth; €15/yr. No credit cards. **Map** p91 A2 ⓱
A former dairy (the name translates as 'Milky Way'), Melkweg has become world renowned as an always innovative home to live music of all styles. The complex also hosts a theatre, cinema, art gallery and café, and holds weekend club nights to boot, so it's no surprise it's a key cultural beacon in the centre of the city. Membership is compulsory for anyone wanting in.

Nachttheater Sugar Factory
Lijnbaansgracht 238 (626 5006/ www.sugarfactory.nl). Tram 1, 2, 5, 7, 10. **Open** 9pm-4am Thur, Sun; 9pm-5am Fri, Sat. No credit cards. **Map** p91 A2/B2 ⓲
This 'night theatre' club has found its niche as a place where performance meets clubbing, catering to both beat freaks and more traditional music fans at the same time. Monthly Vreemd ('Weird') sees various eclectic DJ acts; WickedJazzSounds livens up Sunday evenings; and the cutting edge bash Electronation brings top acts from the worlds of 1980s synthesizer electro and current day minimal techno.

AMSTERDAM BY AREA

Pathé Tuschinski

Paradiso

*Weteringschans 6-8 (626 4521/www.
paradiso.nl). Tram 1, 2, 5, 7, 10.* **Open**
varies. **Membership** €3/mth; €18/yr.
No credit cards. **Map** p91 B3 ㊾
A cornerstone of the live music and
clubbing scene and a name synonymous with quality shows across the
city, this former church is in such
demand that it often hosts multiple
events in one day. The main hall has
a rare sense of grandeur, with multiple
balconies and stained-glass windows
peering down upon performers and
DJs. The smaller hall upstairs is a
fantastic place to catch new talent.
Membership is compulsory. Concerts
by bigger-named stars such as Justin
Timberlake sell out weeks in advance.

Studio 80

NEW *Rembrandtplein 17 (521 8333/
www.studio-80.nl). Tram 4, 9, 14.*
Open 10pm-4am Wed-Thur, Sun;
11pm-5am Fri, Sat. **Map** p91 C1 ㊿
In the midst of Rembrandt Square's
neon glitz and ice-cream eating
crowds lurks this former radio studio,
a black pearl waiting to be discovered.

Dirty disco, deep electronic acid and
gritty hip hop are shown off at very
reasonable prices. The city's progressive techno and minimal crowds find
their home here and bring their record
bag- and synthesizer-wielding friends
from across Europe.

Arts & leisure

De Appel

*Nieuwe Spiegelstraat 10 (625 5651/
www.deappel.nl). Tram 16, 24, 25.* No
credit cards. **Map** p91 C2 ㉛
An Amsterdam institution that
showed its mettle by being one of the
first galleries in the country to
embrace video art. It still has a nose
for things modern, and gives international and rookie guest curators real
freedom to follow their muse.

De Balie

*Kleine Gartmanplantsoen 10 (553 5100/
www.debalie.nl). Tram 1, 2, 5, 6, 7, 10.*
No credit cards. **Map** p91 B3 ㉜
Theatre, new media, photography, cinema and literary events sit alongside
lectures, debates and discussions about

AMSTERDAM BY AREA

Stadsschouwburg

AMSTERDAM BY AREA

social and political issues at this influential centre for the local intelligentsia. Throw in a café and you've got healthy food for both mind and body.

Boom Chicago

Leidseplein Theater, Leidseplein 12 (423 0101/www.boomchicago.nl). Tram 1, 2, 5, 6, 7, 10. **Map** p91 B2 ⑤
This American improv troupe is one of Amsterdam's biggest success stories. With several different shows running seven nights a week (except Sundays in winter), all in English, the group offers a mix of audience-prompted improvisation and sketches.

Koninklijk Theater Carré

Amstel 115-125 (0900 252 5255 premium rate/www.theatercarre.nl). Tram 4, 6, 7, 10/Metro Weesperplein. **Map** p91 E1 ⑤
It's the dream of many to perform in this glamorous space, formerly home to a circus and recently refurbished in grand style. The Carré hosts some of the best Dutch cabaret artists and touring operas, as well as the odd big music name. If mainstream theatre is more

your thing, this is the place to come to see and hear Dutch versions of popular blockbuster like *Grease* and *Cats*.

Pathé Tuschinski

Reguliersbreestraat 26-34 (0900 1458/ www.pathe.nl). Tram 4, 9, 16, 24, 25. **Map** p91 C1 ⑤
This extraordinary cinema is named after Abraham Tuschinski, the city's most illustrious cinematic entrepreneur, who built it in 1921 as a 'world theatre palace'. The Tuschinski's interior and exterior are a striking clash of rococo, art deco and Jugendstil.

Stadsschouwburg

Leidseplein 26 (624 2311/www.ssba.nl). Tram 1, 2, 5, 6, 7, 10. **Map** p91 B3 ⑤
The Stadsschouwburg (or Municipal Theatre) is a seriously impressive 19th-century building, constructed in a traditional horseshoe shape, seating 950 and known primarily for its progressive theatre and opera productions (occasional contemporary music performances are also held). It's currently being renovated, and will eventually link up with the Melkweg.

Jodenbuurt, the Plantage & the Oost

Located south-east of the Red Light District, Amsterdam's old Jewish neighbourhood is a peculiar mix of old and new architectural styles. Enter the skull-adorned gateway between Sint Antoniesbreestraat 130 and 132 to find the Zuiderkerk (South Church), scaling the tower of which allows more energetic tourists to survey the whole scene.

Crossing the bridge at the end of Sint Antoniesbreestraat will lead you to the **Rembrandthuis**. Immediately before this, however, are steps to the **Waterlooplein** flea-market, dominated by the Stadhuis-Muziektheater (the City Hall-Music Theatre). Also close at hand are the **Joods Historisch Museum (Jewish Historical Museum)** and **Hermitage aan de Amstel**.

The largely residential Plantage area lies south-east of Mr Visserplein and is reached via Muiderstraat. The attractive Plantage Middenlaan winds past the **Hortus Botanicus**, passes near the **Verzetsmuseum (Museum of Dutch Resistance)**, and along the edge of zoo **Artis** towards the **Tropenmuseum**.

Jews began to settle here over 200 years ago, and the area was soon redeveloped on 19th-century diamond money. The Plantage is

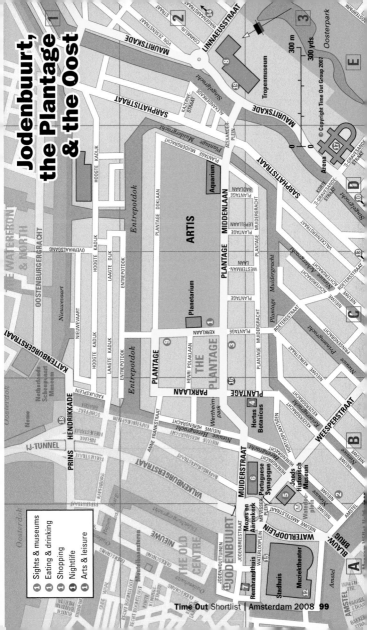

Jodenbuurt, the Plantage & the Oost

Key
- ● Sights & museums
- ● Eating & drinking
- ● Shopping
- ● Nightlife
- ● Arts & leisure

© Copyright Time Out Group 2007

300 m
300 yds

Time Out Shortlist | Amsterdam 2008 **99**

still wealthy, with eminent graceful buildings and tree-lined streets, although its inherent charm has sadly somewhat faded over the years. The area has seen extensive redevelopment, which continues as witnessed along Entrepotdok, where post-hippie houseboats and views of Artis provide a charming contrast to the apartment buildings.

Further south of Mauritskade is Amsterdam Oost (East), where the Arena hotel complex is located on the edge of Oosterpark. Disaster tourists take note: near the corner of Oosterpark and Linneaustraat is the spot where film-maker Theo van Gogh was brutally murdered by an Islamic extremist in 2004 after making a film deemed to be offensive to Muslims. A sculpture in Oosterpark, The Scream, was unveiled in 2007 in his memory.

Sights & museums

Ajax Museum

ArenA Boulevard 29, Amsterdam Zuidoost (311 1336/www.amsterdam arena.nl). Metro Strandvliet or Metro/ NS rail Bijlmer. **Open** 10am-5pm daily. **Admission** museum €3.50; including tour from €8.50.
Great for football fans of all ages, this museum covers the rich history of the club, offering photographs, memorabilia, trophies and videos documenting their greatest players and triumphs.

Artis

Plantage Kerklaan 38-40 (523 3400/ www.artis.nl). Tram 6, 9, 14. **Open** *Summer* 9am-6pm daily. *Winter* 9am-5pm daily. **Admission** €17.50; €16.50 over-65s; €14 4s-11s; free under-4s. No credit cards. **Map** p99 C2 ❶
The first zoo in mainland Europe (and the third oldest in the world) provides a great day out for children and adults. Along with the usual animals, Artis has an indoor 'rainforest' for nocturnal creatures and a 120-year-old aquarium that includes a simulated Amsterdam canal (the main difference is that the

clear water improves your chances of spotting the eels). Yet further extras include savannah land, a geological museum, a zoological museum, an aquarium and, for kids, a petting zoo and playgrounds. A new butterfly greenhouse has also recently opened to set hearts of all ages aflutter.

Hermitage aan de Amstel

Gebouw Neerlandia, Nieuwe Herengracht 14 (530 8751/www.hermitage.nl). Tram 9, 14/Metro Waterlooplein. **Open** 10am-5pm daily. **Admission** €7; €5.60 over-65s; free under-16s, MK. No credit cards. **Map** p99 B3 ❷
Partly opened in 2004 and due for completion in 2008, this 19th-century building is an outpost of the State Hermitage Museum in St Petersburg, the riches of which owe much to the collecting obsession of Peter the Great (1672-1725). Peter himself first came to Amsterdam to learn shipbuilding and how to build a city on a bog – the latter knowledge was applied to his pet project, St Petersburg – and while here he also bought the entire anatomical collection of Dr Frederik Ruysch, perhaps the greatest ever anatomist and preserver of body bits and bobs. With luck, some of Peter's own souvenirs – including Rembrandts – will return for a visit, but so far the collection is focused on Greek jewellery, the last Tsar and Tsarina, Nicolas and Alexandra, and Persian treasures.

Hollandse Schouwburg

Plantage Middenlaan 24 (531 0340/ www.hollandscheschouwburg.nl). Tram 6, 9, 14. **Open** 11am-4pm daily. **Admission** free. **Map** p99 C2 ❸
In 1942, this grand theatre became a main point of assembly for between 60,000 and 80,000 of the city's Jews before they were taken to the transit camp at Westerbork. It's now a monument with a small but very impressive exhibition and a memorial hall displaying 6,700 surnames by way of tribute to the 104,000 Dutch Jews who were exterminated. The façade has been left intact, with most of the inner structure removed to make way for a memorial.

Waterlooplein p109

Hortus Botanicus

Plantage Middenlaan 2A (625 9021/ www.dehortus.nl). Tram 9, 14/Metro Waterlooplein. **Open** *Jan, Dec* 9am-4pm Mon-Fri; 10am-4pm Sat, Sun. *Feb-June, Sept-Nov* 9am-5pm Mon-Fri; 10am-5pm Sat, Sun. *Jul, Aug* 9am-9pm Mon-Fri; 10am-9pm Sat, Sun. **Admission** €6; €3 5s-14s; free under-5s. No credit cards. **Map** p99 B3 ❹

The Hortus has been here since 1682, although it was originally set up more than 50 years earlier when East India Company ships brought back tropical plants and seeds originally intended to supply doctors with medicinal herbs. Some of those same specimens (which include the oldest potted plant in the world, a 300-year-old cycad) are still here on display in the stunning palm greenhouse – which itself dates from 1912 – while three other greenhouses between themselves maintain desert, tropical and subtropical climates. Green-fingered fun for all the family.

Joods Historisch Museum (Jewish Historical Museum)

Nieuwe Amstelstraat 1 (531 0310/www. jhm.nl). Tram 9, 14/Metro Waterlooplein. **Open** 11am-5pm daily. Closed Jewish New Year and Yom Kippur. **Admission** €7.50; €4.50 over-65s, students; €3 13s-17s; free under-12s, MK. No credit cards. **Map** p99 B3 ❺

Housed since 1987 in four erstwhile synagogues in the old Jewish quarter, the Jewish Historical Museum is full of religious items, photographs and paintings detailing the rich history of Jews and Judaism inside the Netherlands. A recent revamping has created more warmth and a sense of the personal in its permanent displays, which concentrate on religious practice and Dutch Jewish culture; among the exhibits is the painted autobiography of Jewish artist Charlotte Salomon, tragically killed at Auschwitz aged 26.

Oosterpark p100

Portuguese Synagogue

Mr Visserplein 3 (624 5351/guided tours 531 0380/www.esnoga.com). Tram 4, 9, 14, 20. **Open** *Jan-Mar, Nov, Dec* 10am-4pm Mon-Thur, Sun; 10am-2pm Fri. *Apr-Oct* 10am-4pm Mon-Fri, Sun. Closed Yom Kippur. **Admission** €6.50; €5 over-65s; €4 10s-17s; free under-10s. No credit cards. **Map** p99 B3 ⑥

Architect Elias Bouwman's mammoth synagogue, one of the largest in the world and reputedly inspired by the Temple of Solomon, was inaugurated in 1675. It's built on wooden piles and is surrounded by smaller annexes (offices, archives, the rabbinate and one of the oldest libraries anywhere in the world). Renovation in the late 1950s restored the synagogue well and the low-key tours are very interesting.

Rembrandthuis

Jodenbreestraat 4 (520 0400/www. rembrandthuis.nl). Tram 9, 14/Metro Waterlooplein. **Open** 10am-5pm daily **Admission** €8; €5.50 students; €1.50 6s-16s; free under-6s, MK. **Map** p99 A2/3 ⑦

You can't help but admire the skill and effort with which craftsmen have tried to re-create this house, bought by Rembrandt in 1639 for ƒ13,000 (around €6,000), a massive sum at the time, and occupied by the artist until bankruptcy forced him to move out in 1656. The presentation is, however, dry and unengaging on the whole. Nagging at you all the time is the knowledge that this isn't really Rembrandt's house, but rather a mock-up of it – which lends an unreal air that is only relieved when guest artists are allowed to use the studio. There's a remarkable collection of Rembrandt's etchings, which show him at his most experimental, but if it's his paintings you're after then make for the Rijksmuseum (see p130).

Tropenmuseum

Linnaeusstraat 2 (568 8200/www. tropenmuseum.nl). Tram 9, 14/bus 22. **Open** 10am-5pm daily. **Admission** €7.50; €6 students, over-65s; €4 6s-17s; free under-6s, MK. **Map** p99 E2 ⑧

Brewing up a storm

The art of brewing runs through Amsterdam's history like alcohol itself does through the human bloodstream, keeping the city's nightlife pumping and vital from as far back as the early 1300s, when hops were first brought to the country from abroad.

As the centuries passed and the local population swelled, the city water became undrinkable. The only way to then revitalise the supply again was to convert it into ale – hence the 17th and 18th centuries' Brouwersgracht ('brewer's canal'). Next up was **Heineken** (p140), invented locally in 1884 and brewed in the city until the 1980s, after which its departure reduced the number of local brewers to a handful. The best known of these is **'t IJ** (p105); free brewery tours take place every Friday at 4pm, and the in-house brews include Zatte, Struis and Columbus.

The **Bekeerde Suster** (p57) is lined with shimmering copper vats and once again allows real aficionados to take tours, while amateurs can sample the house *witbier* and blonde. Elsewhere, brewery-with-a-conscience **De Prael** (www.deprael.nl), is run by a mentally disabled staff and produces beers named after various local singers.

All the local breweries also brew versions of seasonal bock beers, which kick like the deer they're named after. Try them at the **Bock Bier Festival**, held at the Beurs van Berlage every last weekend of October (p33).

Visitors to this handsome building get a vivid glimpse of daily life in the tropical and subtropical parts of the world (a strange evolution for a museum originally erected in the 1920s to glorify Dutch colonialism). Exhibits – from religious items and jewellery to washing powder and vehicles – are divided by region and broad in their catchment. A musical display allows visitors to hear a variety of traditional instruments at the mere push of a button; the walk-through environments include simulated North African and South Asian villages and a Manilan street; and a Latin American exhibit is highlighted by a fun room complete with videos of sporting highlights and a jukebox pumping out tunes.

Verzetsmuseum (Museum of Dutch Resistance)

Plantage Kerklaan 61 (620 2535/www. verzetsmuseum.org). Tram 6, 9, 14. **Open** noon-5pm Mon, Sat, Sun; 10am-5pm Tue-Fri. **Admission** €5.50; €3 7s-16s; free under-6s, MK. No credit cards. **Map** p99 C2 ⑨

The Verzetsmuseum tells the moving story of the Dutch Resistance through a wealth of artefacts: false ID papers, clandestine printing presses and illegal newspapers, spy gadgets and an authentic secret door behind which Jews hid. The exhibits all help to explain the ways people in the Netherlands faced up to and dealt with the Nazi occupation, its disparate exhibits linked by personal testimonies from those who lived through the war. Regular temporary shows explore wartime themes and modern-day forms of oppression, and there's a small research room too.

Eating & drinking

Amstelhaven

Mauritskade 1 (665 2672/www.amstel haven.nl) Tram 3/Metro Weesperplein. **Open** 4pm-1am Mon-Thur, Sun; 4pm-3am Fri, Sat. **Bar. Map** p99 D3 ⑩

Occupying a prime spot on an arterial canal of the Amstel, this bar's cavernous insides are filled with yuppies chowing down posh Dutch food and grooving to weekend DJs. But that's

not the point. Amstelhaven's raison d'être is summer days spent sprawled on the vast deck's sofas and beanbags, watching boats bob as staff serve the resident salty dogs in situ.

Brouwerij 't IJ
Funenkade 7 (320 1786/www.brouwerij hetij.nl). Tram 6, 10. **Open** 3-8pm Wed-Sun. **Bar**.

The famous tasting house at the base of the Gooyer windmill, where wares from award-winning local brewery 't IJ can be sampled. Inside is bare (still retaining the look of the municipal baths it once was) and seating minimal, so if weather permits, plonk down on the pavement outside. Their standard range of tipples is always available for sampling behind the bar, from pale Plzen to the darker, head-poppingly strong brew known as Columbus.

Café de Sluyswacht
Jodenbreestraat 1 (625 7611/http:// sluyswacht.nl). Tram 9, 14/Metro Waterlooplein. **Open** 11.30am-1am Mon-Thur; 11.30am-3am Fri, Sat; 11.30am-7pm Sun. **Bar**. **Map** p99 A2 ⑪

Listing crazily, this wooden-framed bar has been pleasing drinkers for decades, though the building itself has been around since 1695, when it began life as a lock-keeper's cottage. Inside it's snuggly and warm, while outside commands great views of Oude Schans.

Dantzig
Zwanenburgwal 15 (620 9039). Tram 9, 14/Metro Waterlooplein. **Open** 9am-10pm Mon-Thur; 9am-1am Fri, Sat; 10am-10pm Sun. **Café**. **Map** p99 A3 ⑫

The grandness of this vast café on the corner of the Stopera complex belies the fact that it's modern: velvet drapes, Chesterfields and faux oil paintings give the feel of a gentleman's club. The terrace has river views and it's handy after the Waterlooplein fleamarket or before a concert at the Muziektheater.

Dauphine
NEW *Prins Bernardplein 175 (462 1646/www.caferestaurantdauphine.nl). Tram 9/bus 59, 69.* **Open** 10am-midnight Mon-Thur, Sun; 10am-1am Fri, Sat. €€€€. **French**.

This newcomer is located in a former Renault showroom and oozes old school modernism in terms of both design and dining. Indulge in a menu packed with French bistro classics – from seriously swanky burgers to lobster – for breakfast, lunch or dinner.

Hesp

Weesperzijde 130-131(665 1202/www. cafehesp.nl). Tram 12. **Open** 10am-1am Mon-Thur; 10am-2am Fri, Sat; 11am-1am Sun. **Café**.

Hesp has occupied a lovely site on the river near Amstel station for 110 years, offering all the joys of an old-fashioned boozer but moving with the times. The wine list is longer than most bars', the snacks classy and classic (wasabi sits alongside mustard) and entertainment ranges from big bands to latin to lindyhop. In summer, the atmosphere gets boosted when the huge waterside terrace is lit by life-sized electric palm trees.

De Hogesluis

Sarphatistraat 23 (624 1521/www. hogesluis.nl) Tram 3/Metro Weesperplein. **Open** 11am-1am Mon-Sat; 11am-midnight Sun. **Bar**. Map p99 C3 ⑬

From the Taittinger poster and the glowing fittings to the midnight-blue leather seats, this place oozes understated class, though it's not in the least bit snooty and welcomes visitors of all ages and inclinations. Half of the large space overlooking the river is given over to a (pricey) restaurant, but it's best used as the perfect spot for a sly sundowner in the summer months.

De Kas

Kamerlingh Onneslaan 3 (462 4562/ www.restaurantdekas.nl). Tram 9/bus 59, 69. **Open** noon-2pm, 6.30-10pm Mon-Fri; 6.30-10pm Sat. **€€€€**. **Global**.

In Frankendael Park, way out east, is a renovated 1926 greenhouse. It's now a posh and peaceful restaurant that inspires much fevered talk among local foodies. Its international menu changes on a daily basis, and depends on whatever fresh ingredients have been most recently harvested.

Shopping

Dappermarkt

Dapperstraat (no phone). Tram 3, 6, 10 14. **Open** 9am-4pm Mon-Sat. No credit cards. Map p99 E2 ⑭

Portuguese Synagogue p103

Songs in the key of life

Amsterdam Roots

Question: what do artists Youssou N'Dour, Goran Bregovic, Souad Massi, Zap Mama, Ozomatli, Baka Beyond and Ravi Shankar have in common? Answer: they are all world music stars and they have all played at **Amsterdam Roots** (www.amsterdamroots.nl).

The festival is a celebration of world culture and music; one where the forces of the Concertgebouw, Melkweg, Tropentheater and the Paradiso band together every June to mount more than 50 concerts. The climax of the whole thing is Roots Open Air, which sees the Oosterpark transform a Sunday afternoon into a collection of 'villages' full of free performances. Six stages, over 50 local and global acts and around 55,000 city dwellers from all walks of life come together to enjoy the vibes.

World music enthusiasts should also think about taking the hour or so train trip to Park Brakkenstein

in Nijmegen during the first weekend of every June for **Music Meeting** (www.musicmeeting.nl), another cutting-edge WOMAD festival of sorts that has always prided itself on bringing together future taste-definers from around the world. Besides seeing such major musical players as Toumani Diabaté's Symmetric Orchestra, Béla Fleck, Manu Dibango, Trio Mocoto and Balkan Beat Box, visitors might witness Maori songs mixed with wild electro beats (Wai), an accordion quintet whose five nationalities include a blind Austrian who knows his way with Mongolian throat singing sounds (Accordion Tribe), or even a Cuban lumberjack taking music to new and more brazenly flirtatious heights (the late Polo Montañez).

Both Amsterdam Roots and Music Meeting can be seen as refresher courses in all that is good in the world. While other major festivals often raise hackles about how a useful definition like 'crossover' has been appropriated to narrowly describe a generation of dread-locked white kids jumping up and down, volunteer-driven festivals like Amsterdam Roots and Music Meeting – both of which have been doing the good work and spreading the best music for more than two decades – also act as a necessary reminder that when different good things are put together, it often results in ... err, *gooder* things. Either way, thanks to these awesome initiatives, the term 'globalisation' may slowly become less about economic and political irregularities and more about embracing all the potential positives of a world in harmony.

Brouwerij 't IJ p105

Dappermarkt is a locals' market, which means that prices don't rise to match the number of visitors in attendance. It sells all the usual market fodder, plus plenty of cheap clothes.

Waterlooplein

Waterlooplein. Tram 9, 14, 20/Metro Waterlooplein. **Open** 9am-5.30pm Mon-Fri; 8.30am-5.30pm Sat. No credit cards. **Map** p99 A3 ⑮

Amsterdam's top bazaar is basically a huge fleamarket with the added attraction of loads of brand new clothes stalls (though gear can be a bit pricey and, at many stalls, a bit naff). Bargains can be found, but they may be hidden under cheap 'n' nasty toasters and down-at-heel (literally) shoes.

Nightlife

Club 3VOOR12

Studio Desmet, Plantage Middenlaan 4A (035 671 2222/www.3voor12.nl). Tram 9, 14. **Open** *Airs between* 9pm-1am Wed. **Admission** free. **Map** p99 B2 ⑯

This old film theatre bursts into life on Wednesday nights to coincide with a live national radio and TV show. Each broadcast throws up a diverse line-up – one week it's three little-known local acts, the next it's international superstars in town for their sold-out gig. Entry is free, but there's limited capacity, so you must email club3VOOR12@vpro.nl to reserve a place. The catch is not necessarily knowing who you're signing up for, which – needless to say – can work both for or against you.

Hotel Arena

's Gravesandestraat 51 (850 2420/www. hotelarena.nl). Tram 3, 6, 7, 10. **Open** 10pm-4am Fri-Sun. No credit cards.

Once an orphanage, then a youth hostel, now finally finding its feet as a trendy hotel, bar and restaurant. Big city folk already used to trekking long distances will no doubt laugh in the face of its (relative lack of) accessibility, but Amsterdammers tend to forego the small detour eastwards, making it hard

for the Arena to truly kick clubbing butt. That said, monthlies like Salsa Lounge, with its funky Latin bias, provide notable exceptions.

Arts & leisure

Ajax

Amsterdam ArenA, Arena Boulevard 29, Amsterdam Zuidoost (311 1444/ www.ajax.nl). Metro Strandvliet or Metro/NS rail Bijlmer. **Map** p99 D3 ⑰

The country's most famous football club is renowned worldwide for flair on the field and its excellent youth training programme. Battles with main rivals Feyenoord and PSV are fought fiercely each season in the gladiatorial ArenA – and sometimes out of it (see 'hooligans'). Pre-season in July, some of the world's biggest teams are invited to come and take part in the hugely popular Amsterdam Tournament.

ARCAM

Prins Hendrikkade 600 (620 4878/ www.arcam.nl). Tram 9, 14/Metro Waterlooplein/bus 42, 43. **Open** 1-5pm Tue-Sat. **Admission** free. No credit cards. **Map** p99 B1 ⑱

The gallery here at the Architecture Centrum Amsterdam is completely obsessed with the promotion of Dutch contemporary architecture – from the early 20th-century creations of the world-famous Amsterdam School to more modern designs – and as a result organises a wide range of tours, forums, lectures and exhibitions in its fresh new 'silver snail' location.

KIT Tropentheater

Kleine Zaal Linnaeusstraat 2; Grote Zaal Mauritskade 63 (568 8500/www. tropentheater.nl). Tram 7, 9, 10, 14/ bus 22. **Map** p99 E2 ⑲

The Tropeninstituut, next door to the Tropenmuseum (p103), organises performances in both music and dance that are related to various non-Western cultures. The dance programme varies from classical Indian to South African and Indonesian, but always offers shows that are at once engaging and culturally very enlightening.

Post CS

The Waterfront & North

Amsterdam's historic wealth owes a lot to the city waterfront, for it was here that goods were unloaded, weighed and prepared for storage in the warehouses still found locally. At the time, the harbour and its arterial canals formed a whole with the city itself. A drop in commerce slowly unbalanced this unity and the construction of Centraal Station in the late 19th century served as the final psychological cleavage. This neo-Gothic monument to modernity blocked both the city's view of the harbour and its own past.

Today, the area is about moving forward (see itinerary p44). One recent cultural success story was the massive reinvention of Post CS (Oosterdokskade 5), the former post office building just east of Centraal Station (CS). While the surrounding area is being made into a home for the city's music conservatory, the country's largest library and a whole mess of shops and hip hotels, Post CS has been tasked with serving as temporary home until mid 2008 for the Stedelijk Museum of Modern Art, **Mediamatic**, trendy club-restaurant **11** and other creative enterprises.

Directly south of Post CS, the Schreierstoren or 'Weeping Tower' is by far the most interesting relic of Amsterdam's medieval city wall. Built in 1487, it was from this point, on 4 April 1609, that Henry Hudson departed in search of shorter trade routes to the Far East, and in failing discovering New Amsterdam, which

The Waterfront

- Sights & museums
- Eating & drinking
- Shopping
- Nightlife
- Arts & leisure

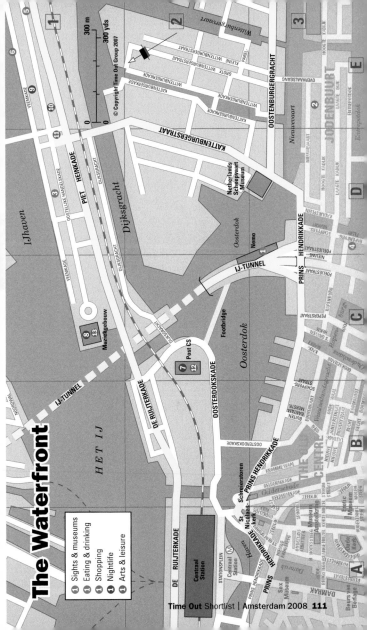

© Copyright Time Out Group 2007

300 m
300 yds

HET IJ

IJhaven

PIET HEINKADE

OOSTELIJKE HANDELSKADE

VEEMKADE

DIJKSGRACHT

Dijksgracht

Muziekgebouw

IJ-TUNNEL

DE RUIJTERKADE

OOSTERDOKSKADE

OOSTERDOKSKADE

Oosterdok

Footbridge

Post CS

Nemo

IJ-TUNNEL

KATTENBURGERSTRAAT

KATTENBURGERKADE

GROTE WITTENBURGERSTRAAT
KLEINE WITTENBURGERSTRAAT
PAREL
WITTENBURGERKADE

WITTENBURGERGRACHT

Witlenburgervaart

OOSTENBURGERGRACHT

Netherlands
Scheepvaart
Museum

Oosterdok

Nieuwevaart

JODENBUURT

OVERHAALSGANG

PRINS HENDRIKKADE

PRINS HENDRIKKADE

NIEUWE
FOELIESTRAAT

FOELIESTRAAT

PEPERSTRAAT

SCHIPPERS-
STRAAT

BUITEN
BANTAM-
MERSTR

Schreierstoren

St
Nicolaas
kerk

Museum
Amstelkring

Erotic
Museum

Sex
Museum

THE
OLD
CENTRE

Haven

Central
Station

STATIONSPLEIN

Centraal
Station

DE RUIJTERKADE

PRINS HENDRIKKADE

DAMRAK

Beurs van
Berlage

later became known as Manhattan. Another eye-opener along the way is the Renzo Piano designed **Nemo**, a science museum whose green building dominates the horizon. It dwarfs the silver shell-shaped ARCAM architecture gallery and the nautically inclined and grand Nederlands Scheepvaartmuseum, currently closed until 2009.

Sights & museums

Nemo
Oosterdok 2 (531 3233/www.e-nemo.nl). Bus 22, 42. **Open** 10am-5pm Tue-Sun (daily in school holidays). **Admission** €11.50; €6.50 students; free under-3s. **Map** p111 D3 ❶

Nemo opened in 1998 and has gone from strength to strength as a kid-friendly science museum. It eschews exhibits in favour of hands-on trickery, gadgetry and tomfoolery (in English and Dutch): you can play DNA detective games, blow mega soap bubbles or explode things in a 'wonderlab'. On top of that, Renzo Piano's mammoth structure (resembling a green ship rising from the water) never fails to raise a gasp from people seeing it for the first time. The outdoor café at the top is a lovely place to while away an afternoon reading and relaxing.

Werf 't Kromhout
Hoogte Kadijk 147 (627 6777/ www.machinekamer.nl/museum). Bus 22, 26. **Open** 10am-3pm Tue. **Admission** €4.50; €2.75 under-15s. **Map** p111 E3 ❷

A nostalgic museum, full of old, silent ship engines and the proper tools for their construction. The shipyard is proud of the fact that it's the oldest remaining original yard still in use, but its 18th-century heritage is no longer very apparent, nor is the yard itself especially active nowadays.

Eating & drinking

Bickers aan de Werf
[NEW] *Bickerswerf 2 (320 2951/www. bickersaandewerf.nl). Tram 3.* **Open** noon-1am Wed-Sun. **Bar**.

The western islands feel like a secluded retreat from the city's bustle, and this modern glass cube is great for a break after aimless exploring. Food ranges from a slice of sponge cake to caviar; coffee becomes an indulgence with a side order of truffles from Jordino. The drinks menu is also outstanding: Japanese iKi beer alongside plenty of specialist whiskies and wines.

Blijburg
Bert Haanstrakade 2004 (416 0330/ www.blijburg.nl). Tram 26/bus 326. **Open** *Summer* 10am-10pm daily. *Winter* 2-10pm Thur, Fri; noon-10pm Sat; 10am-10pm Sun. €€€. No credit cards. **Global**.

Being 25 kilometres (15 miles) from the sea, Amsterdam was hardly anyone's choice for a beach holiday until sand was tipped on to the artificial islands of IJburg, where 45,000 people will eventually come to live. While construction continues, the restaurant/bar Blijburg – which has a regular programme of barbecues, bands and DJs – is on hand to cater to your eating/drinking whims.

Fifteen
Jollemanhof 9 (0900 343 8336/www. fifteen.nl). Tram 16, 26. **Open** noon-1am daily. €€€€. **Global**. No credit cards. **Map** p111 D1 ❸

While Jamie Oliver has only found one gap in his hectic schedule to visit the Amsterdam outpost of his food-based empire, this culinary franchise of sorts – complete with a TV show that documented the transformation of challenged street kids into a well-oiled kitchen brigade – is inspired by his love for dishes honest and fresh. That said, the waterfront location is marred by the graffiti and the fact that there's only one set menu. It's also truly cheeky having a premium rate number as the only telephone contact.

Hotel De Goudfazant
[NEW] *Aambeeldstraat 10H (636 5170/www.hoteldegoudfazant.nl). Ferry from Centraal Station.* **Open** 6pm-1am Tue-Sun. €€€. **Global**.

Deep in the north and yet deeper within a former warehouse, this is the post-industrial dining experience at its atmospheric best. Yes it's all about location, but there's also some genuinely excellent and relatively affordable cookery going down, from fine French food to delicate pizzas.

Kilimanjaro

Rapenburgerplein 6 (622 3485). Bus 22, 43. **Open** 5-10pm Tue-Sun. €€€. **African**. Map p111 D3 ❹
This relaxed and friendly pan-African eaterie offers a reliable assortment of traditional recipes from Senegal, the Ivory Coast, Tanzania and Ethiopia. Once you've eaten your way from the east all the way through to the west coast of Africa, you'll probably need some swift refreshment in the cooling form of fruity cocktails and seriously strong regional beers.

Koffiehuis KHL

Oostelijke Handelskade 44 (779 1575/ www.khl.nl). Tram 25, 26. **Open** noon-midnight Tue, Sun; 10am-midnight Wed, Thur; 10am-2am Fri; noon-2am Sat. No credit cards. **Bar**. Map p111 E1 ❺
This beautiful, light-flooded interior harks back to the days in the early 20th century when it was a canteen serving staff of the Royal Holland Lloyd shipping line. Now it's a café-cum-meeting space serving the local community, with plenty to attract new visitors. There is art on the walls and regular live music for lifting spirits.

Odessa

Veemkade 259 (419 3010/www.de-odessa.nl). Tram 10, 26/bus 26. **Open** 4pm-1am Wed, Thurs, Sun; 4pm-3am Fri, Sat. €€€. **Global**. Map p111 E1 ❻
More dedicated trendsters regularly make the trek to the unlikely environs of an old Ukrainian fishing boat for Odessa's fusion food and tastefully revamped interior – the vibe is 1970s James Bond filtered through a modern lounge sensibility. On warmer nights, dine on the lit deck. DJs raise the tempo by spinning party tunes from 10pm on weekend evenings.

Onassis

NEW *Westerdoksdijk 40 (330 0456/ www.onassisamsterdam.nl).* Tram 3. **Open** noon-1am Mon-Thur, Sun; noon-3am Fri, Sat. **Bar**.
Sleek lines, burnished mahogany, banquettes and voluptuous lounge decks: all create the mood of a yacht fit for a Greek shipping magnate. You'll also need the wealth of one to properly enjoy this place, with lunchtime sandwiches averaging in at €8.50. Best enjoyed as a bar (it's also a restaurant and club), plus in summer a team of in-house masseurs are on hand to ease away that executive stress.

Ot en Sien

Buiksloterweg 27 (636 8233/www.oten sien.nl). Ferry from Centraal Station. **Open** noon-1am Mon-Thur, Sun; noon-3am Fri, Sat. No credit cards. **Bar**.
Just a short ferry hop from Centraal Station, this little bar feels like it's miles away in the heart of the countryside. There are no pretentions here, just friendly service and a fantastic range of Dutch and Belgian beers to get more discerning drinkers sozzled, including a mighty La Trappe Quadrupel and Bourgogne des Flandres.

Pont 13

NEW *Stravangerweg 891 (770 2722/ www.pont13.nl).* Bus 22. **Open** 5-10pm Tue-Sat; 1-10pm Sun. €€€. **Global**.
This renovated old ferry in the western havens – within a neighbourhood of students living in revamped shipping containers – is all-round intriguing if a bit out of the way. Simple, hearty fare prepared with genuine flair.

Wilhelmina-Dok

Noordwal 1 (632 3701/www.wilhelmina-dok.nl). Ferry from Centraal Station. **Open** 11am-midnight daily. €€€. **Mediterranean**.
Through the large windows of this cubic building you get great views of the eastern docklands. Come for soup and sandwiches by day and a daily menu of Mediterranean dishes by night. DJs, a terrace and an open-air cinema spice the place up in summer.

Noord is the word

There was a time when Amsterdam North was right off the map. Even in centuries past, the land on the other side of that big, watery body called the IJ was known as little more than the spot where the remains of freshly executed criminals were hung for public display. Once that practice was stopped, there was really very little of interest to pull short-term visitors northwards – except perhaps cycling routes towards such scenic fishing villages as Volendam and Marken, or the trip on the free ferry from the back of Centraal Station, the latter always good for 20 minutes of seafaring fun. But with the building of the Noord-Zuidlijn metro link (pictured) that will unite this once isolated area with the rest of Amsterdam, and the accompanying (and suitably ambitious) redevelopment plans, things are set to change.

Already the cultural breeding ground of **Kinetic Noord**, located in the former shipping yard NDSM (p117), is by far the largest in the country, with over a hundred artist studios, a skate hall and a whole slew of singular spaces. It sports a wonderful post-apocalyptic vibe that's ideal for parties, concerts and wacky theatre festivals like **Over het IJ** (p36) and **Robodock** (p32). It's got a surrounding district of student container dwellings, a 'clean energy' exhibition, a great restaurant and café (www.noord erlichtcafe.nl), and boasts regular visits from the alternative party boat **Stubnitz** (www.stubnitz.com), an inspired floating zone that books bands, DJs and artists.

And now this new ground zero for Dutch subculture is also home to the Benelux headquarters of MTV networks, which moved into a wildly revamped former woodwork factory in 2007. It's the hope of the powers-that-be to reinvigorate Amsterdam as a 'creative capital' – that MTV and the other similarly commercially oriented creative industries currently setting up shop will cross-fertilise with the more squat-edged original artistic denizens. They also hope that much inspiration and money will be made by all – but as far as that goes, only time will tell.

Shopping

Pols Potten

KNSM-laan 39 (419 3541/www.
polspotten.nl). Tram 10, 26. **Open**
10am-6pm Tue-Fri; 10am-5pm Sat;
noon-5pm Sun.

'Pol's Pots'. Quite why a shop stocking
innovative furnishings and domestic
accessories should wish to associate
itself with one of history's most notorious mass murderers remains a mystery, but it does have lots of pots, plus
a design team to help you catch the
latest trends while they're hot.

Nightlife

11

Post CS building, Oosterdokskade
3-5 (638 9901/www.mediamatic.net).
Tram 16. **Open** 10pm-4am Fri, Sat.
No credit cards. **Map** p111 C2 ⑦

Scheduled for demolition in 2008, the
industrial building hosting 'temporary' club 11 has most likely been
saved by the success of the club itself,
as well as its adjoining restaurant,
offices and gallery. Home to Joost van
Bellen and his rock 'n' rave evening
Rauw, 11 also boasts the finest in techno, electro and minimal music, pre-
senting both top DJs and cutting-edge
music producers every week.

Bimhuis

Piet Heinkade 3 (788 2188/www.bim
huis.nl). **Open** *Telephone reservations*
noon-7pm Mon-Fri. *Box office* 7-11pm
show nights; most shows start 9pm.
Map p111 C1 ⑧

The name Bimhuis is familiar to jazz
fans the world over, and musicians
queue up for a chance to grace its
stage. Even its transplant to a bizarre
glass box jutting oddly out of the
Muziekgebouw complex (p117) hasn't
tarnished its reputation. Instead, the
eye-catching building and familiar
interior layout have provided the
Bimhuis with a healthy future.

Student sea container housing

Café Pakhuis Wilhelmina

Veemkade 576 (419 3368/www.cafe pakhuiswilhelmina.nl). Tram 26. **Open** hours vary Wed-Sun. No credit cards. **Map** p111 E1 ❾

Wilhelmina is still often overlooked by casual clubbers. Is it the club's IJ location? The absence of bouncers? Or the bottles of beer for only €2? Regardless, don't miss it if your heart lies with today's leftfield music scene. Professor Nomad does weekly improv and theme nights, Ichi One drops dubstep and filthy drum 'n' bass, and the eRRorKREW brings the underground bubbling to the surface.

Panama

Oostelijke Handelskade 4 (311 8686/ www.panama.nl). Tram 26. **Open** 9pm-3am Thur, Sun; 9pm-4am Fri, Sat. **Map** 111 E1 ❿

An increasing force in the Amsterdam nightlife, restaurant/theatre/nightclub Panama overlooks the IJ in one of the city's most booming areas. Monthly Rush and Bold evenings bring the best in national DJs, while enormous international artists such as Danny Howells and Sander Kleinenberg also find their way here. On Sunday, bring your kids to an intimate concert by the likes of Ellen ten Damme.

Arts & leisure

Galerie Paul Andriesse

Withoedenveem 8 (623 6237/www. galeries.nl/andriesse). Tram 13, 14, 17. No credit cards. **Map** p111 D1 ⓫

Recently relocated, the Galerie Paul Andriesse may no longer be all that innovative, but there's still a very selective savvy at work that embraces both older and wiser artists (Marlene Dumas often shows new works here) and up-and-coming names such as Rineke Dijkstra, Hellen van Meene, Thomas Struth and Jan van de Pavert.

Mediamatic

Post CS building, Oosterdokskade 3-5 (638 9901/www.mediamatic.net). Centraal Station then 10min walk. **Open** varies. No credit cards. **Map** p311 C2 ⓬

This bleeding-edge organisation dedicated to the outer reaches of technology and multimedia is now housed in the happening Post CS building and has an exhibition space on the ground floor. Also poke your head in on their neighbours, Horse Move Project Space (www.horsemove.nl), where exhibiting artists choose the ones to follow them.

Muziekgebouw

Piet Heinkade 1 (788 2010/tickets 788 2000/www.muziekgebouw.nl). Tram 16, 26. **Map** p111 C1 ⓭

Designed by noted Danish architects 3xNielsen, this is one of the most innovative musical complexes in Europe, befitting of previous incarnation the IJsbreker's long-lasting ethos to promote modern variants of classical, jazz and world music. Never afraid to take risks, its weekly schedule typically bustles with delights, from cutting-edge multimedia works to celebrations of composers from the last 150 years.

NDSM

TT Neveritaweg 15 (330 5480/www. ndsm.nl). Ferry from Centraal Station/ bus 35, 94.

NDSM was a shipbuilding yard at the beginning of the last century. Today it's a cultural complex that's yet to be completed, something that is rather in step with the constantly mutating needs of Amsterdam's vibrant artistic community. Apart from two stages (one of which is to be made completely out of recycled materials), the facility has a more general function in serving as a 'breeding ground' for artists. Small-scale workshops and performances are held almost daily in the studios here.

Theater Fabriek Amsterdam

Czaar Peterstraat 213 (522 5260/www. theaterfabriekamsterdam.nl). Tram 10, 26/bus 42, 43. No credit cards.

In an old factory that originally built ship engines, Theater Fabriek organises big musical shows, popular operas and post-Cirque de Soleil-style performances for people who like a mix of avant-garde and spectacle.

Brouwersgracht

The Jordaan

The Jordaan area emerged when the city was extended in the 17th century, originally designated for the working classes and smelly industrial enterprises (although it also provided a haven for victims of religious persecution, such as Jews and Huguenots). But despite its working class associations, properties are now highly desirable, and while the residents are mainly fiercely proud, community-spirited Jordaaners, the nouveaux riches have moved in to yuppify the 'hood.

The Jordaan has no major sights; it's more of a place to just stumble across things. The area north of the shopping-dense Rozengracht, the Jordaan's approximate mid-point, is more interesting and picturesque, with the area to the south being more commercial. You will also stumble upon some of Amsterdam's

more unusual and interesting galleries peppered liberally around the area (see box p121).

Between scenic coffee breaks or decadent daytime beers, check out some of the specialist shops tucked away on these adorable side streets. Apart from the shops, many of the best of the outdoor markets are also found nearby: Monday morning's bargain-filled **Noordermarkt** and Saturday's organic foodie paradise **Boerenmarkt** are held around the **Noorderkerk**, the city's first Calvinist church, built in 1623. Adjacent to the Noordermarkt is the bargain-packed Westermarkt, while another general market fills Lindengracht on Saturdays.

Between Brouwersgracht and the blisteringly scenic Westelijk Eilanden, more quirky shopping opportunities can be found on

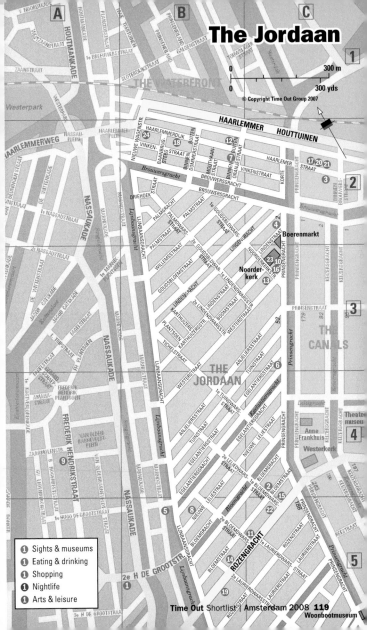

Haarlemmerstraat and its westerly extension Haarlemmerdijk, which is where you'll see Haarlemmerpoort city gate, built in 1840. Behind it is wanderful Westerpark, which in turn connects to the happening arts complex **Westergasfabriek**.

Eating & drinking

De Aardige Pers

NEW *2e Hugo de Grootstraat 13 (400 3107). Tram 10.* **Open** 1-11pm daily. **€€€**. No credit cards. **Iranian**. **Map** p119 B5 ❶
'The Nice Persian' sums it up. Iranian cuisine served up family style and with family warmth. *Fesenjoon* – chicken in a walnut and pomegranate sauce – is a house speciality, rich and delicious.

Amsterdam

Watertorenplein 6 (682 2666/www. cradam.nl). Tram 10. **Open** 10.30am-midnight Mon-Thur, Sun; 10.30am-1am Fri, Sat. **€€€**. **Dutch**.
This spacious monument to industry just west of the Jordaan pumped water from the coast's dunes for around a century. Now it pumps out honest Dutch and French dishes – from *krokketten* to caviar – under a mammoth ceiling and floodlighting rescued from the old Ajax stadium. A unique experience in a capital not known for its cuisine.

Café Chris

Bloemstraat 42 (624 5942/www.cafe chris.nl). Tram 13, 14, 17. **Open** 3pm-1am Mon-Thur; 3pm-2am Fri, Sat; 3pm-9pm Sun. No credit cards. **Bar**. **Map** p119 C4 ❷
Not much has changed since 1624 at the oldest bar in town, where builders from the Westerkerk would come to receive their pay after a hard day's graft. Local workers still come to unwind in unpretentious surroundings teeming with charming bric-a-brac.

Harlem

Haarlemmerstraat 77 (330 1498). Tram 3/bus 18, 22. **Open** 10am-1am Mon-Thur; 10am-3am Fri, Sat; 11am-1am Sun. No credit cards. **Bar**. **Map** p119 C2 ❸

A good-looking bar with friendly staff and a funky soundtrack. The house 'soul food' can be a little hit-and-miss in terms of quality (though it's always filling and reasonable), but drinking is as important here as eating.

Proust

Noordermarkt 4 (623 9145/www. goodfoodgroup.nl). Tram 1, 2, 5, 13, 17, 20. **Open** 9am-1am Mon; 5pm-1am Tue-Thur; noon-3am Fri; 9.30am-3am Sat; 11am-1am Sun. **Bar**. **Map** p119 C2 ❹
Still trendy after all these years, and great for market pit-stops or bar crawl kick-starts. Inside it's sleek and pared down in style – like the punters. If full, try heading over to Finch next door, which is cut from the same cloth; on warm days both bars' terraces merge into one convivial whole.

Semhar

Marnixstraat 259-261 (638 1634/www. semhar.nl). Tram 10. **Open** 4-10pm daily. **€€**. **African**. **Map** p119 B5 ❺

The frame game

Galerie Fons Welters

A person could easily fill up an entire holiday studying the many displays in the 40-odd galleries dotted around the Jordaan. Since they occupy places that were once homes or shops, none are big, and most specialise in just one medium – photography, for example, or modern Dutch art. Almost all sell works on display.

Rockarchive (110 Prinsengracht, 423 0489, www.rockarchive.com) is one of just four outlets (the others are in London and Dublin) owned by photographer Jill Furmanovsky. There's always a selection of iconic pictures showing from cameras of the calibre of Gered Mankowitz, Sheila Rock and the owner herself, and digital through to rare silver gelatine prints can be bought on site.

There are more high quality photos at **Gallery Vassie** (1e Tuindwarsstraat 16, 489 4042), run by an ex-V&A curator. Artists from Lee Miller to Antoni & Alison have been shown here, as well as unearthed treasures from the likes of photographer Walfred Moisio.

If you're feeling seriously flush, then head to the less well-known **Arthouse Marc Chagall** located at Bloemgracht 134 (330 7577, www.chagallkunst.com). So exclusive that it's only open for a few hours every day (noon-6pm Mon-Fri), it houses a collection of lithographs, graphic works and woodcuts by the Russian master, many of them signed.

Over at the opposite end of the spectrum is **KochxBos Gallery** (1e Anjeliersdwarsstraat 3, 681 4567, www.kochxbos.nl), which specialises in art from the dark, mean and dirty side – queasy surrealist Ray Caesar, whom they regularly show, is a case in point.

Other Jordaanese peddlers of more out-there art include the **Stedelijk Museum Bureau Amsterdam** (Rozenstraat 59, 422 0471, www.smba.nl), **Torch** (Lauriergracht 94, 626 0284, www.torchgallery.com), **Galerie Diana Stigter** (Hazenstraat 17, 624 2361, www.dianastigter.nl) and the **Galerie Fons Welters** (Bloemstraat 140, 423 3046, www.fonswelters.nl).

If you want to see the stuff being made rather than just ogling it, **Open Ateliers Jordaan** (www.openateliersjordaan.nl) offers a chance to poke your nose into more than 70 artists' studios.

AMSTERDAM BY AREA

A great spot to tuck into the *injera* (a type of tasty sourdough pancake) and veggie-friendly food of Ethiopia (best washed down with a calabash of cold beer) after an afternoon wandering the wild streets of the Jordaan.

't Smalle

Egelantiersgracht 12 (623 9617). Tram 13, 14, 17, 20. **Open** 10am-1am Mon-Thur, Sun; 10am-2am Fri, Sat. No credit cards. **Bar**. Map p119 C3 ❻
This charming bar boasts one of the most scenic terraces on one of the prettiest canals in the city, so it's hardly surprising that its waterside seats are snared early in the day: patience – or an alarm clock in good working order – is essential. Interior decor is cute, with gleaming brass and candles harking back to the 18th century, when it was the Hoppe distillery.

Small World Catering

Binnen Oranjestraat 14 (420 2774/ www.smallworldcatering.nl). Bus 18, 22. **Open** 10.30am-8pm Tue-Sat; noon-8pm Sun. No credit cards. **Café**. Map p119 B2 ❼

The base for this catering company is a tiny deli that feels like the home kitchen of the proprietors themselves. Besides superlative coffee and fresh juices, enjoy salads, lasagnes and truly sublime gourmet sandwiches.

De Vliegende Schotel

Nieuwe Leliestraat 162 (625 2041/ www.vliegendeschotel.com). Tram 13, 14, 17. **Open** 5-11.30pm daily. €€. **Vegetarian**. Map p119 B5 ❽
The venerable Flying Saucer serves up a splendid array of innovative meat-free dishes in a hearty buffet format. If it's booked up, the nearby De Bolhoed (Prinsengracht 60-62, 626 1803) offers lovely vegan dishes as a consolation.

Yam-Yam

Frederik Hendrikstraat 90 (681 5097/ www.yamyam.nl). Tram 3. **Open** 6-10.30pm Tue-Sun. €€. No credit cards. **Italian**. Map p119 A4 ❾
Unparalleled and inexpensive pastas and wood oven pizzas in a hip, casual atmosphere: no wonder Yam-Yam is a firm favourite with both hungry post-clubbers and locals alike.

Noordermarkt p124

Shopping

Boerenmarkt

Westerstraat/Noorderkerkstraat (no phone). Tram 3, 10. **Open** 9am-3pm Sat. No credit cards. **Map** p119 C3 ⑩
Every Saturday, the Noordermarkt turns into an organic farmers' market. Groups of singers or medieval musicians sometimes make a visit feel more like a day trip than a grocery shop.

Broer & Zus

Rozengracht 104 (422 9002/www.broerenzus.nl). Tram 13, 14, 17. **Open** noon-6pm Mon; 10.30am-6pm Tue-Fri; 10am-6pm Sat. **Map** p119 C5 ⑪
For the baby or toddler who has it all, Broer & Zus makes gift-giving a cinch with its handmade toys and adorable T-shirts with goofy slogans. Playful fun for kids with a sense of style.

Crumpler

NEW *Haarlemmerdijk 31 (620 2454/www.crumpler.nl). Tram 1, 2, 4, 5, 13, 14, 16, 17, 24, 25.* **Open** 11am-6pm Tue-Fri; 11am-5pm Sat; 1-5pm Sun. **Map** 119 B2 ⑫

Bags for boys – OK, the girls love 'em too, but oh how the fellas fall for trendy laptop containers from Crumpler.

Delicious Food

Westerstraat 24 (320 3070). Tram 3. **Open** 10am-7pm Mon, Wed-Fri; 9am-6pm Sat; 11am-3pm Sun. **Map** p119 C3 ⑬
Organic produce has reached the self-contradictory pinnacle of urban rustic chic at what can only be described as a bulk food boutique. Come here for an enticing spread of the finest pastas, nuts, spices, oils and vinegars.

De Kasstoor

Rozengracht 202-210 (521 8112/www.dekasstoor.nl). Tram 13, 14, 17. **Open** 10am-6pm Tue-Sat. **Map** p119 B5 ⑭
De Kasstoor is not your average Dutch interior design shop; it also has hand-picked collectors' pieces from the likes of Le Corbusier, Eames and Citterio, as well as a very extensive upholstery and fabrics library. Plan on paying excess baggage charges when you find yourself hauling your purchases back to the airport.

AMSTERDAM BY AREA

Reprezent

Kitsch Kitchen

Rozengracht 8 (622 8261/www.kitsch kitchen.nl). Tram 13, 14, 17. **Open** 10am-6pm Mon-Sat. **Map** p119 C4/5 ⑮
Mexican Mercado with a twist. Even the hardiest denouncers of tat will love the colourful culinary and household objects here, wacky wallpapers included.

Noordermarkt

Noordermarkt (no phone). Tram 3, 10. **Open** 7.30am-1pm Mon. No credit cards. **Map** p119 C3 ⑯
North of Westermarkt, Noordermarkt is frequented by the serious shopper. The stacks of (mainly second-hand) clothes, shoes, jewellery and hats need to be sorted with a grim determination, but there are real bargains to be had. Arrive early to nab the best stuff.

Reprezent

Haarlemmerstraat 80 (528 5540/www. reprezent.nl). Tram 3/bus 18, 22. **Open** 10.30am-6.30pm Mon-Wed, Fri, Sat; 10.30am-9pm Thur. **Map** p119 C2 ⑰
Custom skateboards, snowboarding threads from Volcom, Grenade and Special Blend and various ass-kicking accessories. The staff also organise in-house surf and snowboard tours.

Schaak en Go het Paard

Haarlemmerdijk 173 (624 1171/www. schaakengo.nl). Tram 3/bus 18, 22. **Open** 1-5.30pm Mon; 10am-5.30pm Tue, Wed, Fri, Sat; 10am-8pm Thur. **Map** p119 B2 ⑱
This is the place to come for a truly glorious selection of handmade chess sets, from African to ultra-modern.

SPRMRKT

Rozengracht 191-193 (330 5601/www. sprmkt.nl). Tram 13, 14, 17. **Open** By appt only Mon; 10am-6pm Tue-Sat. **Map** p119 B5 ⑲
A whopping 450sq m (that's really big for Amsterdam) of exceptionally cool duds. The prize is the shop-within-the-shop, SPR+, featuring picks from Margiela, Rick Owens, the Acne Jeans collection, Wendy & Jim and more. A very tasty selection of vintage 1960s and '70s furniture, coffee table design books and a wide range of accessories round off the experience.

Unlimited Delicious

Haarlemmerstraat 122 (622 4829/ www.unlimiteddelicious.nl). Tram 3/ bus 18, 22. **Open** 9am-6pm Mon-Sat. **Map** p119 C2 ⑳

Known for such twisted treats as their balsamic vinegar and tomato bonbons and a crazy caramel-balsamic-chocolate pie with a brownie bottom, Unlimited Delicious also offers courses in bonbon making for enthusiasts.

Vlaamsch Broodhuis

NEW *Haarlemmerstraat 108 (528 6430/www.vlaamschbroodhuys.nl). Tram 3/bus 18, 22.* **Open** 11am-6.30pm Mon; 8.30am-6.30pm Tue-Fri; 9am-5pm Sat. No credit cards. **Map** p119 C2 ㉑
The name may be a mouthful, but it's worth a visit just to wrap your gums around their tasty sourdough breads, fine French pastries and fresh salads from restaurant/greenhouse De Kas (p106), among other treats.

Wegewijs

Rozengracht 32 (624 4093/www. wegewijs.nl). Tram 13, 14, 17. **Open** 8.30am-6pm Mon-Fri; 9am-5pm Sat. No credit cards. **Map** p119 C5 ㉒
The Wegewijs family started running this shop more than a century ago. On offer are around 50 foreign cheeses and over 100 different domestic varieties of caseus, including *graskaas*, a grassy-tasting cheese that is available in the summer months only. For those nervous about buying a strange cheese, Wegewijs allows you to sample Dutch varieties beforehand.

Nightlife

Flexbar

NEW *Pazzanistraat 1 (www.flexbar.nl). Tram 3, 10/bus 18, 21, 22.* **Open** 10pm-4am Thur, Sun; 10pm-5am Fri, Sat.
Barely just opened and already packed – it's unavoidable in a city that craves new impulses. Especially when electro music's own Eva Maria, house legend Wannabeastar and quintessential hip hoppers Rednose Distrikt have set up camp. Flexbar consists of two spaces, often with different programmes.

Strand West

Stavangerweg 900 (682 6310/www. strand-west.nl). Bus 22, 48. **Open** varies. No credit cards.

Following Blijburg's lead, *stranden-ten* (beach hangouts) have popped up all over the city. This one promotes progressive house music in one-off events approximately every month. The surrounding area is well known for boasting a wealth of arty ad hoc student housing in sea containers.

Arts and leisure

Noorderkerk

Noordermarkt 48 (620 3119/www. noorderkerkconcerten.nl). Tram 3, 10. No credit cards. **Map** p119 C3 ㉓
Sure, the wooden benches in this early 17th-century church are a little on the hard side, but all is soon forgiven thanks to their comprehensive programme of recitals, which attracts accomplished musicians and features performances of countless classical favourites. Reservations recommended.

The Movies

Haarlemmerdijk 161 (624 5790/www. themovies.nl). Tram 3. **Map** p119 B2 ㉔
The oldest cinema still being used in Amsterdam has been circulating celluloid since 1912, and still exudes a genteel atmosphere as a result of its elegant old-fashioned interior. The adjoining Wild Kitchen serves decent set dinners that cost between €26 and €36.50; prices include a ticket for a film.

Westergasfabriek

Haarlemmerweg 8-10 (586 0710/ www.westergasfabriek.com). Tram 10/bus 18, 22.
With a plethora of old industrial areas being cleverly re-invented as performance, event and exhibition spaces, this former gas works is quickly evolving into one of Amsterdam's premier cultural and creative hubs (as it was during the 1990s, when it served as a happening underground squat village). It's also the new home base for Cosmic (606 5050, www.cosmictheater.nl), an inspired theatre troupe that has long been addressing the multicultural realities of the modern world. Sporadic club nights, concerts, art exhibitions and various festivals are also held.

Rijksmuseum p129

The Museum Quarter, Vondelpark & the South

The heart of the late 19th-century Museum Quarter is Museumplein, the city's largest square, bordered roughly by the **Rijksmuseum**, the **Stedelijk Museum of Modern Art**, the **Van Gogh Museum** and **Concertgebouw**. However, the heart will be beating fainter in the coming few years, what with the Rijksmuseum partially closing and the Stedelijk relocating to the Post CS building. Museumplein itself is not really an authentic Amsterdam square, but recent additions include grass, a wading pool, a skate ramp, a café and a wacky new amendment to the Van Gogh Museum.

As you'd expect in such cultural surroundings, property doesn't come cheap, and the affluence is apparent. Housing covers more than its fair share of overly elegant 19th-century mansions, while Van Baerlestraat and PC Hooftstraat are as close as Amsterdam gets to Rodeo Drive, their boutiques offering solace to ladies who might otherwise lunch.

Vondelpark is the city's largest and most central park, and the last few years have seen much renovation as the park has sunk two to three metres (seven to ten feet) since it was first built – some of the larger trees are in fact 'floating' on huge

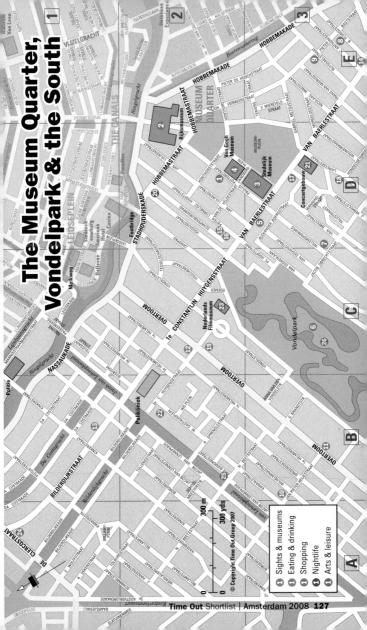

The Museum Quarter, Vondelpark & the South

Legend:
- Sights & museums
- Eating & drinking
- Shopping
- Nightlife
- Arts & leisure

300 m
300 yds

© Copyright Time Out Group 2007

blocks of styrofoam or are slyly reinforced with underground poles. There are several ponds and lakes in the park – no boating, though – plus a number of play areas and cafés; most pleasant are **'t Blauwe Theehuis** and Café Vertigo at the **Nederlands Filmmuseum**. Vondelpark gets fantastically busy on sunny days and Sundays, when bongos abound, dope is toked and football games take up any space that happens to be left over. Films, plays and public concerts are also put on, with a festival of free open-air performances in summer.

Stretching out in the rough shape of a ring beneath Vondelpark is a fairly indeterminate region known as Nieuw Zuid (New South), which is itself bordered to the north by Vondelpark, to the east by the Amstel and to the west by the 1928 Olympisch Stadion (www.olympisch-stadion.net).

Museumplein p126

Sights & museums

CoBrA Museum of Modern Art

Sandbergplein 1, Amstelveen (547 5050/www.cobra-museum.nl). Tram 5/Metro 51/bus 170, 172. **Open** 11am-5pm Tue-Sun. **Admission** €7; €4 over-65s; €3 5s-16s; free under-5s, MK.
The CoBrA group (an acronym of Copenhagen, Brussels and Amsterdam) attempted to radically reinvent the language of paint in 1948, preaching an ethos of participation and believing everyone should make art, regardless of ability or education. Artists such as Karel Appel, Eugene Brands and Corneille were once regarded as little more than eccentric troublemakers; they've now been absorbed into the canon. This museum, way out south in the people's suburb of Amstelveen, provides a sympathetic environment in which to trace the development of one of the most influential Dutch art movements of the 20th century.

Electrische Museumtramlijn Amsterdam

Haarlemmermeerstation, entrance at Amstelveenseweg 264 (618 8528/www. museumtram.nl). Tram 16. **Open** *Jan-Apr, Oct-Dec* 11am-5pm Sun. *July, Aug* special timetable Wed. **Tickets** €4; €2 4-11s, over-65s; free under-4s. No credit cards.
The pride and raison d'être of the Electrische Museumtramlijn, housed in a beautiful 1915 former railway station, is its rolling stock. For its one-and-a-half-hour round trips, colourful antique street-cars from several cities take you along a traditional track through the nearby Amsterdamse Bos.

House of Bols

NEW *Paulus Potterstraat 14 (570 8575/www.houseofbols.nl). Tram 2, 3, 5, 12.* **Open** noon-6pm Mon, Wed-Sun. **Admission** €10 (over-18s only, includes free cocktail). **Map** p127 D2 ❶
The Bols were one of the first producers of fine jenever – the original gin – and began it all in 1575. Besides a

'World of Bartending', they also have a 'Hall of Taste' where you can taste with your eyes, hands and nose. Kind of cheesy, but a lot of fun if you are in the right mood. Hell, you even get a free cocktail in the 'Mirror Bar' after the tour. It's only too bad they don't serve absinthe – that might combine nicely with a visit to the Van Gogh Museum directly across the street.

Rijksmuseum

Stadhouderskade 42 (674 7047/www. rijksmuseum.nl). Tram 2, 5, 6, 7, 10. **Open** 9am-6pm Mon-Thur, Sat, Sun; 9am-10pm Fri. **Admission** €10; free under-19s, MK. **Map** p127 D2/E2 ❷

Designed by PJH Cuypers and opened in 1885, the Rijksmuseum holds the country's largest collection of art and artefacts, including 40 Rembrandts and four Vermeers. However, most of its million exhibits will be out of the public eye until after the summer of 2010 while the Rijksmuseum gets a €227 million facelift. The closure may turn out to be a blessing in disguise: instead of overdosing on the vastness of the place, visitors will be able to see the 400 most masterful masterpieces in the Philips Wing. Some of the collection will meanwhile be in exhibitions organised by other museums throughout the Netherlands. In short: there will still be plenty of Golden Age art to look at, but you'd do well to check in with the museum's excellent website before you turn up.

Stedelijk Museum of Modern Art

Paulus Potterstraat 13 (573 2911/ www.stedelijk.nl). Tram 2, 3, 5, 12. **Open** 10am-6pm daily (Post CS). **Admission** €9; €4.50 7s-16s; free under-7s, MK. **Map** p127 D3 ❸

It's moved. Until summer 2008, temporary modern art exhibitions organised by the Stedelijk are on display on the second and third floors of the Post CS building near Centraal Station. But since the Stedelijk's rebuilding will take until at least 2009, there may be yet another transfer before the vast

Blades of glory

It's 9pm on a Friday night. Most of the locals are slumped in front of the telly or drinking in a bar – but not the people currently assembling in the Vondelpark. Unless it's raining, every Friday a group of skate fanatics meets to snake the 20-kilometre (12.4-mile), three-hour-long **Friday Night Skate** through central Amsterdam (www.fridaynightskate.com).

It all started in 1997, when three friends decided to do something special to kick off the weekend. Ten years later, that same group varies from a small handful of die-hards in winter to hundreds in summer, but whatever the cause they all have one thing in common: a love of skating around the city. Forget tracing circles around boring parks – it's high bridges, car parks, tunnels and noisy roads this lot are after.

Things never get stale. Each week there is a new route but the start and finish is always in Vondelpark, directly opposite the Filmmuseum (p136). There are teams of 'blockers', who block the roads so cars and cyclists can't get in the way, plus 'flying nurses' who'll come to your assistance if ever you have an unscheduled meeting with the hard tarmac. Some skaters even carry sound systems on their backs, providing tunes to help people move with purpose. It's free, it's fun and it's a great way to make new friends.

collection returns to Paulus Potterstraat. Wherever it finds itself, the museum has an amazing collection to draw from. Pre-war highlights include works by Cézanne, Picasso, Matisse and Chagall, plus a collection of paintings and drawings by Malevich. Post-1945 artists represented include De Kooning, Newman, Ryman, Judd, Stella, Lichtenstein, Warhol, Nauman, Middleton, Dibbets, Kiefer, Polke, Merz and Kounellis.

Van Gogh Museum

Paulus Potterstraat 7 (570 5200/www. vangoghmuseum.nl). Tram 2, 3, 5, 12. **Open** 10am-6pm Mon-Thur, Sat, Sun; 10am-10pm Fri. **Admission** €10; €2.50 13s-17s; free under-13s, MK. Temporary exhibition prices vary. **Map** p127 D2 ❹

After a major and impressive refurbishment, the enlarged Rietveld building remains home base to the 200 paintings and 500 drawings by Van Gogh forming the museum's permanent collection, while the new wing by Japanese architect Kisho Kurokawa is usually home to temporary exhibitions that focus on Van Gogh's contemporaries and his influence on other artists. These shows are assembled from both the museum's own extensive archives and private collections. Do yourself a favour and get there early in the morning, though: the queues in the afternoon can get frustratingly long, and the gallery unbearably busy. It's also well worth noting that Friday evenings at the museum often feature lectures, concerts and films.

Eating & drinking

Bagels & Beans

Van Baerlestraat 40 (675 7050/www. bagelsbeans.nl). Tram 3, 5, 12. **Open** 8am-6pm Mon-Fri; 9.30am-6pm Sat, Sun. **Café**. **Map** p127 D3 ❺

An Amsterdam success story, this branch of B&B also boasts a wonderfully peaceful back patio. Perfect for an economical breakfast, lunch or snack; sun-dried tomatoes are a speciality, always employed with particular skill.

Van Gogh Museum

't Blauwe Theehuis

Vondelpark 5 (662 0254/www.blauwe theehuis.nl). Tram 1, 2, 6. **Open** 9am-11pm Mon-Thur, Sun; 9am-1am Fri, Sat. No credit cards. **Bar**. **Map** p127 C3 ❻

One of the few local landmarks that you can nestle down inside with a beer, HJAB Baanders' extraordinary 1930s teahouse – a sort of UFO-hat hybrid – is a choice spot for fair-weather drinking. In summer there are DJs and barbecues, though it's a romantic spot for dinner and drinks all year round.

Café Gruter

Willemsparkweg 73-75 (618 3249). Tram 3, 5, 12, 24. **Open** noon-1am Mon-Thur, Sun; noon-2am Fri, Sat. **Café**. **Map** p127 D3 ❼

The area around the museums is surprisingly pretty low on cafés and bars, so those that are there get packed. Take a short stroll into the residential heart of the district and you'll come across decent cafés like this one, providing you with everything you need, including six draught beers.

Caffe Oslo

NEW *Sloterkade 1A (669 9663/www.caffeoslo.nl).* Tram 1. **Open** 9am-1am Mon-Thur, Sun; 9am-3am Fri, Sat. **Bar**.

So slick a bar comes as a surprise, plonked as it is canal-side in an unremarkable residential area not far from the Vondelpark. Inside it's all blond wood, cool creamy colours and a beautiful crazy-paving floor. Punters are slightly older, style-hungry locals who come early for the breakfasts and stay late for the fashionable menu.

Eetcafé I Kriti

Balthasar Floriszstraat 3 (664 1445/ www.ikriti.nl). Tram 3, 5, 12, 16. **Open** 4pm-1am daily. **€€€**. **Greek**. **Map** p127 E3 ➑

Eat and party Greek style in this evocation of Crete. Bouzouki-picking music legends drop in on occasion and pump up the frenzied atmosphere, further boosted by plate-lobbing antics.

Le Garage

Ruysdaelstraat 54-56 (679 7176/www.restaurantlegarage.nl). Tram 3, 5, 6, 12, 16. **Open** noon-2pm, 6-11pm Mon-Fri; 6-11pm Sat, Sun. **€€€€**. **French**. **Map** p127 E3 ➒

Don your glad rags to blend in at this extremely fashionable brasserie, which is a great place for emptying your wallet while watching a cross-section of Dutch glitterati do exactly the same thing. The authentic French regional cuisine – and 'worldly' versions thereof – is pretty damn good, as you'd expect.

Kashmir Lounge

Jan Pieter Heijestraat 85-87 (683 2268). Tram 1, 6, 7, 11, 17. **Open** 10am-1am Mon-Thur; 10am-3am Fri, Sat; 11am-1am Sun. No credit cards. **Coffeeshop**. **Map** p127 B3 ➓

Lit with little beyond candlelight, Kashmir may seem too dark at first, but once your eyes adjust it's an opulent cavern of Indian tapestries, ornate tiles, hand-carved walls and comfy cushions swathed in zebra and cheetah prints. With a multitude of obscure corners and partially enclosed tables, you can feel like a VIP at no extra charge.

De Peper

Overtoom 301 (779 4913/www.de peper.org). Tram 1, 6. **Open** 6pm-1am Tue, Thur-Sat. **€**. No credit cards. **Vegetarian**. **Map** p127 B3 ⓫

This purveyor of the cheapest and best vegan food in town is a collectively organised, non-profit project combining culture with an awesome kitchen.

De Peperwortel

Overtoom 140 (685 1053/www.peper wortel.nl). Tram 1, 6, 7, 10. **Open** 4-9pm daily. **€€**. No credit cards. **Global**. **Map** p127 C2 ⓬

One could survive for weeks on takeaways from the Pepper Root, with its range of dishes that embrace Dutch, Mexican, Indian and Spanish cuisines.

Riaz

Bilderdijkstraat 193 (683 6453/www. riaz.nl). Tram 3, 7, 12, 17. **Open** 11.30am-9pm Mon-Fri; 2-9pm Sun. **€€**. No credit cards. **South American**. **Map** p127 B1 ⓭

This Surinamese joint is where Ruud Gullit scores his rotis when he's in town.

Vakzuid

Olympisch Stadion 35 (570 8400/www. vakzuid.nl). Tram 16, 24/bus 15, 23. **€€€**. **Global**.

Vakzuid, with its view over the Olympisch Stadion and modish cons, is popular with local working trendies. Thursday to Saturday nights it transforms into a club, while Sunday afternoons are more child-friendly.

Vis aan de Schelde

Scheldeplein 4 (675 1583/www. visaandeschelde.nl). Tram 5, 25. **Open** noon-2.30pm, 5.30-11pm Mon-Fri; 5.30-11pm Sat, Sun. **€€€€**. **Fish**. This eaterie out near the RAI convention centre has become a real culinary temple for the connoisseur of fine fish from all around the world.

Wildschut

Roelof Hartplein 1-3 (676 8220/www. goodfoodgroup.nl). Tram 3, 5, 12, 24. **Open** 9am-1am Mon-Thur; 9am-3am Fri; 10.30am-2am Sat; 9.30am-1am Sun. **Bar**. **Map** p127 E3 ⓮

AMSTERDAM BY AREA

Amsterdam rocks

Amsterdam's diamonds are world famous, with the city having been a major centre of the gem trade since the 16th century. From the very beginning, the industry was a big employer for the city's Jewish population, which began expanding thanks to Amsterdam's (relative) tolerance of other religions. Nor was it necessary to be a member of a guild to work in the diamond business – and with all Jews barred from joining guilds anyway, the gem trade inevitably came to employ many Jewish cutters and polishers as it developed.

The 19th century was boom time thanks to huge quantities of South African diamonds being unearthed, and so Amsterdam maintained its role as top dog in the diamond trade until business started dwindling during the Great Depression. The real end to the honeymoon, however, came with World War II, when most of those cutters remaining in Amsterdam were deported and killed during the Nazi occupation.

Although the European focus for gemstones is now in Antwerp, the industry never totally left Amsterdam, and diamonds still rate as a top five tourist attraction. Those who want to find out more should head to the new **Diamant Museum Amsterdam**, which covers every aspect of this most cherished of jewels – starting with their geological formation three billion years ago and winding up with the business today. The museum is split into two parts: the collection, which includes a small permanent gallery of sparklers, and a special space for a programme of changing temporary exhibitions. On top of all that, visitors can gawp at the Dutch royal family's own jewels (only reproductions, alas) alongside interesting multimedia exhibits on such subjects as infamous diamond robberies and tried and trusted methods of spotting a fake. There's also a gift shop, but bear in mind that falling head-over-heels in love with a small piece of crushed carbon in the shop is the easy part; working out how you're going to pay for it may prove to be a little more tricky in the long run.

Diamant Museum Amsterdam

Paulus Potterstraat 8 (305 5300/ www.diamantmuseumamsterdam. nl). Tram 2, 5. **Open** 9am-5pm daily. **Admission** €6; €4 students/65+; free under-12s.

A stunning example of Amsterdam School architecture, this elegant semi-circular building puts the 'grand' into grand café and positively drips with nouveau detail. The drink and food menu mirrors the upmarket surroundings, as does the regular clientele, which includes flush locals, loud yuppies and art-weary tourists.

Shopping

Azzurro Due

Pieter Cornelisz Hooftstraat 138 (671 9708). Tram 2, 3, 5, 12. **Open** 1-6pm Mon; 10am-6pm Tue, Wed, Fri; 10am-9pm Thur; 10am-5.30pm Sat; noon-5pm Sun. **Map** p127 D2 ⑮
If you've got to splurge on cutting-edge fashion, this is as good a spot as any. Saucy picks from Anna Sui, Blue Blood, Chloé and Stella McCartney attract the usual hordes of mediacrities.

Bertram & Brood

NEW *Maasstraat 82-84 (670 2597/ www.bertrambrood.nl). Tram 5.* **Open** 9am-5.30pm Mon-Fri; 9am-5pm Sat. No credit cards.
After 20 years of working in the baking industy, Nol Bertram branched out to open a mini-chain of swish bakeries throughout North Holland. There's a big range of breads stuffed with health boosting ingredients like linseed and sunflower seeds. The pleasant, rustic-looking shop also boasts a café.

Bits and Pieces

Cornelis Schuytstraat 22 (618 1939). Tram 16. **Open** noon-6pm Mon; 10am-6pm Tue-Fri; 10am-5pm Sat.
Innovative purchasing mixes new designers with established names such as Martine Sitbon, Clements Ribeiro and Earl Jean. Often features in Dutch magazines next to A-list 'what is she wearing/where did she get it' taglines.

For Our Friends

NEW *Pieter Cornelisz Hooftstraat 142 (676 6220/www.bluebloodbrand. com). Tram 2, 5.* **Open** 10am-6pm Mon-Wed, Fri; 10am-9pm Thur, 10am-5.30pm Sat; noon-5pm Sun. **Map** p127 D2 ⑯
All the gear any upwardly mobile trendster could ever want, from denim, scooters, sneakers and toys to gold-embossed Smythson journals and treats beyond imagining.

Intertaal

Van Baerlestraat 76 (575 6756/www. intertaal.nl). Tram 3, 5, 12, 16. **Open** 10am-6pm Tue-Fri; 10am-5pm Sat. **Map** p127 D3 ⑰

Friday Night Skate p129

Dealing in language books, CDs and teaching aids, Intertaal will be of use to all learners of a new foreign language, whether they're grappling with basic Dutch or improving their English.

Lairesse Apotheek

Lairessestraat 40 (662 1022/www.de lairesseapotheek.nl). Tram 3, 5, 12, 16. **Open** 8.30am-6pm Mon-Fri; 10am-4pm Sat. **Map** p127 D3 ⓲

One of the largest suppliers of alternative medicines in the country, from chemist Marjan Terpstra. The shop is out of the way if you're just popping in for haemorrhoid cream, but the interior is inspiring enough to be on any design junkie's must-see list.

Marlies Dekkers

NEW *Cornelis Schuytstraat 13 (471 4146/www.marliesdekkers.nl). Tram 16.* **Open** noon-6pm Mon; 10am-6pm Tue-Fri; 10am-5pm Sat.

Local lingerie wizard Marlies Dekkers' wildly wonderful flagship store won't disappoint, whatever you're looking for. Besides her lingerie and swimwear lines, there's a variety of treats to help set the mood: scented candles, local handmade bonbons and beautifully boxed sets of champagne.

Pied-à-Terre

Overtoom 135-137 (627 4455/www. piedaterre.nl). Tram 1, 2, 5. **Open** 10am-6pm Mon-Wed, Fri; 10am-9pm Thur; 10am-5pm Sat. No credit cards. **Map** p127 C2 ⓳

Travel books, international guides and maps for active holidays. Adventurous walkers should talk to the helpful staff before making a trip out of town.

Waterwinkel

Roelof Hartstraat 10 (675 5932/www. springwater.nl). Tram 3, 24. **Open** 1-6pm Mon; 10am-6pm Tue-Fri; 10am-5pm Sat.

Mineral water everywhere, and every drop to drink. The variety of native and imported water in this unusual store will charm many, but may induce an unfortunate emergency in the more weak-bladdered among us.

Nightlife

The Mansion

NEW *Hobbemastraat 2 (616 6664/ www.the-mansion.nl). Tram 2, 5.* **Open** 6pm-1am Wed, Thur, Sun (restaurant only Sun); 6pm-3am Fri, Sat. **Map** p127 D2 ⓴

This restaurant/bar/club is less Hugh Hefner and more elegant gentleman's club with chicks allowed. The staff are decked in outfits designed by Europe's answer to Donna Karan, René Lezard, and the decor is plush chinoiserie. Expect DJs, dancing and a space in your wallet where the money used to be.

OCCII

Amstelveenseweg 134 (671 7778/www. occii.org). Tram 1, 2. **Open** 9pm-2am Mon-Thur, Sun; 10pm-3am Fri, Sat. No credit cards.

Formerly a squat, this friendly bar and concert hall is tucked away at one end of Vondelpark. Mainly home to touring underground rock, experimental and reggae acts, if you turn up with an open mind then there's a very good chance of witnessing something special.

Arts & leisure

Amsterdam RAI Theater

Europaplein 8-22 (549 1212/www. raitheater.nl). Tram 4/Metro Amstel.

This huge convention and exhibition centre by day turns into an enormous theatre by night and on weekends. Musicals, operas, comedy nights, ballets, spectacular shows – all can be enjoyed in a venue created to make each visit an inspiring experience.

Concertgebouw

Concertgebouwplein 2-6 (reservations 671 8345/24hr information in Dutch and English 573 0511/www.concert gebouw.nl). Tram 2, 3, 5, 12, 16, 20. **Map** p127 D3 ㉑

With its beautiful architecture and clear acoustics, the Concertgebouw is a favourite venue of many of the world's top musicians, and is home to its very own world famous Royal Concertgebouw Orchestra. As you'd expect, the sound in the Grote Zaal

Delicious Amsterdam

These days, mention Dutch food and most serious gastronomes will barely be able to repress a snigger. And yet once upon a time, according to über-food critic Johannes van Dam, the national dishes were serious stuff indeed.

'Dutch cuisine was as rich as Belgian or French until the end of the 19th century,' he says. That was when *huishoudscholen* – 'household schools', whose noble intention was teaching impoverished Amsterdammers to make more easy, affordable meals – ended up stripping the native cuisine of its many riches, leaving nothing in its wake except meat, vegetables and potatoes. The rest, as they say, is history.

Recent years, however, have seen a fiercely renewed interest in traditional food across the city. Johannes praises **Greetje** (Peperstraat 23, 779 7450) for reinventing old favourites like eel soup, blood sausage and liquorice ice-cream, and singles out **De Roode Leeuw** (Damrak 93-94, 555 0666) and **Moeders Pot** (Vinkenstraat 119, 623 7643) as the best places to taste real home-style Dutch cooking.

Geographical phenomena have also shaped the national fare: tasty North Sea shrimps flavour *kroketten* – try it for youself at **Holtkamp** (Vijzelgracht 15, 624 8767), whose luxury lines also include fresh lobster and calves' sweetbreads with mushrooms. The other standard snack is raw herring, of which van Dam cautions: 'If you don't watch out, you will undoubtedly be served onion with your fresh fish. It is unnecessary and even harmful. Good herring is ruined by onion.' Don't say we didn't warn you.

Most people, however, tend to say 'cheese' if they need to name a staple. The most famous cheese is gouda, but van Dam says that fans should avoid factory-made versions. Look instead for *boeren* (farmers') gouda. This can be bought at more specialist cheese retailers (such as **De Kaaskamer**, Runstraat 7, 623 3483), and at most markets. Yet more tasty variations include eminently spicy leidsekaas with cumin seeds and Friesland's nagelkaas with cloves, both unusual and utterly delicious.

While Dutch cuisine hasn't fully recovered from the misguided intentions of the past, the city is at least doing well enough for the arch critic himself to have recently written a book in English about local cuisine. Its name? *Delicious Amsterdam*, of course.

Concertgebouw p134

(Great Hall) is excellent. The Kleine Zaal (Recital Hall) is perhaps less comfortable, but is the perfect size for both chamber groups and soloists.

Fenomeen
Schinkelstraat 14 (671 6780/http:// saunafenomeen.nl). Tram 1, 2. No credit cards.
Effortlessly embodying the very liberal spirit of Amsterdam, Fenomeen is a relaxed, legalised squat sauna, housed in old horses' stalls, that's popular with (but not limited to) the gay and lesbian crowd. It houses a sauna, steam bath, cold bath, and a chill-out room with mattresses and showers in the courtyard. Professional massages are also available, and there's a café offering vegetarian and vegan dishes.

Gasthuis Werkplaats & Theater
Marius van Bouwdijk Bastiaansestraat 54 (616 8942/www.theatergasthuis.nl). Tram 1, 3, 6, 12. No credit cards. **Map** p127 B2 ㉒

The Gasthuis emerged from a group of squatters who became critical darlings in just a few years. Even when their home, a former hospital, was threatened with demolition, their artsy activities contributed a great deal towards the building's ultimate salvation. The rolling programme is, as you might expect, mainly youthful and experimental. Some productions are in English; be sure to check the website beforehand to guarantee a comprehensible evening's entertainment.

Nederlands Filmmuseum (NFM)
Vondelpark 3 (589 1400/www.film museum.nl). Tram 1, 2, 3, 5, 6, 12. No credit cards. **Map** p127 C2 ㉓
This stylish building overlooking the Vondelpark is both a cinema and a museum. The most important centre of cinematography in the Netherlands, it collects films to add to its vast catalogue and restores copies that have been ravaged by the passage of time. It also regularly screens silent films,

authentically accompanied by an old-fashioned pianola, and specialises in major retrospectives and edgier contemporary fare. In the summer, be sure to take in an outdoor screening on the terrace of the in-house Café Vertigo.

Platform 21

NEW *Prinses Irenestraat 19 (301 8000/www.platform21.com). Tram 5.* **Open** noon-6pm Wed-Sun. No credit cards.

Organising a variety of activities and exhibitions, Platform 21 is indeed a platform where the effect of art, design, fashion and business in shaping our world is explored. Its location in a round modernist chapel is worth the visit alone – as will be their nature-themed restaurant, serving its first customers at time of going to press.

Serieuze Zaken Studioos

NEW *Bilderdijkstraat 66 (427 5770/http://serieuzezaken.photo net.nl). Tram 10, 12.* No credit cards. **Map** p127 A1 ㉔

Rob Malasch was already known as a quirky theatre type and journalist before opening this gallery. Shows here might feature anything from Brit Art to work by modern Chinese painters.

Smart Project Space

Arie Biemondstraat 101-11 (427 5951/www.smartprojectspace.net). Tram 1, 3, 6, 12. No credit cards. **Map** p127 B2 ㉕

Relocated in a former pathology lab and reopening in 2007, Smart will no doubt remain loyal to 'hardcore art' in its huge new exhibition space, which also has two cinemas, a media centre, a lecture hall, and a decent in-house café and restaurant for hungry Bohos.

Theater Het Amsterdamse Bos

Amsterdamse Bos (643 3286/www.bos theater.nl). Bus 66, 170, 172, 176, 199. No credit cards.

What better way to spend a dreamy midsummer night than by picnicking beneath the stars in a sultry sylvan setting while classic drama – Shakespeare included (translated into Dutch) – is performed before you? No wonder the trees are talking. Get to the Bos early with your hamper, bag a place, settle back, open the wine and enjoy.

Toomler

Breitnerstraat 2 (670 7400/www. toomler.nl). Tram 2, 5, 16, 24. No credit cards.

Located next to the Hilton, this café hosts acts four nights a week. Most programming is stand-up in Dutch, but it's the English-language Comedy Train International, in January, July and August, that has come to be most closely associated with the venue. On weekends there is (predominantly jazz) music during Friday Night Live (11pm) and Super Sundays Live (4pm).

Vondelpark Openluchttheater

Vondelpark (673 1499/www.openlucht theater.nl). Tram 1, 2, 3, 5, 7, 10, 12. No credit cards. **Map** p127 C3 ㉖

Theatrical events have been held in Vondelpark since 1865, and the tradition continues each summer with a variety of shows. Wednesdays offer a lunchtime concert and a mid-afternoon children's show; Thursday nights find a concert on the bandstand; there's a theatre show every Friday evening and various events (many of them more child-friendly) on both Saturday and Sunday afternoons. Bear in mind the place gets especially packed in summer.

Vondeltuin

Vondelpark 7 (664 5091/www.vondel tuin.nl). Tram 1, 2, 3, 5, 6, 12. No credit cards.

Rollerblades, skates and accessories are rented to those looking to make the most of the surrounding area's potential for concrete cruising. Those seeking less sedate thrills should head for the more youth-orientated and ramp-happy Skatepark Amsterdam (www.skateparkamsterdam.nl) at the NDSM yard (p117), which also plays host to a hugely popular monthly rollerdisco featuring live DJs for more coordinated dancers.

Albert Cuypmarkt p143

The Pijp

While hardly a historical treasure trove of sights, the Pijp's time is the present, with well over 150 different nationalities keeping its global village vibe alive and the recent economic boom seeing the opening of more upmarket eateries and bars than ever before. The gentrification process, it seems, is in full effect. This trend will be heightened over the next few years by the construction of the Metro's controversial new Noord-Zuidlijn, the route of which will run pretty much directly beneath bustling Ferdinand Bolstraat.

The Pijp is the best known of the working-class quarters built in the late 19th century. Harsh economics saw the building of long, narrow streets, which led to its appropriate nickname, 'the Pipe'. Because rents were high, many tenants were forced to sublet rooms to students and artists, who then gave the area its Bohemian character.

The Pijp today houses a mix of nationalities, providing locals with halal butchers, Surinamese, Spanish, Indian and Turkish delicatessens, and restaurants offering authentic Syrian, Moroccan, Thai, Pakistani, Chinese and Indian cuisine. Thanks to these low-priced exotic eats, the Pijp is quite simply the best place in town for quality snacking treats, the many ingredients for which are almost always bought fresh from the single largest daily market in all of the Netherlands: Albert Cuypmarkt, the hub around which the Pijp turns. The market attracts thousands of customers every day to the junctions of Sweelinckstraat, Ferdinand Bolstraat and 1e Van der Helststraat, north into the lively

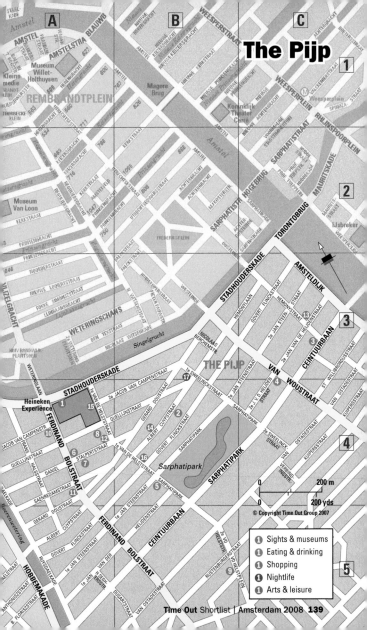

The Pijp

A **B** **C**

AMSTEL

AMSTELSTRA

BLAUWB

WEESPERSTRAAT

1

Museum Willet-Holthuysen

REMBRANDTPLEIN

Magere Brug

Koninklijk Theater Carré

WEESPERSTR

Weesperplein

SARPHATISTRAAT

RHIJNSPOORPLEIN

MAURITSKADE

Museum Van Loon

SARPHATISTR HOGEBRUG

TORONTOBRUG

2

IJsbreker

FREDERIKSPLEIN

VIJZELGRACHT

WETERINGSCHANS

Singelgracht

AMSTELDIJK

STADHOUDERSKADE

HEMONYLAAN

GOVERT FLINCKSTRAAT

HEMONYSTRAAT

2e JAN STEEN

2e JAN VAN DE HEIDENSTRAAT

❶13

VAN WOUSTRAAT

CEINTUURBAAN

3

NICOLAAS BERCHEMSTR

THE PIJP

2e JAN STEENSTRAAT

1e J.V. HEIREN STRAAT

ST. WILLIBRORDUSSTRAAT

2e OSTADESTRAAT

KUIPERSTRAAT

❶17

❹4

1e SWEELINCKSTRAAT

SARPHATIPARK

STADHOUDERSKADE

2e JACOB VAN CAMPENSTRAAT

Heineken Experience

❶1

❶15

QUELLIJNSTRAAT

GERARD DOUSTRAAT

❷2

ALBERT CUYPSTRAAT

GOVERT FLINCKSTRAAT

SARPHATIPARK

1e J.V. HEIREN STRAAT

SARPHATIPARK

2e SWEELINCK STRAAT

VAN OSTADESTRAAT

KUIPERSTRAAT

VERENIGINGSTRAAT

FERDINAND BOLSTRAAT

WETERINGLAAN

1e V.D. HELSTSTRAAT

❶10

❶8 ❶12

❶14

❸16

Sarphatipark

SARPHATIPARK

JACOB VAN CAMPENSTR

JAN FRANS

QUELLIJNSTRAAT

DANIEL

❶6

STALPERTSTRAAT

❶7

HALSTRAAT

SAENREDAMSTRAAT

❶11

GERARD DOUSTRAAT

ALBERT CUYPSTRAAT

GOVERT FLINCKSTRAAT

1e JAN STEENSTRAAT

❺5

1e V.D. HELSTSTRAAT

1e JAN STEENSTRAAT

CEINTUURBAAN

HEIJDENSTRAAT

2e JAN STEENSTRAAT

2e V.D. HELSTSTRAAT

FERDINAND BOLSTRAAT

RUSTENBURGERSTRAAT

4

HOBBEMAKADE

RUYSDAALKADE

ANTHONISZSTRAAT

B. FLORISZSTRAAT

1e SEGL STRAAT

2e JAN STEENSTRAAT

VAN DER

DUSARTSTRAAT

VAN OSTADESTRAAT

5

0 200 m
0 200 yds

© Copyright Time Out Group 2007

❶ Sights & museums
❶ Eating & drinking
❶ Shopping
❶ Nightlife
❶ Arts & leisure

Gerard Douplein, and also south towards Sarphatipark. Another particularly pretty street, and also one rich with cafés and bars, is the always lovely Frans Halsstraat.

Sights & museums

Heineken Experience

Stadhouderskade 78 (523 9666/www. heinekenexperience.com). Tram 6, 7, 10, 16, 24, 25. **Open** 10am-6pm (no entry after 5pm) Tue-Sun. **Admission** €10. **Map** p139 A4 ❶

After Heineken stopped brewing here in 1988, the company kept the building open for endearingly unflashy tours: for a charitable donation of *f*2 (less than €1 in today's money), you got an hour-long guided walk followed by as much Heineken as you could humanly consume. Unfortunately, the company cottoned on to the fact that most people were there for the booze rather than the educational benefits, and recently renovated the huge building as the Heineken Experience. And while it's a lot flashier, it's a little less illuminating and a lot less fun. Plus points: the quasi-virtual reality ride through a brewery from the perspective of a Heineken bottle is easily the most ludicrous exhibit in all of Amsterdam, and you still get three free beers plus a surprise free gift at the end. But all in all, you're probably better off just going to a bar.

Eating & drinking

Bazar

NEW *Albert Cuypstraat 182 (675 0544/www.bazaramsterdam.com). Tram 16, 24, 25.* **Open** 9am-1am Mon-Thur; 9am-2am Fri-Sun. €€. **North African**. **Map** p139 B4 ❷

If you can't find Bazar, look up at the sky and search there for an angel. This former church, now downgraded to an Arabic-kitsch café, is one of the glories of Albert Cuypmarkt. Sticking to the winning formula set by its Rotterdam mothership, it has a menu that travels the world but lingers lovingly in the environs of North Africa. Breakfast, lunch or dinner, Bazar is a real winner.

Bloemers

Hemonystraat 70 (400 4024). Tram 3, 4, 25. **Open** 10am-1am Mon-Thur, Sun; 10am-3am Fri, Sat. **Bar**. **Map** p139 C3 ❸

A justifiably popular neighbourhood bar on the eastern fringes of the Pijp, with a dark wood interior enlivened by old posters and chandeliers. A kitchen pumps out well-priced international classics for lunch and dinner. Capacity doubles when the terrace, complete with swing seats, opens for summer.

Buna Bet

NEW *Van Woustraat 74 (673 9449/ www.bunabet.nl). Tram 25.* **Open** Mon-Sat 8am-5pm. **Café**. **Map** p139 C4 ❹

No booze here, but plenty of coffee with a conscience on Amsterdam's up-and-coming foodie street. Choose from a range of fairtrade coffees and cakes.

Café Krull

Sarphatipark 2 (662 0214). Tram 3, 4, 16, 24, 25. **Open** 3.30pm-1am Mon-Thur; 2pm-3am Fri; noon-2am Sat; noon-1am Sun. **Bar**. **Map** p139 B4 ❺

Statue of singer André Hazes

The Amsterdam School

Museum Het Schip

Amsterdam's monuments are not products of imperial imaginations imposing their stone wills on an unwilling populace, but rather the homes of merchants and working men and women. And it was also for those same workers that the Amsterdam School built its gentler versions of Gaudí-style buildings, working with a socialist vision in the early 20th century.

While due credit can be given to the stonemasons who perforce had to practise non-geometrical brickwork when repairing houses slowly sinking into the mud, it was Hendrik Berlage who pioneered the main movement by not only stripping things down, rejecting all the neo-styles that had defined 19th-century Dutch architecture, but also by providing a much-needed opportunity to experiment with new forms by starting **Plan Zuid**, an urban development meant to provide housing for the working classes south of the Pijp.

Although the Amsterdam School was short lived – the money ran out – examples of its work remain liberally dotted around the city. Located along the waterfront, the eerie and epic **Scheepvaarthuis** (Prins Hendrikkade 108-114) is most usually considered to be the school's first ever work and has just reopened as the Hotel Amrâth (see box p169). The school's real playground is at Plan Zuid, on the border of the Pijp and Rivierenbuurt. **Josef Israelkade**, located between 2e Van der Helststraat and Van Woustraat, is a pleasant stretch along the Amstelkanaal; enter PL Takstraat and then encircle Burg Tellegenstraat without forgetting to pop your head into the courtyard of **Cooperatiehof**. It's the school at its hallucinatory best, at once incongruous with its surroundings and yet utterly inspired.

It's a different story elsewhere, though. Backtrack and cross the Amstelkanaal, and then walk down **Waalstraat**; here you'll find later examples of the school's work, where tightening purse strings led to greater restraint. Conclude your tour at **Wildschut** (p133) to best enjoy its panorama of goodies. It's also worth visiting the extraordinary **Spaarndammer** neighbourhood over on the other side of town near the Westerpark. One of the school's most frolicsome works, the Ship, as the locals like to call it, is now home to the **Museum Het Schip** (Spaarndammerplantsoen 140, 418 2885, www.hetschip.nl, 1-5pm Wed-Sun), which operates Amsterdam School boating and walking tours, and also boasts an exhibition space devoted to its architectural legacy.

Heineken Experience p140

Light from the enormous windows floods this delightful locals' café that's busy at all hours, with lap-toppers taking advantage of Wi-Fi, parents treating offspring to a hot chocolate, and – later on – evening imbibers of every stripe. The barman's music choice is exquisite (disco, Motown, easy listening, rockabilly), plus the outdoor picnic tables are a drinker's dream.

Café de Pijp
Ferdinand Bolstraat 17-19 (670 4161/www.goodfoodgroup.nl). Tram 16, 24, 25. **Open** 3.30pm-1am Mon-Thur; 3.30pm-3am Fri; noon-2am Sat; noon-1am Sun. No credit cards. **Bar.** **Map** p139 A4 ⑥

Popular with the neighbourhood's more affluent young bucks, there's a modish retro feel here – lacquered walls, 1970s lamps, school chairs – and weekends are livelied up with DJs. There's also a full menu and snacks.

Gollem
NEW *Daniel Stalpertstraat 74 (676 7117/www.cafegollem.nl). Tram 16, 24, 25.* **Open** 4pm-1am Mon-Thur, Sun; 2pm-2am Fri, Sat. No credit cards. **Café.** **Map** p139 A4 ⑦

An outstanding place to get sozzled, this dark and very cosy Belgian beer specialist offers more than 150 bottled brews – including 42 abbey beers and 14 trappists – and 14 on tap. The helpful menu lists the strengths of the suds.

Mamouche
Quellijnstraat 104 (673 6361/www. restaurantmamouche.nl). Tram 3, 12, 24, 25. **€€€.** **Morrocan.** **Map** p139 A4 ⑧

In the heart of the multicultural Pijp is this Moroccan restaurant with a real difference: it's posh, stylish (in a sexy, minimalist sort of way) and provides a groovy kind of background soundtrack music that can only be described as 'North African lounge'.

Renato's Trattoria
NEW *Van der Helstplein 31 (673 2300). Tram 12, 25.* **Open** 5.30-11pm daily. **€€.** No credit cards. **Italian.** **Map** p139 B5 ⑨

Dropping in here is like briefly stepping into Italy itself, with hearty hospitality and raw kitchen action to match. Pizza – heavily loaded but with a delicious crispy crust – is the house speciality, popular with all ages.

De Taart van m'n Tante

Ferdinand Bolstraat 10 (776 4600/ www.detaart.nl). Tram 16, 24, 25. **Open** 10am-6pm daily. No credit cards. **Café**. Map p139 A4 ⑩

The café affectionately known as My Aunt's Cake started life as a purveyor of over-the-top cakes (which they still produce) before becoming the campest tea-room in town. Set in a glowing pink space filled with mismatched furniture, it's particularly gay-friendly (note the Tom of Finland cake).

Warung Spang-Makandra

Gerard Doustraat 39 (670 5081/www. spangmakandra.nl). Tram 6, 7, 10, 16. **Open** 11am-10pm Tue-Sat; 1-10pm Sun. **€**. **Global**. Map p139 A4 ⑪

An Indonesian-Surinamese restaurant where the Indo influence always comes up trumps thanks to their addictive Javanese rames. The decor is kept very simple, but the relaxed vibe and beautifully presented dishes will make you want to sit down and linger over a meal rather than take it away.

Wijnbar Boelen & Boelen

1e van der Helststraat 50 (671 2242/ www.wijnbar.nl). Tram 3, 4, 16, 24, 25. **Open** 6pm-midnight Tue-Sun. **Bar**. Map p139 A4 ⑫

Many of the regulars come here for the Frenchified food, but as the name implies, the wine's the real star of the show at this compact yet airy bar on the edge of the Pijp's main nightlife strip. The emphasis is on old world tipples, but there are also well-edited selections from both the Antipodes and the Americas, and the friendly owners can offer suggestions for those less well versed in the ways of the grape.

Yo-Yo

2e Jan van der Heijdenstraat 79 (664 7173). Tram 3, 4. **Open** noon-7pm Mon-Sat. No credit cards. **Coffeeshop**. Map p139 C3 ⑬

Located on a leafy residential street near Sarphatipark and the Albert Cuypmarket, this chill spot lacks the commercialism and crowds found in more central shops. The herb is all-organic,

and it's run by a very pleasant lady who bakes fresh apple pie every day – a truly awesome cure for the chronic munchies if ever there was one.

Shopping

Albert Cuypmarkt

Albert Cuypstraat (no phone). Tram 4, 16, 24, 25. **Open** 9.30am-5pm Mon-Sat. No credit cards. Map p139 B4 ⑭

Amsterdam's largest general market sells everything from pillows to prawns at great prices. The clothes on sale tend to be run-of-the-mill cheapies.

Dirk van den Broek

Marie Heinekenplein 25 (673 9393/ www.lekkerdoen.nl). **Open** 9am-9pm Mon-Fri; 9am-8pm Sat. No credit cards. Map p139 A4 ⑮

Suddenly fashionable – its red bags are now must-haves for the town's designer lemmings and have even been spotted on the arms of the fashion ratpack overseas – Dirk remains cheaper than Albert Heijn, while its choice has improved, although it's not the most glamorous of supermarkets.

Runneboom

1e Van der Helststraat 49 (673 5941). Tram 16, 24, 25. **Open** 7am-5pm Mon-Sat. No credit cards. Map p139 B4 ⑯

This Pijp bakery is a staunch favourite with locals, who queue far into the street come rain or shine. A huge selection of French, Russian, Greek and Turkish loaves is offered, with rye bread the house speciality. Delicious cakes and pastries are also sold.

Nightlife

Badcuyp

1e Sweelinckstraat 10 (675 9669/www. badcuyp.nl). Tram 4, 16, 24, 25. **Open** 11am-1am Tue-Thur, Sun; 11am-3am Fri, Sat. Map p139 B3 ⑰

Small and friendly, the focus at this popular night spot is firmly placed on world and jazz. Besides the intriguing range of international talents in the main hall, the cute café plays host to regular salsa, African, jazz and open jam evenings that are always a hoot.

Eramsburg Bridge, Rotterdam

Day Trips

There's more to the Netherlands than just its capital city, of course, and for a relatively compact country it boasts an astonishing variety of landscapes, from beaches and dykes to thick woods and forests to real urban jungles, all of which can be reached simply by taking a short train journey from Centraal Station. Amsterdam itself is part of one of the most densely populated areas in the world: no fewer than 40 per cent of the country's entire population inhabit the built-up sprawl known as the Randstad or 'Edge City'. It's made up of Delft, Haarlem, the Hague, Leiden and Utrecht, as well as bitter urban rivals Amsterdam and Rotterdam. Each of the destinations below can easily be explored in day trips undertaken from the capital, although they also stand up to more leisurely and sustained exploration.

Delft

Imagine a miniaturised Amsterdam – those canals reduced to dinky proportions, bridges narrowed, merchants' houses shrunk – and you have the essence of Delft. Though it's small and often scoffed at for its sleepiness, Delft is a student town with plenty going on. Its bars and cafés may appear to outsiders to be survivors of a bygone era – white-aproned waiters, high-ceilinged interiors and all – but it's the norm in Delft. Other cities offer hot chocolate finished with aerosol cream; cafés here use real cream and accompany it with a fancier brand of biscuit. It's truly appropriate that this is the home of 'Royal Blue'.

Everything you're likely to want to see is in the old centre. As soon as you cross over the road from the

station towards the city centre, you encounter an introduction to Delft's past: a representation of Vermeer's famous *Milkmaid* in stone.

Delft was traditionally a centre for trade, producing and exporting butter, cloth, Delft beer – at one point in the past, almost 200 breweries could be found alongside its canals – and, later, pottery of course. Its subsequent loss in trade has been Rotterdam's gain, but the aesthetic benefits can be seen in the city's centuries-old gables, hump-backed bridges and shady canals. To appreciate how little has changed, walk to the end of Oude Delft, the oldest canal in town (it almost had to make way for a tramline in the 1920s), cross the busy road to the harbour and compare the view to Vermeer's *View of Delft*, now on display in the Mauritshuis in the Hague (p150).

But though the city's museums and churches are grand, it's fun simply to stroll around town. The historic centre has more than 600 national monuments. Pick up a guide from the VVV office and see what the town has to offer.

Sights & museums

De Delftse Pauw
Delftweg 133 (015 212 4920/www. delftsepauw.com). Open Apr-Oct 9am-4.30pm daily. *Nov-Mar* 9am-4.30pm Mon-Fri; 11am-1pm Sat, Sun. **Admission** free.
Delft is most famous for its blue and white tiles and pottery, known as Delft Blue (or internationally as Royal Blue). This is one of the few factories that is open to visitors.

Legermuseum
Korte Geer 1 (015 215 0500/www.leger museum.nl). Open 10am-5pm Tue-Fri; noon-5pm Sat, Sun. **Admission** €6; €3 seniors, 4-17s; free under-4s, MK.
Gun nuts take note: the 'Army Museum' houses the country's largest military collection.

Museum Lambert van Meerten
Oude Delft 199 (015 260 2199). **Open** 10am-5pm Tue-Sat; 1-5pm Sun. **Admission** €6; free under-12s.
This museum offers an overview of the Delft Blue industry and includes a huge range of tiles, depicting everything from battling warships to randy rabbits – contrasting dramatically with today's mass-produced trinkets.

Nieuwe Kerk
Markt 80 (015 212 3025/www.nieuwe kerk-delft.nl). Open Apr-Oct 9am-6pm Mon-Sat. *Nov-Mar* 11am-4pm Mon-Fri; 10am-5pm Sat. **Admission** €3; €1.50 under-12s. (Tower €2.50; €1 under-12s).
The 'New Church' took almost 15 years to construct and was finished in 1396. It contains the mausoleums of lawyer-philosopher and founder of 'natural law' theory Hugo de Groot (better known to anglophone readers as 'Grotius') and William of Orange (interned alongside his dog, which faithfully followed him into death by refusing food and water), in a black and white marble mausoleum designed by Hendrick de Keyser. De Keyser also designed the epic 1620 Stadhuis (or City Hall) across the Markt.

Oude Kerk
Heilige Geestkerkhof 25 (015 212 3015, www.oudekerk-delft.nl). Open Apr-Oct; 9am-6pm Mon-Sat; *Nov-Mar* 11am-4pm Mon-Fri, 10am-5pm Sat. **Admission** €3; €1.50 under-12s.
The town's other splendid house of worship, the Gothic 'Old Church' (c1200), is known as 'Leaning Jan' because its tower stands two metres (over six feet) off-kilter. Art-lovers should note that it's the final resting place of Vermeer.

De Porceleyne Fles
Rotterdamseweg 196 (015 251 2030/ www.royaldelft.com). Open Apr-Oct 9am-5pm Mon-Sun. *Nov-Mar* 9am-5pm Mon-Sat. **Admission** €4.50 guided tour.
Another look behind the scenes of a Delft Blue pottery factory.

Embrace the cliché

Despite the official mantra 'there's more to Holland than this', the Dutch clichés – yep, that's windmills, tulips and clogs – continue to beguile most visitors, no matter how cool they may think they are. And rightly so. They're part of the Netherlands' DNA, and while you can stroll into a gallery anywhere and see a Van Gogh, there aren't many places where you can sip beer beneath a windmill.

Clogs, which are sold in every tourist shop, make groovy wall-decorations and are even seen on feet: mostly workmen's (they're EU-recognised safety shoes), kids' and occasionally those of hicks from the sticks. Just outside town is the improbably fascinating **Klompenmakerij De Zaanse Schans** (Kraaienest 4, Zaandam, 075 617 7121, www. zaanseschans.nl) a clog-making museum detailing the shoe's unique history and symbolism.

Tulips, meanwhile, are ubiquitous – flowers play a crucial role in the Dutch economy. The most famous place to buy them is the **floating flower market** (Singel, between Koningsplein and Muntplein). It's less dazzling than it sounds, but still pretty. For real action, you need to head out to Aalsmeer's **flower auction** (Legmeerdijk 313, 0297 392185, www.vba-aalsmeer.nl), a vast complex shifting 19 million blooms daily in a nail-biting Dutch auction.

Eight windmills remain to this day in Amsterdam; most famous of these is **De Gooyer** (Funenkade 5), abutting the award-winning brewery 't IJ. There are also photogenic examples on Haarlemmerweg: **De 1200 Roe** (No.701) was built in 1632, while **De Bloem** (No.465) is a mere whippersnapper dating from 1878. Both were used until the 1950s. Grab a chance to see the improbably urban **De Otter** (Gillisvan Ledenberchstraat 78) in Westerpark while you can. Its future is now being wrangled over by the highest court in the land, no less, which is currently deciding whether it should be allowed to move, brick by brick, to a place where wind can actually get to it.

Het Prinsenhof Municipal Museum

Sint Agathaplein 1 (015 260 2358/www.prinsenhof-delft.nl). **Open** 10am-5pm Tue-Sat; 1-5pm Sun. **Admission** €5; €4 students, 12-16s, 65+; free under-12s.

Located in the former convent of St Agatha, this castle-like structure holds ancient and modern art exhibitions along with displays about Prince William of Orange, who was assassinated here in 1584 by one of many keen to earn the price put on his head by Philip II of Spain during Holland's 80-year fight for independence. The bullet holes are still visible on the stairs.

Reptielenzoo Serpo

Stationsplein 8 (015 212 2184/www. serpo.nl). **Open** 10am-6pm Mon-Sat; 1-6pm Sun. **Admission** €7.50; €6.50 seniors; €5.50 4-11s; free under-4s.

Europe's largest collection of poisonous snakes is here, along with whole herds of other scaly creatures.

Getting there

Delft is 60 kilometres (37 miles) south-west of Amsterdam on the A4. Trains from Amsterdam Centraal Station take just under an hour, though you may need to change at the Hague.

Tourist information

Toeristische Informatie Punt (Tourist Information Point)

Hippolytusbuurt 4 (0900 515 1555/ www.delft.nl). **Open** *Apr-Oct* 10am-4pm Mon; 9am-6pm Tue-Fri; 10am-5pm Sat; 10am-4pm Sun. *Nov-Mar* 11am-4pm Mon; 10am-4pm Tue-Sat; 10am-3pm Sun.

Haarlem

Although Amsterdam is also located in Noord-Holland, it's Haarlem, just 15 minutes away by train, which serves as the provincial capital.

Positioned a mere cycle ride away from the lovely beaches of Zandvoort- and Bloemendaal-aan-Zee, Haarlem serves as a smaller, gentler and older version of Amsterdam. Unfortunately, all traces of the city's origins as a tenth-century settlement on an inland sea disappeared with the draining of the Haarlemmermeer in the mid 19th century. That doesn't mean that the place has lost its appeal, though: the historic centre, with its lively main square and canals, not to mention some of the country's most charming almshouses, is beautiful.

Sights & museums

Frans Halsmuseum

Groot Heiligland 62 (023 511 5775/ www.franshalsmuseum.nl). **Open** 11am-5pm Mon-Sat; noon-5pm Sun. **Admission** €7; free under-18s.

Housed in what used to be an elderly men's almshouse and orphanage which are well worth a visit in themselves, this museum is a magnificent collection of 16th- and 17th-century portraits, still lifes, genre paintings and landscapes. The highlight is a group of eight portraits of militia companies and regents from the brush of Frans Hals himself. The museum also has vast collections of period furniture, Haarlem silver and an 18th-century apothecary with Delftware pottery.

De Hallen

Grotemarkt 16 (023 5115775/www. dehallen.com). **Open** 11am-5pm Mon-Sat; noon-5pm Sun. **Admission** €5; free under-18s.

This is a genuinely up-to-the-minute modern art museum housed in two rather interesting old buildings, the Verweyhal (a 19th-century gentleman's club) and the atmospheric Vleeshal or 'meat hall', an early 17th century butcher's market. Exhibitions tend to focus on cutting-edge international artists, and have recently featured Tracey Emin, Sarah Lucas and the German Jonathan Meese.

St Bavo

Grotemarkt (023 553 2040/www. bavo.nl). **Open** 10am-4pm Mon-Sat. **Admission** €2; free under-12s.

This truly enormous church, dominating Grotemarkt, the main square, provides an excellent point to begin exploring Haarlem's long history. Built around 1313, it suffered fire damage in 1328 and rebuilding lasted another 150 years. It's surprisingly bright inside: cavernous white transepts stand as high as the nave and make a stunning sight. The floor is made up of 1,350 gravestones, including one featuring only the word 'Me' and another long enough to hold a famed local giant. In the interests of balance, there's also a dedication to a local midget who died of injuries from a game of dwarf-tossing. Ironic really, as it was a sport he'd invented himself. The centrepiece is the famous Müller organ (1738) – the most photographed organ in the world. An extraordinary gold and red instrument, it boasts an astonishing 5,068 pipes. In its time it has been played by Handel, as well as the ten-year-old Mozart, who squeezed out a few tunes in 1765 while he was on a tour of the Netherlands with his family. The boy genius's visit is marked with a plaque.

Teylers Museum

Spaarne 16 (023 516 0960/www.teylers museum.nl). **Open** 10am-5pm Tue-Sat; noon-5pm Sun. **Admission** €7; €2 6-18s; free under-5s, MK.

Though somewhat in the shadow of the Frans Halsmuseum, the Teylers is nevertheless a good example of an old-fashioned Age of Enlightenment museum of everything. Founded in 1784, it's the oldest museum in the Netherlands. Fossils and minerals sit beside antique scientific instruments here, and in addition there is a superb collection, spanning the 16th to the 19th centuries, of more than 10,000 drawings by Old Masters including the likes of Rembrandt, Michelangelo and Raphael. There's also a new wing to explore that hosts temporary art and science exhibitions.

Getting there

By car, Delft is ten kilometres (six miles) west on the A5. Trains from Amsterdam Centraal Station take roughly 15 minutes.

Tourist information

VVV

Stationsplein 1 (0900 616 1600 premium rate/www.vvvzk.nl). **Open** Oct-Mar 9.30am-5pm Mon-Fri; 10am-3pm Sat. Apr-Sept 9.30am-5pm Mon-Fri; 9.30am-3pm Sat.

The Hague

Beginning life in the 13th century as a hunting ground for Dutch counts, its full name, 's Gravenhage, means 'the Count's Hedge'. But the Hague (*Den Haag* in Dutch) is not in fact officially a city. In days of yore, the powers that be did not want to offend its more ancient neighbours, Leiden and Utrecht, and so never granted the Hague a status beyond that of a mere town. Nevertheless, it is the nation's hub of power and a centre for international justice.

Sights & museums

Binnenhof

Binnenhof 8A (070 364 6144/www. binnenhofbezoek.nl). **Open** 10am-4pm Mon-Sat. **Admission** €5-€7; €4-€6 under-13s.

The Hague's history begins right here, where, in 1248, William II built a castle. Now parliament buildings occupy the site, and every September Queen Beatrix arrives in a lovely golden coach for the pomp and ceremony of the annual state opening of parliament. Guided tours are organised daily around the Knights' Hall, the place where the ceremony takes place.

Escher in Het Paleis

Lange Voorhout 74 (070 42 77730/ www.escherinhetpaleis.nl). **Open** 11am-5pm Tue-Sun. **Admission** €7.50; €5 7-15s; free under-7s.

AMSTERDAM BY AREA

The Hague

The Gemeentemuseum's new sister museum, Escher in het Paleis, is filled with further examples of the artist's mind-melting work.

Gemeentemuseum Den Haag

Stadhouderslaan 41 (070 338 1111/ www.gemeentemuseum.nl). **Open** 11am-5pm Tue-Sun. **Admission** €8.50; free under-18s.

The star of this gallery is Piet Mondrian's *Victory Boogie Woogie*, which sold for €36 million in 1998. It's now on display here, in a museum which holds the world's largest collection of Mondrians, plus several pieces by MC Escher – not to mention one of the best fashion collections in the world.

Madurodam

George Maduroplein 1 (070 416 2400/ www.madurodam.nl). **Open** *Mid Mar-June* 9am-8pm daily. *July, Aug* 9am-11pm daily. *Sept-mid Mar* 9am-6pm daily. **Admission** €13; €12 over-65s; €9.25 3-11s; free under-3s.

An insanely detailed miniature city that dishes up every Dutch cliché in the book: windmills turn, ships sail and trains speed around on the world's largest model railway. If you visit on a summer's evening, when the models are lit from within by 50,000 miniature lamps, be prepared for your ironic appreciation to evaporate completely and be replaced by unalloyed, child-like wonder.

Mauritshuis

Korte Vijverberg 8 (070 302 3456/www.mauritshuis.nl). **Open** *Apr-Aug* 10am-5pm Mon-Sat; 11am-5pm Sun; *Sept-Mar* 10am-5pm Tue-Sat; 11am-5pm Sun. **Admission** €9.50 incl audio tour; €4.75 seniors; free under-18s.

Once a home for local counts, like much of the Hague, the Mauritshuis is now open to the public and houses one of the most famous art collections in the world, boasting works by Rubens, Rembrandt and Vermeer, among others.

Panorama Mesdag

Zeestraat 65 (070 364 4544/www. mesdag.nl). **Open** 10am-5pm Mon-Sat; noon-5pm Sun. **Admission** €5; €4 over-65s; €2.50 3-13s; free under-3s.

This building houses the largest painting in the country, measuring 120 metres (400 feet) in circumference, from which the museum takes its name. Painted by Hendrik Willem Mesdag (and with the assistance of the great Amsterdam painter George Hendrik Breitner, then still a student) it's a view of the landscape of Scheveningen, which visitors examine from an observation platform. The museum also displays works from the Hague (with mainly seascapes by Roelof and Mauve) and Barbizon (peasant life and landscape by the likes of Alma-Tadema) Schools.

Getting there

By car, the Hague is 50 kilometres (31 miles) south-west of Amsterdam on the A4, then the A44. Trains from Amsterdam Centraal Station to Den Haag station take 50 minutes; you may need to change at Leiden.

Tourist information

VVV
Hofweg 1, outside Centraal Station (0900 340 3505 premium rate/www. denhaag.com). **Open** 10am-6pm Mon-Fri; 10am-5pm Sat; noon-5pm Sun.

Leiden

Canal-laced Leiden derives a good deal of its undeniable charm from the fact that it is home to the Netherlands' oldest university. It was founded here in 1575 and boasts such notable alumni as the philosopher René Descartes, sixth president of the United States John Quincy Adams and many a Dutch royal. The old town teems with students, bikes and bars, has the highest concentration of historic monuments per square metre of anywhere in the country, and is consequently a most rewarding place to visit, ideal for a charming weekend away from comparatively frenetic Amsterdam.

Sights & museums

Hortus Botanicus Leiden
Rapenburg 73 (071 527 7249/www. hortusleiden.nl). **Open** *Apr-Oct* 10am-6pm daily. *Nov-Mar* 10am-4pm Mon-Fri, Sun. **Admission** €5; €2.50 4-12s; free under 4s, MK.
Over 6,000 species of flora are represented here at one of the world's oldest botanical gardens, including descendants of the country's first tulips.

Molenmuseum de Valk
2e Binnenvestgracht 1 (071 516 5353/ http://home.wanadoo.nl/molenmuseum). **Open** 10am-5pm Tue-Sat; 1-5pm Sun. **Admission** €3; €1.70 6-15s, concessions; free under-6s, MK.
If Dutch clichés are the things that you came here to see, head straight to the 'Falcon Windmill Museum', an erstwhile mill turned museum where you can see the old living quarters, machinery and also a picturesque view over Leiden. (A better panorama, though, can be had from the top of the Burcht, a 12th-century fort on an ancient artificial mound in the city centre.)

Naturalis
Darwinweg (071 568 7600/www. naturalis.nl). **Open** 10am-5pm Tue-Fri; 10am-6pm Sat, Sun. **Admission** €9; €6 13-17s; €5 4-12s; free under-3s.
The ten million fossils, minerals and assorted stuffed animals exhibited at this museum of natural history make it the largest collection of any museum in the Netherlands.

Rijksmuseum van Oudheden
Rapenburg 28 (0900 6 600600/www. rmo.nl). **Open** 10am-5pm Tue-Fri; noon-5pm Sat, Sun. **Admission** €8.50; €5.50 4-17s; €7.50 over-65s; free under-4s, MK.
Perhaps Leiden's most noteworthy museum, the National Museum of Antiquities houses the largest collection of archaeological artefacts in the Netherlands. Of particular interest are the unique display of Egyptian mummies, which should not be missed, and an exhibition of bog finds.

Rijksmuseum voor Volkenkunde

Steenstraat 1 (071 516 8800/www. rmv.nl). **Open** 10am-5pm Tue-Sun. **Admission** €7.50; €4 concessions; free MK.

The National Museum of Ethnology showcases cultures of Africa, Oceania, Asia, the Americas and the Arctic.

Stedelijk Museum de Lakenhal

Oude Singel 28-32 (071 516 5360/www.lakenhal.nl). **Open** 10am-5pm Tue-Fri; noon-5pm Sat, Sun. **Admission** €4; €2.50 over-65s; free under-18s, MK.

In the Golden Age of the late 16th and 17th centuries, Leiden grew fat on textiles. It also spawned three great painters: Rembrandt van Rijn, Jan van Goyen and Jan Steen. Although few works by these masters remain in Leiden today, the Lakenhal Municipal Museum does have a painting by Rembrandt, as well as works by other Old Masters and collections of pewter, tiles, silver and glass.

Getting there

By car, Leiden is 40 kilometres (24 miles) south-west of Amsterdam on the A4. Trains from Amsterdam Centraal Station take 35 minutes.

Tourist information

VVV

Stationsweg 2D (0900 222 2333 premium rate/www.leidenpromotie.nl). **Open** 11am-5.30pm Mon; 9.30am-5.30pm Tue-Fri; 10am-4.30pm Sat.

Rotterdam

The antithesis of Amsterdam both visually and in vibe, this port city – its nickname is the Havenstad or 'harbour city' – brings a bit of urban grit to the pretty Dutch landscape. Almost completely flattened during World War II, it has blossomed into a concrete-

and-glass jungle, and what it lacks in charm it makes up for with creativity and innovation. In fact, the city remains in an almost continuous state of regeneration: a fine example of this is Rotterdam Centraal Station, currently being rebuilt. It may mean your entry point into the city is a building site, but the changes promise to be breathtaking – and well worth the long wait – when the station finally opens in 2010.

Sights & museums

Euromast

Parkhaven 20 (010 436 4811/www. euromast.nl). **Open** *Apr-Sept* 9.30am-11pm daily. *Oct-Mar* 10am-11pm daily. **Admission** €8.30; €5.40 4-11s; free under-4s.

A bird's eye view of the whole city and its docklands – and way beyond – can be had from the nearby Euromast, if you can handle the precipitous height of 185 metres (607 feet). A hundred metres up there's a café/restaurant and even two hotel suites. There are also three rather vertiginous thrills: Euroscoop is a rotating lift, and the foolhardy can abseil or take a death-slide from 100 metres.

Historical Museum Rotterdam

Korte Hoogstraat 31 (010 217 6767/ www.mr.rotterdam.nl). **Open** 10am-5pm Tue-Sun. **Admission** €3; €1.50 4-16s; free under-4s.

This vast historical centre includes the Dubbelde Palmboom ('Double Palm Tree'), housed in an old granary in Delfshaven and exploring life in the Meuse delta from 8000 BC to the present, and Het Schielandshuis, a palatial 17th-century mansion, another of few buildings spared in the bombing.

Kijk-Kubus

Overblaak 70 (010 414 2285/www. cubehouse.nl). **Open** *Jan, Feb* 11am-5pm Sat, Sun. *Mar-Dec* 11am-5pm daily. **Admission** €2; €1.50 concessions; free under-4s.

Cube houses in Oude Haven

Rotterdam's Oude Haven (Old Harbour) is now a work of imaginative modernism, the pinnacle of which is Piet Blom's witty bright yellow cubic houses. Built in the 1970s, Kijk-Kubus remains a modernist monument open to visitors. Other cubes are private homes. One is currently being converted into a hostel, and is due to open in 2008.

Kunsthal

Westzeedijk 341 (010 440 0301/www. kunsthal.nl). **Open** 10am-5pm Tue-Sat; 11am-5pm Sun. **Admission** €8.50; €8 seniors; €5 students; €2 6-18s; free under-6s.

Designed by Rem Koolhaas's locally based OMA bureau, the Kunsthal offers more than 3,000 square metres of art, design and photography, with regular travelling exhibitions.

Museum Boijmans van Beuningen

Museumpark 18-20 (010 441 9400/ www.boijmans.rotterdam.nl). **Open** 11am-5pm Tue-Sun. **Admission** €9; free under-18s; free on Wed.

The city's principal art museum is home to a quite magnificent collection

of traditional and contemporary art, including works by Bruegel, Van Eyck and Rembrandt.

Netherlands Architecture Institute

Museumpark 25 (010 440 1200/www. nai.nl). **Open** 10am-5pm Tue-Sat; 11am-5pm Sun. **Admission** €8; €5 seniors, students, 12-18s; €1 4-12s; free under-4s.

Favourite city son and architectural wizard Rem Koolhaas designed Rotterdam's cultural heart, the Museumpark, where you'll find outdoor sculptures and five museums. This one, which opened in 1993, gives an overview of the history and development of architecture, with particular emphasis on Rotterdam itself. It also hosts regular temporary exhibitions on architecture-related subjects and has an extensive archive.

Getting there

By car, Rotterdam is 73 kilometres (45 miles) south of Amsterdam on the A4, then the A13. Direct trains from Amsterdam Centraal Station take roughly one hour.

AMSTERDAM BY AREA

Utrecht

Tourist information

Use-it

Schaatsbaan 41-45 (010 240 9158/
www.use-it.nl).
A kind of 'young person's VVV', this
place offers loads of tips for trips to
the city, plus some free lockers to ditch
your backpack.

VVV

Coolsingel 5 (0900 403 4065 premium
rate/www.rotterdam.info). **Open** 9am-
5.30pm Mon-Thur, Sat; 9am-9pm Fri;
10am-5pm Sun.

Utrecht

Utrecht is one of the oldest cities
in the Netherlands. And during its
Middle Ages salad days, it was the
biggest. A religious and political
centre for hundreds of years, at one
point there were around 40 houses of
worship in the city, all with towers
and spires. From a distance, it must
have looked like a holy pincushion.
But there's more to Utrecht than just
history: the university is one of the

largest in the Netherlands – still
expanding and employing architects
like Rem Koolhaas (who designed
the Educatorium) – and the centre
bustles with trendy shops and
cafés. Happily, too, the Hoog
Catharijne, the country's biggest
shopping mall, will soon be knocked
down. But until then, you'll have to
negotiate the labyrinthine layout,
following signs to 'Centrum' to exit
Centraal Station.

Utrecht is in an area rich in
castles, forests and arboretums.
Slot Zuylen (Zuylen Castle,
Tournooiveld 1, Oud Zuilen, 030 244
0255, www.slotzuylen.com)
overlooks exquisite waterfalls and
gardens. Check out the concerts and
shows in **Kasteel Groeneveld**'s
gorgeous gardens (Groeneveld
Castle, Groeneveld 2, Baarn, 035 542
0446, www.kasteelgroeneveld.nl), to
the north-east of Utrecht. Take a
stroll in the **Arboretum von
Gimborn** (Vossensteinsesteeg 8,
030 253 1826/www.bio.uu.nl/
bottuinen) in Doorne, then pop over

to **Kasteel Huis Doorn** (Doorn Castle, Langbroekerweg 10, 034 342 1020, www.huisdoorn.nl). This will answer a question that's probably been puzzling you for ages: what happened to the Kaiser after World War I? Wilhelm II lived here in exile for 20 years before eventually passing away in 1941.

Sights & museums

Centraal Museum

Nicolaaskerkhof 10 (030 236 2362/ www.centraalmuseum.nl). **Open** 11am-5pm Tue-Thur, Sat, Sun; noon-9pm Fri. **Admission** €8; €6 seniors, 13-17s; €2 under 12s, MK.

This museum houses a varied collection, from paintings by Van Gogh to contemporary art and fashion. One wing is dedicated to illustrator Dick Bruna, who was born and still lives in Utrecht, and who created that always charming bunny, Miffy.

Domtoren

Domplein (030 236 0010). **Open** noon-5pm Mon, Sun; 10am-6pm Tue-Fri; 10am-5pm Sat. **Admission** €7.50; €4.50 concessions; free under-4s.

A good starting point for exploring the town is the cathedral tower that dominates the skyline for miles around. At over 112 metres (367 feet), it's the highest tower in the country. You can climb up it and the panorama is worth the 465 steps: vistas stretch 40 kilometres (25 miles) to Amsterdam on a clear day. The space between the tower and the Domkerk was originally occupied by the nave of the huge church, which was destroyed by a freak tornado in 1674. Many other buildings were damaged and the exhibition inside the Domkerk shows interesting 'before' and 'after' sketches.

Museum Catharijneconvent

Lange Nieuwstraat 38 (030 231 3835/ www.catharijneconvent.nl). **Open** 10am-5pm Tue-Fri; 11am-5pm Sat, Sun. **Admission** €8.50; €7.50 over-65s; €4.50 6-17s; free under-5s.

The St Catharine Convent Museum is located in a beautiful late-medieval building. Mainly dedicated to Dutch religious history, it also has a great collection of paintings by Old Masters, including Rembrandt.

Nationaal Museum van Speelklok tot Pierement

Steenweg 6 (030 231 2789/www. museumspeelklok.nl). **Open** 10am-5pm Tue-Sun. **Admission** €7; €4 4-12s; €6 over-65s; free under-4s.

Though it sounds as if it's only for hurdy-gurdy fanciers and organ grinders, this museum, the world's biggest collection of automated musical instruments, is actually great fun, especially the regular guided tours which bring the street organs, cuckoo clocks and rabbits in hats to life for visitors of all ages.

Rietveld-Schröderhuis

Prins Hendriklaan 50 (030 236 2310/ www.rietveldschroderhuis.nl). Tour bus from Centraal Museum, leaving Thur-Sun hourly between 11.45am and 2.45pm. **Open** 11am-5pm Thur-Sun. **Admission** €16; €13 12-18s, over-65s; €8 under-12s.

Another Utrecht-born celebrity in the Centraal Museum's collection is De Stijl architect and designer Gerrit Rietveld, best known for his rectangular chairs and houses, of which the Rietveld-Schröderhuis, on the outskirts of the city centre, can be reached on the Centraal Museum's tour bus.

Getting there

Utrecht is 40 kilometres (25 miles) south-east of Amsterdam. Direct trains from Amsterdam Centraal Station take half an hour.

Tourist information

VVV

Domplein 9 (0900 128 8732 premium rate/www.utrechtyourway.nl). **Open** noon-6pm Mon; 10am-6pm Tue-Wed, Fri; 10am-8pm Thur; 9.30am-5pm Sat; noon-5pm Sun.

AMSTERDAM BY AREA

Your best bed in low budget!

Exiting Amsterdam right on your doorstep

You will find the 3 Stayokay hostels in the lively city centre of Amsterdam. No matter where, you will find the same informal relaxed atmosphere, giving you an opportunity to meet fellow travellers. From a Stayokay hostel, the world is yours for the taking!

The hostels

dorms & private rooms • prices from € 20,50 including breakfast • € 2,50 discount per night for HI member • open 24 hours • bar • restaurant • WIFI and internet desks • luggage lockers • bicycle rent • and more

Information
Stayokay Amsterdam Vondelpark
Tel: +31 (0)20 589 89 96
www.stayokay.com

30 hostels in the Netherlands

Essentials

timeout.com

Over 50 of the world's greatest
cities reviewed in one site.

't Hotel p167

Hotels

Over the last year or so, there's been a building frenzy in the hotel sector, with an outbreak of rather large, seriously high-class additions. In keeping with the city's push to redevelop the area around the waters of the IJ, this has been – and will be for some time yet – the main focus of the boom. A highly handsome branch of the Swiss Mövenpick chain recently opened next door to the Muziektheater; just a few short minutes' walk away over on Oosterdokseiland, near the station, digging has already begun on what will be the biggest (550 rooms) hotel in town, at a cost of €150 million. Operated by the UK's City Inn chain, it's due to open in 2010.

Across the road, the Grand Hotel Amrâth Amsterdam (see box p169) opened in July 2007, converting one of the city's true landmark monuments, the Scheepvaarthuis, into an extremely smart hotel.

Lower down the budget scale it's business as usual, with fewer facilities, smaller rooms, compact bathrooms (showers are standard; baths a luxury, even at the top end) and vertiginous stairwells making things occasionally awkward for disabled travellers. This is a fair reflection of an across-the-board lack of accommodation and land in a country conjured out of the sea.

Nor is Amsterdam, hotel-wise at least, the place to come for a cheap weekend away – and prices continue to creep up and up without respite.

For some reason, boutique hotels haven't really caught on here; we've listed the finest of the few there are below. Perhaps the best way to experience a local version of the

OUR CLIMATE NEEDS
A HELPING HAND TODAY

Be a smart traveller. Help to offset your carbon emissions
from your trip by pledging Carbon Trees with Trees for Cities.

All the Carbon Trees that you donate through Trees for Cities
are genuinely planted as additional trees in our projects.

Trees for Cities is an independent charity working with local
communities on tree planting projects.

www.treesforcities.org   Tel 020 7587 1320

Trees for Cities
Charity registration number 1060154

phenomenon is to stay in a B&B. Far from the dowdy, seaside images the term usually conjures up, B&Bs are often designed to their stylish owners' very high specifications, but be warned: bed-and-breakfasting is seldom a budget option.

Hotels cluster around particular areas of Amsterdam: the Museum District and the Canals have plenty, while the Pijp and Jordaan, alas, contain few. A general rule of thumb should be to avoid – with a couple of noteworthy exceptions – hotels near the station or Red Light District.

Money matters

Credit card payment isn't always accepted in this quaint old city, particularly in smaller places, so check first. A hotel's rate may or may not include the city tax of five per cent, which could be added onto your final bill. Before booking, it's always worth checking for special deals on hotels' own websites, or on more commercial hotel websites – www.bookings.nl (also in English) is a good place to start.

The Old Centre

Amstel Botel

Oosterdokskade 2-4 (626 4247/www. amstelbotel.nl). Tram 1, 2, 5, 9, 13, 17, 24, 25. €
Convenient for Centraal Station, the Docklands and Noord, this is good, clean accommodation with a few frills like in-house movies. The early opening, late closing bar (9am-1am) has pinball, pool and a jukebox – very good for teenagers on rainy days. Major rebuilding of the area means that views aren't as nice as they've been in the past.

Barbizon Palace

Prins Hendrikkade 59-72 (556 4564/ www.nh-hotels.com). Tram 1, 2, 4, 5, 9, 13, 14, 16, 17, 24, 25. €€€
This flash branch of the reliable home-grown NH chain is right opposite Centraal Station, and therefore ideal if

SHORTLIST

Best newcomers
- Grand Hotel Amrâth Amsterdam (p169)

Boutique experiences
- Bilderberg Jan Luyken (p174)
- Hotel Vondel (p175)
- Kamer01 (p171)

Essential Amsterdam
- Greenhouse Effect (p163)
- Van Ostade Bicycle Hotel (p175)
- Xaviera Hollander Bed & Breakfast (p175)

Nests for culture vultures
- Ambassade Hotel (p166)
- Between Art and Kitsch (p174)
- Lloyd Hotel (p162)

Views from on high
- Dikker & Thijs Fenice Hotel (p170)
- Hotel Okura Amsterdam (p175)
- Mövenpick Hotel Amsterdam City Centre (p172)

Cheap and cheerful
- Hotel Brouwer (p167)
- Hotel Leydsche Hof (p170)
- Hotel Prinsenhof (p170)

Movie star treatment
- Dylan (p166)
- Hotel 717 (p170)
- InterContinental Amstel Amsterdam (p170)
- Sofitel the Grand Amsterdam (p165)

Most stylish interiors
- College Hotel (p175)
- 't Hotel (p167)
- Ideaal II (p172)
- Residence Le Coin (p165)
- Seven Bridges (p172)
- Stayokay Amsterdam Zeeburg (p172)

Staying dead centre
- RHO Hotel (p165)

ESSENTIALS

Cultural cooking with Lloyd

The basic idea was simple: they aimed to create as much space and freedom as possible. The reinvention of a youth prison into a hotel and self-styled 'cultural embassy' – complete with 120 rooms, running the range from one to five stars – took over eight long years before the Lloyd Hotel finally opened amid the up-and-coming eastern docklands area in 2004.

Its roots can be traced back to an underground group of cultural prime movers being inspired to take full advantage of the global arts scene and the 'eternal immigration' of its participants. Only then did the idea of a hotel begin – one that would also act as a showcase of sorts for not only visitors but also the local creative arts scene at large.

But this is no mere designer hotel. MVRDV, the insanely inspired architects who gave the world the unrealised Pig City (a strange skyscraper for pig breeding), have turned a once claustrophobic hell-hole into a bastion of light while respectfully retaining such original elements as stained glass windows, tiled walls, exposed timbers and jail doors re-invented as linen storage units. Meanwhile, some of the more high-profile names in the Dutch design world – Atelier van Lieshout, Bureau Lakenvelder, Richard Hutten, Marcel Wanders and Hella Jongerius, for example – duly took responsibility for the interiors of the rooms themselves.

Many rooms are best described via their bathrooms: some are shared, some fold away, some have strange translucent walls and some only exist as an open shower in the middle of the room. Besides the requisite bar and two restaurants (one 'fast', the other 'slow'), there's almost always something special going on for guests to join in with, be it an artist's party or happenings like 2006's Full Llove Inn, the latter a room in an Opel Kadett atop a four-and-a-half-metre-high pole. In short, expect the unexpected – in the nicest possible way, of course.

Lloyd Hotel

Oostelijke Handelskade 34 (561 3604/www.lloydhotel.com). Tram 10, 26. €-€€€€

you're hopping off the train laden with luggage. Public areas are decked out in sleek monochrome, making the rooms themselves (in bland hotel beige) a bit disappointing. That said, facilities could never be called run-of-the-mill: they include conference rooms in a 15th-century chapel and a rather upmarket Michelin-starred restaurant that makes eating in a genuine experience.

Flying Pig Downtown

Nieuwendijk 100 (420 6822/group bookings 421 0583/www.flyingpig.nl). Tram 1, 2, 3, 5, 13, 17. €

Not so much a hostel, more a way of life, and a stalwart of the Inter-railing scene. Young (they don't accept guests over 40 or under 16) backpackers flock here from around the world, as much for the social life as the accommodation. You can see why: the hostel organises walking tours and in-line skating for free, and there are regular parties and consistent cheap beer. There are also branches near to the Vondelpark and on the beach at Noordwijk-aan-Zee; the latter is open all year but comes into its own in the summer, when water sports, beach activities and barbecues become the order of the day. A regular daily shuttle bus ferries guests between the beach and uptown branches of the hostel for free.

Grand Hotel Krasnapolsky

Dam 9 (554 9111/www.nh-hotels.com). Tram 1, 2, 4, 5, 9, 13, 14, 16, 17, 24, 25. €€€€

Slap bang in the centre of Amsterdam, right opposite the Royal Palace, facilities here are really excellent: restaurants, bars, a ballroom, beauty salon and a winter garden for relaxing weekend brunch. Accommodation ranges from suites to compact rooms at the back (what you'll get if you book a deal). Less expensive rooms lack baths, but come with truly invigorating multi-head showers.

Greenhouse Effect

Warmoesstraat 55 (624 4974/www. greenhouse-effect.nl). Tram 4, 9, 17, 24, 25. €

If you're planning to disappear in a cloud of cannabis smoke, this is the place to rest your addled head. Above the coffeeshop of the same name (p60), some rooms feature shared facilities, several are kitted out in very trippy styles and others are just plain, old-fashioned nice with good canal views. Breakfast is served until midday and the attached bar has an all-day happy hour and DJ nights. You'll feel most comfortable here if you are young and/or very into smoking; otherwise, it might all seem a bit surreal.

Hotel des Arts

Rokin 154-156 (620 1558/www.hoteldes arts.nl). Tram 4, 9, 14, 16, 24, 25. €€

A snug hotel exuding a touch of faded glamour, rooms here tend to be decorated with clunky, polished period furniture and highly ornate chandeliers – although some of them are also a little dark. Most are very spacious, however, and are geared towards groups and families. The hotel is near the main shopping street and most sights are within easy walking distance.

RHO Hotel p165

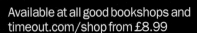

Hotel de l'Europe

Nieuwe Doelenstraat 2-8 (531 1777/ www.leurope.nl). Tram 4, 9, 14, 16, 24, 25. €€€€

Another luxury landmark hotel with views across the Amstel, this is the place for indulgent splurges or honeymoon hideaways. Every detail here is taken care of – think marble bathrooms and Bulgari toiletries. The bridal suite has a four-poster bed and a two-person jacuzzi in the room; it's also one of the few hotels in Amsterdam to boast a swimming pool, and there's a highly rated restaurant, Excelsior.

Ibis Amsterdam Centre

Stationsplein 49 (638 9999/www.ibishotel.com). Tram 1, 2, 5, 9, 13, 17, 24, 25. €€

If you're arriving in town late or leaving first thing, this place is ideal. Right next to Centraal Station, there's a 24-hour bar and very early (4am onwards) breakfast. There's nothing fancy – just the reliable Ibis formula of basic but comfortable rooms and reasonable if not cutting-edge facilities.

Nova

Nieuwezijds Voorburgwal 276 (623 0066/ www.novahotel.nl). Tram 2, 5. €€

The five charming town houses that make up Nova are comfortable, plainly furnished (yet good-looking in an IKEA sort of way), and smell fresh as daisies since the place went totally no-smoking in February 2007. The hotel is also handily located for the Nieuwezijds nightlife as well as the main cultural sights.

Renaissance Amsterdam

Kattengat 1 (621 2223/www.marriott.com). Tram 1, 2, 4, 5, 9, 13, 14, 16, 17, 24, 25. €€€

An upmarket option for exploring the highly Bohemian charms of both the nearby Harlemmerstraat and Jordaan areas, this 400-roomed place compensates for its flowery decor with top-end hotel luxuries like in-house movies, interactive videos and DVDs, and even PlayStations, making it a good bet for flush families with recalcitrant kids.

There's also a babysitting service. In 2007, single rooms were all renovated and the hotel spruced up.

Residence Le Coin

Nieuwe Doelenstraat 5 (524 6800/www.lecoin.nl). Tram 4, 9, 14, 16, 24, 25. €€

On a quiet, café-lined street between the Old Centre and the central shopping district, this medium-sized hotel arranged across seven buildings has spacious, very stylish rooms in muted colours – with minimal fussy extras. Drenched in light thanks to big windows, furnishings are a classy mix of old and new, with designer chairs and lots of shiny wood. The attic rooms are particularly full of character, and many rooms come with kitchenettes, making this a good bet for families and guests aiming at longer stays.

RHO Hotel

Nes 5-23 (620 7371/www.rhohotel.nl). Tram 1, 2, 4, 5, 9, 13, 14, 16, 17, 24, 25. €€

If your budget doesn't stretch as far as the swankier and more expensive hotels on and around Dam Square, this one matches on location, if not on interior design or style. On a back-street bustling with bars, restaurants and theatres, the art deco lobby harks back to the days when it was a gold merchant's, although the rooms themselves are surprisingly plain.

Sofitel the Grand Amsterdam

Oudezijds Voorburgwal 197 (555 3111/ www.thegrand.nl). Tram 4, 9, 14, 16, 24, 25. €€€€

Centuries of history in a luxurious courtyard hotel. Rooms are spacious and airy thanks to big windows; bathrooms are embellished with Roger & Gallet smellies and the suites range from junior to royal. Not exactly a bargain getaway destination, but there are nevertheless deals like the appropriately-named Dream Package, which includes champagne, dinner and use of the spa. Indulgent Sunday brunch (€45) in the Council Chamber is open to non-guests also.

Swissotel

Damrak 96 (522 3000/www.amsterdam. swissotel.com). Tram 1, 2, 4, 5, 9, 13, 14, 16, 17, 24, 25. €€€

One of the best-looking of the big international chains, this place is geared towards the business market, but it's still a good destination for the purely pleasure seeking. First of all, it's right next to Dam square and near department store De Bijenkorf. Secondly, all rooms have big beds, on-demand film and music and are soundproofed. Pricier rooms come with espresso machines and swish interior design, and suites overlook Dam Square.

Victoria

Damrak 1-5 (623 4255/www.parkplaza. com/amsterdamnl_victoria). Tram 1, 2, 4, 5, 9, 13, 14, 16, 17, 24, 25. €€

A stalwart of the city hotel scene, the Victoria has recently been spruced up; the public areas of this big, 300-roomed hotel opposite Centraal Station now look very dapper indeed, decked out in browns, creams and reds. Rooms themselves are good in size, and come with all the expected trappings. A big plus is the excellent health club and pool, which are open to non-guests, for a fee.

Winston Hotel

Warmoesstraat 129 (623 1380/www. winston.nl). Tram 4, 9, 14, 16, 24, 25. €

The legendary Winston has a youthful, party-loving atmosphere and arty rooms decorated in eccentric, eclectic style by local businesses and artists, ranging from monochrome to kinky S&M den decor. Cheaper dormitory beds are available, but are much less fun. There's also a bar and club (p81).

Western Canal Belt

Ambassade Hotel

Herengracht 341 (555 0222/www. ambassade-hotel.nl). Tram 1, 2, 5. €€€

Come to this literary hotel if you want to bump into your favourite author. Staff are discreet and attentive, and rooms – which stretch from single to suite to apartment – are decorated in

Louis Quatorze style. There's also a library, the many shelves of which are loaded with signed tomes by illustrious previous guests, which residents are free to peruse at their leisure.

Amsterdam Wiechmann

Prinsengracht 328-332 (626 3321/ www.hotelwiechmann.nl). Tram 1, 2, 5, 7, 17. €€

From a suit of armour in reception to teapots and toasters in the breakfast room, retro touches adorn this long-established hotel that's an ideal base for getting to know the Jordaan. Room decoration errs towards the chintzy, but it's cosy nevertheless, and some rooms look onto the canal (though these cost more). There's a strict non-smoking policy enforced throughout.

Belga

Hartenstraat 8 (624 9080/www. hotelbelga.nl). Tram 1, 2, 5. €€

Accommodation that is at the same time both family friendly and affordable is rare in Amsterdam, so thank heavens for cosy Belga. In contrast to the stealth wealth of the surrounding Nine Streets, rooms here are functional but clean and tidy, and the downstairs breakfast-cum-lunchroom is a kitsch, colourful delight. There are two resident felines, so avoid if allergic.

Dylan

Keizersgracht 384 (530 2010/www. dylanamsterdam.com). Tram 1, 2, 5. €€€€

Outrageous elegance is the keyword in the Dylan's raspberry, turmeric or coal colour-coded chromatherapy rooms, detail-obsessed bar and restaurant boasting chef Dennis Kuipers' African inspired menu. Everything, from the alignment of the cushions to the service itself, is fully thought out.

Estherea

Singel 303-309 (624 5146/www. estherea.nl). Tram 1, 2, 5. €€€

Spread over several elegant houses at the spectacular epicentre of the canals, this private hotel has been run by the same family for decades. The emphasis

Winston Hotel

here is on understated luxury: rooms are swathed in Fortuny-style fabrics and come equipped with DVD players and marble bathrooms, ensuring that once you're in, you won't want to stray back out of your front door.

't Hotel
Leliegracht 18 (422 2741/www.thotel.nl). Tram 1, 2, 5, 13, 14, 17. €€
A stylish bolthole on a beautiful canal in the Jordaan, this prosaically named place is fitted throughout in 1920s-inspired style. Bauhaus prints adorn the walls, the colour scheme is muted and the armchairs are design classics. All rooms have great views onto the canal or the rear garden and all are spacious. Split-level room eight, tucked away up in the eaves of the building, is especially full of character.

Hotel Brouwer
Singel 83 (624 6358/www.hotel brouwer.nl). Tram 1, 2, 5. €
These eight neat, en-suite rooms all look onto the Singel canal, but this is not the place to come if you expect rafts of extras. If you want honest, well-priced accommodation sited in a long-standing family-run hotel, though,

you're in for a treat. The whole place is non smoking and, unusually for a hotel in the budget class, there's a lift.

Hotel Pulitzer
Prinsengracht 315-331 (523 5235/www. pulitzer.nl). Tram 13, 14, 17. €€€€
Sprawling across 25 canal houses, rooms are naturally big and stylish in this glamorous hotel that's due to get an outpost of the Gordon Ramsay empire in late 2007. There's a lovely garden at the back and, in August, the major classical music Grachtenfestival (p36) takes place in and around the grounds, making the hotel an excellent choice for serious music fans.

Singel Hotel
Singel 13-17 (626 3108/www.singel hotel.nl). Tram 1, 2, 5. €
This medium-sized, 32-roomed place is ideally located for canal and Jordaan hikes, and for arrival and departure by train (it's a five-minute walk from Centraal Station). Inside its solid 17th-century walls, rooms are plain and are furnished in a modern, basic style; they are generally clean and tidy, and all are en-suite. Front-facing rooms have been known to get a bit noisy.

ESSENTIALS

Toren

Keizersgracht 164 (622 6352/www.
hoteltoren.nl). Tram 13, 14, 17. €€€
Bursting with extraordinary history,
over the years this building has been a
Golden Age mansion, a prime minis-
ter's home, a university and even a
hiding place for numerous persecuted
Jews during World War II. Now it's a
family-run hotel and comes with all the
usual posh trappings: truly opulent
fabrics, grand public rooms and attentive staff. Standards are a bit of a
cramp, but deluxe rooms have jacuzzis,
and the bridal suites even come with
elegant double whirlpool baths.

Southern Canal Belt

American Hotel

Leidsekade 97 (556 3000/www.
amsterdamamerican.com). Tram
1, 2, 5, 6, 7, 10. €€€€
This dazzling art nouveau monument
looks extra spruce now that a fountain
has been added to its terrace, and its
public areas – like the buttressed in-
house Café Americain – are all eye-
pleasing. Rooms (not including suites)
are pretty cramped, although they do

enjoy pleasant views of the canal
or public square below. The decor is
smart-but-bland hotel standard.

Amsterdam Marriott Hotel

Stadhouderskade 12 (607 5555/www.
marriott.com). Tram 1, 2, 5, 6, 7, 10.
€€€€
Set right next to the green lungs of
Amsterdam – the lovely Vondelpark –
the Marriott has just been given an over-
haul, so it's goodbye to the dowdy green
and brown gentleman's club styling and
hello to soothing yellows and modern
furnishings. All 392 rooms now come
equipped with Revive beds, six pillows,
high-thread-count linen and luxury
duvets. Bathrooms have also gone similarly upmarket, with cherry wood and
granite surfaces and cascade shower
heads. The onsite restaurant, Quoy, is
regarded as something of a well-kept
secret on the city's dining scene.

Banks Mansion

Herengracht 519-525 (420 0055/
www.banksmansion.nl). Tram
16, 24, 25. €€€
Once you check into this grand hotel in
a former bank building, everything is
for free – yep, drinks in the lounge,

Kamer01 p171

ESSENTIALS

Shipshape at the Amrâth

The latest addition to the Amrâth mini-chain looks set to become one of Amsterdam's landmark residences. Due to open in mid 2007, the **Grand Hotel Amrâth Amsterdam** is the first luxury opening in 15 years and arguably the most significant hotel in the city. Sure, plenty of Amsterdam's hotels have monument status and are historically noteworthy, but the Amrâth nods not only to the launch of Dutch seafaring supremacy (Cornelis Houtman and Peter de Keyser sailed from this spot to the East Indies in 1595), but also to the birth of an architectural movement.

Considered to be the first true example of Amsterdam School architecture, the Scheepvaarthuis ('Maritime House'), which houses the hotel, was built between 1913 and 1916 by Johan van der Mey. Also involved were two other leading lights of Dutch modernism: Piet Kramer and Michel de Klerk. The carvings that cover the façade – of fish, animals and the busts of Dutch explorers – were the first commission for Hildo Krop, later the official city sculptor.

Upon originally opening, the Scheepvaarthuis was home to several shipping offices, a function it fulfilled for the best part of the 20th century – the last of its old tenants, the KNSM, finally set sail from the building in 1981. After that, it fulfilled a rather more prosaic role as offices for public transport and the city's parking services, while the exigencies of office life meant that all the remarkable quirks disappeared beneath hoardings and boarding.

Happily, a brand new chapter in the Scheepvaarthuis' history is unfolding, and the opening of the Amrâth has seen all those same gloriously fine details restored to glowing health. Now the building consists of 137 rooms and 26 suites – one of which is three storeys high, set in the imposing tower at the front. In addition to the usual embellishments, the Amrâth subscribes to that growing deluxe trend of a free mini bar. It also joins the exclusive club of Amsterdam hotels boasting pools.

Grand Hotel Amrâth Amsterdam

Prins Hendrikkade 108-114 (552 0000/www.amrathamsterdam.nl). Tram 1, 2, 5, 9, 13, 17, 24. €€€

movies in your room, and even the minibar is help-yourself too. This classy form of an all-inclusive holiday also involves a pillow menu, cascade showerheads, plasma TVs and DVD players. Needless to say it's hardly bargain basement stuff, but do look out for special deals on the website.

Bridge Hotel

Amstel 107-111 (623 7068/www.the bridgehotel.nl). Tram 4, 6, 7, 9, 10. €€
Gloriously isolated on the eastern bank of the Amstel, this privately run hotel in a former stonemason's workshop is actually just a few minutes from the bright lights of Rembrandtplein, and is also well situated for exploring the Plantage and Jodenbuurt. Rooms are simple and bright; river views cost more. There are apartments and also a studio for stays longer than three days.

Dikker & Thijs Fenice Hotel

Prinsengracht 444 (620 1212/www. dtfh.nl). Tram 1, 2, 5, 6, 7, 10. €€€€
A well-established and respectable name on the city hotel scene, this upmarket place is owned by a publisher, so authors often drop in. Set in an 18th-century warehouse building near Leidseplein, rooms are plain but smart, while the highly glamorous penthouse has walls made of glass for unsurpassed views over the city rooftops. At breakfast time, guests are bathed in jewel-coloured light from the stained-glass windows.

Hotel 717

Prinsengracht 717 (427 0717/www. 717hotel.nl). Tram 1, 2, 5. €€€€
The epitome of understated glamour, this small, flower-filled place emphasises searching the globe for the best accoutrements: linens from the USA, bespoke blankets from Wales, spring mattresses from London. There is afternoon tea daily and a garden. Guests are the type who shed euros on antiques in the Spiegelkwartier.

Hotel Agora

Singel 462 (627 2200/www.hotel agora.nl). Tram 1, 2, 5. €€

Ideal for botanists looking to stock up on bulbs, this homely little place is in an 18th-century house on a canal near the floating flower market. What Agora lacks in extras, it more than makes up for with nice touches like conservatory breakfasts and a garden. Rooms are plain but very neat and comfortable and all of them enjoy some lovely canal or garden views.

Hotel Leydsche Hof

Leidsegracht 14 (623 2148/www.free webs.com/leydschehof). Tram 1, 2, 5, 6, 7, 10. €
A hidden gem of a hotel on a genteel canal just minutes from Leidseplein, the Piller family lovingly care for the seven bright, simply decorated rooms in their charming 17th-century house. All are simple but nicely decorated in dark wood and the high-ceilinged breakfast chamber boasts a rather striking marble fireplace.

Hotel de Munck

Achtergracht 3 (623 6283/www.hotel demunck.com). Tram 4. €€
This higgledy-piggledy place in an old Dutch East India Company captain's house is perched on a secluded little canal near the river. Rooms here are plain and basic (and some are looking a little tired), though they are clean and neat. The breakfast room is a delight, though, with a 1950s jukebox and walls plastered with old album covers.

Hotel Prinsenhof

Prinsengracht 810 (623 1772/www. hotelprinsenhof.com). Tram 4. €
Good for travellers simply after a place to kip at night, this dinky, ten-roomed hotel is near the nightlife and foodie Utrechtsestraat and has helpful staff. Rooms themselves (some have canal views) are simple, some share facilities, and they're all clean and tidy. Those physically less able should note that the stairs are very steep.

InterContinental Amstel Amsterdam

Professor Tulpplein 1 (622 6060/www. interconti.com). Tram 6, 7, 10. €€€€

Mövenpick Hotel Amsterdam City Centre p172

They don't come much posher than this: if movie stars or royalty are in town, they almost always lay their heads in one of the huge, soundproofed rooms or even bigger luxury suites here. Everything is superlative: staff are liveried, the restaurant Michelin-starred, and every service imaginable is present, swimming pool included. If money is no object or you want to indulge in a once-in-a-lifetime splurge, then this is the place to do it.

Kamer01

3e Weteringdwarsstraat 44 (625 6627/ www.kamer01.nl). Tram 7, 10, 16, 24, 25. €€
A stylish, gay-friendly B&B designed by Atelier Hertogh. The aptly-named Red Room comes with a huge shower (big enough for two – or more), while the equally descriptive Blue Room – with its circular bed and private roof terrace – will be redesigned in late 2007. Both come with iMacs, flat-screen TVs and DVD players. There's a minimum two-night stay.

Marcel van Woerkom

Leidsestraat 87 (622 9834/www.marcel amsterdam.com). Tram 1, 2, 5. €€

Artist Marcel has been letting rooms in his stylish 'creative exchange' since 1970. Chances are you'll run into other artists or designers admiring the art on the walls. Despite it being classed as a B&B, you only get the bed, but there are plenty of breakfasting choices nearby. The place is understandably popular, so book well in advance.

Mercure Hotel Arthur Frommer

Noorderstraat 46 (622 0328/www. mercure.com). Tram 4. €€€
On a residential street within walking distance of the sights and the local nightlife, this courtyard hotel is in one of the nicest locations in town by far, near Amstelveld and with restaurant-lined Utrechtsestraat also very close at hand. Rooms are spacious and smart, though not overburdened with fancy extras. There's also a bar that's popular with guests and non-guests.

Nicolaas Witsen

Nicolaas Witsenstraat 4 (623 6143/ www.hotelnicolaaswitsen.nl). Tram 4. €€
One of the few hotels to fill the gap between museums and the Pijp, this place, though plain, functional (and a

ESSENTIALS

tad overpriced for what you get), is well placed for both serious culture vultures and fun-seekers. Ground-floor rooms can get noisy but plusses include free Wi-Fi and a lift. The excellent delicatessen on the corner encourages in-room midnight feasting.

Seven Bridges

Reguliersgracht 31 (623 1329/ www.sevenbridgeshotel.nl). Tram 16, 24, 25. €€
The ideal destination for hermits who want a luxury hidey-hole far from the madding crowd, this hotel is also convenient for the museums and trips into the city centre. There are no public spaces, just eight antique-packed rooms. Breakfast is served in bed on Villeroy and Boch crockery. One of Amsterdam's best-kept secrets.

Jodenbuurt, the Plantage and the Oost

Arena

's Gravesandestraat 51 (850 2400/www. hotelarena.nl). Tram 3, 6, 9, 10, 14. €€
A hotel, restaurant and club in an old orphanage, a ten-minute tram ride from town, it's the one-stop-shop of food, booze and boogie. Standard and larger rooms are a bit boring, but (pricier) extra large ones and suites are kitted out by leading local designers.

Eden Lancaster

Plantage Middelaan 48 (535 6888/www. edenhotelgroup.com). Tram 6, 9, 14. €€
If you're planning on taking the kids to the excellent Artis zoo (p100) then this hotel is just across the road, and their triple and quad rooms are very much aimed at families. Even though it's a little out of the way of the more central sights, the main railway station is a short tram ride or 20-minute walk away, and there are several good cafés in the immediate vicinity.

Hotel Adolesce

Nieuwe Keizersgracht 26 (626 3959/ www.adolesce.nl). Trams 4, 6, 7, 10/ Metro Weesperplein. €

You won't get any breakfast at this unfussy place near the Skinny Bridge, but guests can help themselves to drinks, fruit and chocolate in the lounge. Rooms are plain – the attic room is nicest – but it's close to both the Hermitage Museum (p100) and Waterlooplein fleamarket (p109), and enjoys a close proximity to the river.

Stayokay Amsterdam Zeeburg

Timorplein 21 (551 3190/www. stayokay.com). Trams 7, 10. €
This new branch of the reliable hostel chain in a grand old school building is aimed at families and discerning hostellers. Rooms sleep two to eight; there are no dorms. Designed by Edward van Vliet in warm reds with mosaic floors and sleek furniture, hostelling never looked so good.

The Waterfront & North

Ideaal II

Opposite Levantkade 51 (419 7255/ www.houseboats.nl). Tram 10, 26. €€
An inspired and deeply indulgent option for those seeking waterborne accommodation, this converted cargo boat near the up-and-coming cultural quarter sleeps up to five sybarites, and comes with two bathrooms, jacuzzi, state-of-the-art stainless steel kitchen and decks dedicated to sunbathing and swimming. At night, you'll sleep on (what else?) a waterbed. Overnight stays are possible, but longer ones make far more economic sense. Check the website for some excellent last-minute deals.

Mövenpick Hotel Amsterdam City Centre

Piet Heinkade 11 (519 1200/www. moevenpick-hotels.com). Tram 25, 26. €€€
A glamorous multi-storey branch of the Swiss chain recently opened on the banks of the IJ. Rooms are decorated in muted modern greys and woods. The

ESSENTIALS

Soft architecture for sale

Golfstromen Studio

Joop De Boer, a 29-year-old part-time city planner, and Jeroen Beekmans, a 21-year-old political science student, aren't architects in the technical sense of the word, but they do have a real passion for buildings. They are the team behind **Golfstromen Studio** (www.golfstromen.nl), a bureau that creates what they have termed 'soft architecture'; fully immersive experiences in the likes of vacated offices, abandoned factories, under bridges and in low-key courtyards.

Their efforts have now come to the attention of Buma Cultuur, the people behind organising the **Amsterdam Dance Event** (ADE; p33). For the next instalment of ADE, Golfstromen will be drawing on Buma's support to create the city's first ever indoor campsite. If all goes to plan, the site will also launch their 'reconstruction hotel'

– in fact, the original idea behind Golfstromen Studio's inception.

Golfstromen Studio tries to act as a bridge between Amsterdam's underground, its local adventure seekers and the people with the property. 'Basically, we create possibilities,' says De Boer. 'What we want is to run a website listing temporary sleeping spaces in empty buildings throughout town. It would entice adventurous tourists. We'll then price it below the budget hotels and get people to the weirdest places.'

This sort of underground scene is already extremely vibrant in Amsterdam, but the rules are unusually restrictive ('Amsterdam is a tough environment compared to other cities,' complains De Boer), and devising the plans for rethinking sites demands cunning, strategy and fiery vigour. For the ADE event, they need a place that is at once empty, inspiring and creative, but can also happily host around 100 to 250 sleeping mats or hammocks. On their list for consideration so far is an abandoned office building, the former Shell tower Overhoeks and a decrepit residential block over in Zuid that's currently waiting in line for imminent demolition.

With 60,000 people visiting last year's ADE – the biggest club event in the world – Beekmans and De Boer have got their work cut out for them. They need to create something that will turn sleeping into an imaginative experience. 'It's got to be really, really fun,' says Beekmans with a smile. 'Experiencing the ordinary in new ways is what people want more than anything else.'

Truelove Antiek
and Guesthouse

more expensive rooms include access to the 'executive lounge' and have great views over the water and the city.

The Jordaan

Frederic Rentabike
Brouwersgracht 78 (624 5509/www.frederic.nl). Bus 18, 22. No credit cards. €€
This bike shop also does a nice little sideline in renting out nine houseboats all around town, ranging from sleek vessels to eminently more homely numbers. Houseboat No.5, located on the Prinsengracht, is big, stylish, central and comes with internet access.

Truelove Antiek and Guesthouse
Prinsenstraat 4 (320 2500/06 248 056 72 mobile after 6pm/www.truelove.be). Tram 1, 2, 5. €€
Above an old antique shop (itself now serving as the hotel's reception), this dinky place is nicely decorated with the odd piece from downstairs. There's no smoking throughout, and the attic room is best of the bunch, and all come with a CD player and a kettle. There's also an apartment on Langestraat.

The Museum Quarter, Vondelpark & the South

Between Art and Kitsch
Ruysdaelkade 75 (679 0485/www.between-art-and-kitsch.com). Tram 16, 24, 25. €
Technically speaking it's between the museums and the Pijp, actually. This B&B has just two rooms: one is decorated in mock art deco with authentic period knick-knacks, the other in faux Baroque, and yes, rooms do live up to the name's promise. On a nice canal, it's great for culture vultures keen to get out there and explore.

Bilderberg Jan Luyken
Jan Luykenstraat 58 (573 0730/www.bilderberg.nl). Tram 2, 5, 6, 7, 10. €€
One of the city's most stylish secrets, this place – complete with spa and a wine bar – is just a kitten-heeled skip from the upmarket shops dotted along PC Hooftstraat. Rooms feature plenty of designer touches and wall-mounted CD players, and are truly something of a bargain for a place boasting these looks and facilities. Check for special packages: the Amsterdam Beauty

ESSENTIALS

Arrangement, for example, gets you a cocktail, bed and breakfast for the night, and an hour and a half in the spa for under €110 per person.

College Hotel

Roelof Hartstraat 1 (571 1511/www.the collegehotel.com). Tram 3, 12, 25. €€€
An unusal one this, in that it's part of the city's own hotel and catering college and thus staffed by students training in situ. Boutique styling and some glam touches ensure that prices reach far from pocket-money. Some rooms, though lovely, are small; pay top dollar to get oodles of space (the TCH suite is far bigger than most Amsterdam flats). There's also a bar and an ambitious modern Dutch restaurant. Perhaps because of the hotel's educational function, service can sometimes be a bit unpredictable.

Hotel V

Victorieplein 42 (662 3233/www. hotelv.nl). Tram 4, 12, 25. €€
The Hotel V is a bit of a hike from the sights and the centre, but tram No.4 stops right outside to whisk you into town within ten minutes, and the less mainstream lures of the Pijp are barely a 15-minute walk away. This boutique B&B-style hotel is ideal for business travellers sick of corporate sterility: it's near the RAI and business areas of Zuid. There's sleek decor in all rooms, but you won't find much in the way of extras. That said, the lounge, with its pebbly fireplace and furry pouffes, looks genuinely lovely.

Hotel Vondel

Vondelstraat 28-30 (612 0120/www. hotelvondel.nl). Tram 2, 5, 6, 7, 10. €€€
Another well-hidden gem near the museums and Amsterdam's more upmarket shopping district, this chic little place is covered with art and boasts a lovely decked garden. Rooms, from small to extra large via a junior and family suite, are designer driven, with Burberry-check blankets, chandeliers and swanky bathrooms. Unusually for such a trendy hotel, families are encouraged.

Xaviera Hollander Bed & Breakfast

Stadionweg 17 (673 3934/www.xaviera hollander.com). Tram 5, 24. €€
Prudes avert your eyes, since you won't want to stay in the home of the original Happy Hooker. Rooms, upstairs in Xaviera's own banker-belt villa or in a hut at the bottom of her garden, are nice, but guests come here mainly for a truly outrageous anecdote – or several – from the lady herself.

The Pijp

Hotel Okura Amsterdam

Ferdinand Bolstraat 333 (678 7111/ www.okura.nl). Tram 12, 25. €€€€
This multi-storey, multi-tasking, very smart business-class stopover has everything captains of industry need: a top-floor, top of the range French restaurant, Le Ciel Bleu; a full-size pool and health club; and sushi bars. Rooms are done up in suitably masculine style and range from small standards to the huge (and hugely expensive) presidential suite on the 21st floor.

Hotel Savoy

Ferdinand Bolstraat 194 (644 7445/ www.hampshirehotels.com/savoy). Tram 3, 12, 16, 24, 25. €€€
One of a limited number of accommodation options in this rather ill-served area, this hotel in an imposing red-brick Amsterdam School building came under new ownership in autumn 2006, and has since been restyled as a swanky concept hotel, which should suit the increasingly gentrified Pijp right down to the ground.

Van Ostade Bicycle Hotel

Van Ostadestraat 123 (679 3452/www. bicyclehotel.com). Tram 12, 16, 24, 25. €
This staging post for pedal-pushers was one of the first (and is still one of the few) places to stay in the Pijp. Staff can suggest trips and rent out bikes. Rooms are comfy and there are loads of excellent places nearby to refuel for the day ahead or wind down after a long, hard ride around town.

ESSENTIALS

PUB CRAWL

DO YOU LIKE TO PARTY and meet other travellers ?

SUNDAY to Friday 6 nights a week!

- 6 Dance Bars and Clubs
- 6 Free drinks
- Unlimited free shots 8:30-9:00 pm
- Vodka shots between venues
- Drink specials
- No cover charge for bars and clubs
- Professional guides

all for just:
€19,95

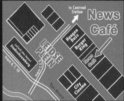

ULTIMATE PARTY XXX AMSTERDAM

The Ultimate Party starts between 8.30 pm and 9.00 pm @
NEWS CAFÉ (Korte Leidsedwarsstraat 77)

4 doors down from Burger King
TRANSPORTATION:
Tram 1,2,5,6,7 or 10 to Leidseplein

The Ultimate Party Hotline: +31 (0)641221163

BRING THIS AD AND RECEIVE A €1,- DISCOUNT
No reservation required,
just show up @ News Café between 8.30 pm and 9.00 pm

FOR MORE INFO CHECK: WWW.JOINULTIMATEPARTY.COM

A night you won't remember...
...but never forget!

Getting Around

Arriving & leaving

By air

Schiphol Airport

0900 0141/www.schiphol.nl
Amsterdam's airport is located 18
kilometres (11 miles) south west of
the city. There is only one terminal
building, and within that are four
separate departure and arrival halls.

Connexxion Airport Hotel Shuttle

*Connexxion counter, Section A7,
Arrivals, Schiphol Airport (038 339
4741/www.airporthotelshuttle.nl).*
This bus service from Schiphol
to Amsterdam departs every 30
minutes between 6am and 9pm for
anyone who buys a ticket (€12.50
single/€19.50 open return), not just
hotel guests. Drop-off points are the
hundred-odd allied hotels and, as
the bus stops at them all, it's easy
to get off near your destination.
Schedules and the expanding list of
destination hotels are on the website,
which also has a booking service.

Airport trains

Trains leave approximately every
ten minutes between 4am and
midnight (after which they are
hourly), at 12, 18, 23, 30, 42 and 48
minutes past the hour, as well as on
the hour and half-hour. The journey
to Centraal Station takes about 20
minutes. Buy your ticket (€3.60
single, €6.10 return) before you
board, otherwise you're highly
likely to incur a €35 fine.

By taxi

A fixed fare from the airport to the
south and west of the city is about
€25, and to the city centre is about
€35. Bear in mind that there are
always plenty of licensed taxis
beside the main exit.

By bus

Long-distance international
Eurolines coaches (560 8788/
www.eurolines.nl) stop at Amstel
station, Julianaplein 5, in the south
east of the city, which is connected
to Centraal Station by Metro.

By train

A range of national service trains
(operated by NS) and international
services all stop at Centraal Station
in the city centre.

In town

Getting around Amsterdam is very
easy: there are efficient, cheap and
integrated trams, metros and buses
and, moreover, in the centre most
places are reachable on foot. Locals
tend to get around by bike, and
there are also boats and water taxis.
Public transport provision for those
with disabilities, however, is dire.

The best way of getting around
is by tram, which runs a network
of routes through the centre (buses
and the Metro are more for serving
outlying suburbs).

GVB

*Stationsplein CS, Old Centre: New Side
(0900 8011/www.gvb.nl). Tram 1, 2, 4,
5, 9, 13, 16, 17, 24, 25.* **Open** *Phone
enquiries* 8am-10pm daily. *In person*
7am-9pm Mon-Fri; 8am-9pm Sat, Sun.
The GVB runs Amsterdam's Metro,
bus and tram services, and can also
provide detailed information and
departure and arrival times on all
of them, as well as selling tickets.

ESSENTIALS

Fares & tickets

A *strippenkaart* (strip ticket) system operates across trams, buses and metros: prices begin at €1.60 for a strip of two units (one journey in one zone) bought on the tram/bus or purchased from machines for the Metro. Cheaper are 15-unit (€6.80) or 45-unit (€20.10) cards, bought from GVB offices, post offices, train stations, and many supermarkets and tobacconists. Kids under three travel free; older children (four-18) and seniors (65+) pay reduced fares. *Strippenkaarten* must be stamped on boarding trams/buses or entering Metro stations. For convenience's sake, Amsterdam is divided up roughly into five separate zones: Noord (north), West, Centrum, Oost (east) and Zuid (south); most of central Amsterdam falls within the main Centrum zone.

Journeys all work on the basic principle of one unit for the journey plus one unit for each zone, so for a single zone, stamp two units; for two zones stamp three and so on.

If the tram is conductorless, then stamp the *strippenkaart* with the yellow box near the doors: fold it so that the unit you need to stamp is at the end. On conducted trams and buses, the *strippenkaart* is stamped for you. On the Metro, stamping machines are located near the entrance. More than one person can travel on one strip ticket, but the correct number of units must be stamped per person.

Stamped cards are valid for an hour and allow transfer to other buses/trams/metros, or across all three. *Strippenkaarten* are valid for a year from the date of first stamping. Unlimited day tickets costing €6.50, and the I amsterdam Pass valid for one, two or three days costing €33-€53, can also be purchased from either the GVB or Amsterdam Tourist Board. Don't even think about travelling without a ticket: inspectors aren't always on board, but they do check regularly and passengers without tickets will receive €35 on-the-spot fines.

Trams & buses

Trams run from 6am Monday to Friday, 6.30am on Saturday and 7.30am on Sunday. Night buses (numbered from 351 to 363) take over later (1am-5.30am Mon-Fri, to 6.30am weekends) and all go to Centraal Station. Night bus stops are indicated by a black square at the stop with the bus number printed on it. During off-peak hours and at quiet stops, stick out your arm to let the driver know that you want to get on. Signs at tram and bus stops show the name of the stop and line number, while boards will indicate the full route.

The yellow and decorated trams are synonymous with Amsterdam, but the newer, bluer and higher-windowed ones are becoming more common. Other road users should be warned that they will only stop if absolutely necessary. Cyclists should listen for tram warning bells and be careful to cross tramlines at an angle that avoids the front wheel from getting stuck. At the same time, motorists in the city should avoid blocking tramlines: cars are allowed to venture on to them only if they're turning right.

Metro

The Metro uses the same ticket system as trams and buses (see above) and serves suburbs to the south and east. Three separate lines, 51, 52 and 53, terminate at Centraal Station (sometimes abbreviated to CS). Trains on the city Metro run from 6am Mon-Fri (6.30am Sat, 7.30am Sun) to around 12.15am on a daily basis.

Taxis

Most taxis are operated by the central office TCA. They're hard to hail on the street, but ranks are found around the city – most central are the ones at Centraal Station, by the bus station at the junction of Kinkerstraat and Marnixstraat, on Rembrandtplein and Leidseplein. Cabs can be ordered on 677 7777. Wheelchairs only fit in taxis folded, but there is a service for wheelchair users (633 3943, 7am-5pm daily); be sure to book journeys at least one or two days in advance.

Fares

Getting a taxi in Amsterdam is relatively straightforward, but check that the meter starts at the minimum charge (€3.40) and ask the rough cost of the journey before setting out. Even short journeys are expensive: on top of the minimum charge, it costs €1.94 per kilometre for the first 25 kilometres, €1.45 per kilometre thereafter.

If you feel you've been ripped off (relatively rare), ask for a receipt, and contact the TCA on 650 6506 (9am-5pm Mon-Fri) or the police.

There are now companies out to break the monopoly of TCA. One such company is the popular **Tulip Taxi** (636 3000) which offers a minimum charge of €2.55, with €0.85 for the first 15 kilometres and €1.50 per kilometre thereafter, saving up to 50% on inner-city rides. Bear in mind that it's sadly a very small fleet, so there are often long waiting times for taxis.

Driving

If you absolutely must bring a car to the Netherlands, join a national motoring organisation beforehand. This should then issue you with booklets that explain what to do in the event of a breakdown in Europe. To drive a car within the Netherlands, you also need a valid national driving licence, although ANWB (see below) and many car hire firms favour photocard licences (Brits need the paper version as well for this to be legal; the photocard takes a couple of weeks to come through if you're applying from scratch). You'll need proof that the vehicle has passed a road safety test in its country of origin, as well as an international identification disk, a registration certificate, and – needless to say – any and all relevant insurance documents.

Car hire

Local car hire (*autoverhuur*) firms generally expect at least a year's experience and demand a valid national driving licence (with photo) and passport, and drivers to be over 21. All require a credit card deposit with hire.

Adam's Rent-a-Car
685 0111/www.adamsrentacar.nl

Dik's Autoverhuur
662 3366/www.diks.net

Hertz
612 2441/www.hertz.nl

Parking

Parking is a nightmare: the centre is metered from 9am until at least 7pm (to midnight in many places), setting you back up to €4.60 an hour and with clamping and ticketing both extremely common. Parking during the day (9am to 7pm: €27.60) or evening (7pm to midnight: €18.40) passes, plus weekly (€165.60 9am-7pm, €248.40 24 hours) can be bought from Stadstoezicht offices (www.stadstoezicht.amsterdam.nl). Bear in mind that after controlled hours, parking at meters across the city is completely free.

ESSENTIALS

Car parks

Car parks are indicated by a white 'P' on a blue square sign. **ANWB Parking Amsterdam Centraal** (Prins Hendrikkade 20A in the Old Centre: New Side, 638 5330) is open 24 hours daily and charges €3.50 per hour. Many nearby hotels offer a 10% discount on parking here. **Europarking** (Marnixstraat 250, 0900 446) in Oud West is cheaper, charging €2.80 per hour, but is only open 6.30am-1am Mon-Thur; 6.30am-2am Fri, Sat; 7am-1am Sun. Both accept payment by credit card. When leaving your car, make sure to empty it of valuables: cars with foreign number plates are particularly vulnerable to break-ins both inside and out of the centre.

Clamping & fines

If you're clamped, a sticker on your windscreen tells you to phone 251 2222 (24 hours pay and go service). Someone will come to remove the clamp for the €103.60 fine (payable by credit card). During business hours, go to any of the clamping offices listed on www.stadstoezicht. amsterdam.nl and hand over your money; if you have to pay in cash after usual business hours, go to the pound at Daniel Goedkoopstraat 7-9, then back to the car to wait for someone to remove the clamp.

If you don't pay within 24 hours, you'll be towed: this costs €150 or more, plus a parking fine, plus a tariff per kilometre to reclaim it from the pound within 24 hours, plus €58 for every 12 hours after. Take your passport, licence number and cash or major credit card.

Petrol

There are 24-hour petrol stations (*tankstations*) at Gooiseweg 10, Sarphatistraat 225, Marnixstraat 250 and Spaarndammerdijk 218.

Water transport

Amsterdam is best seen – and even better understood – from the water. Sure there are canal cruises, but they do not offer the freedom to do your own exploring. You can try to bond with a local boat owner; otherwise your options are limited to the pedal-powered canal bike or pedalo. Upon rental, don't ignore the introductory run-down of the rules of the water (put at its most basic: stick to the right and be very wary of canal cruisers, who always assume that size makes right).

Pedaloes

Canal Bike

Weteringschans 24, Southern Canal Belt (626 5574/www.canal.nl). **Open** *Summer* 10am-6pm; in good weather until 9.30pm daily. *Winter* 10am-5.30pm daily at Rijksmuseum; weekends also at Westerkerk and Leidseplein.

Canal buses

Canal Bus

Weteringschans 27, Southern Canal Belt (623 9886/www.canal.nl). Tram 6, 10. **Open** 10am-7pm daily.

Water taxis

Water Taxi Centrale

Stationsplein 8, Old Centre: New Side (535 6363/www.water-taxi.nl). Tram 1, 2, 4, 5, 9, 13, 16, 17, 24, 25. **Open** 8am-midnight daily.

Cycling

The best way to get from A to B in a country made for cycling. There are bike lanes on most roads, marked by white lines and bike symbols. Never leave a bike unlocked – it will get stolen – and use two locks. Most bikes have pedal-backwards (as opposed to handlebar-mounted) brakes, which take getting used to.

Resources A-Z

Accident & emergency

In the case of minor accidents, you can just turn up at the outpatient departments at the following city hospitals (*ziekenhuis*). All are open 24 hours a day, seven days a week, and remain open all year round.

Academisch Medisch Centrum
Meibergdreef 9, Zuid (566 9111/first aid 566 3333). Metro Holendrechp/ bus 59, 60, 120, 126, 158.

Boven IJ Ziekenhuis
Statenjachtstraat 1, Noord (634 6346/ first aid 634 6200). Bus 34, 36, 37, 39, 171, 172.

Onze Lieve Vrouwe Gasthuis
's Gravesandeplein 16, Oost (599 9111/ first aid 599 3016). Tram 3, 6, 10/ Metro Weesperplein or Wibautstraat.

St Lucas Andreas Ziekenhuis
Jan Tooropstraat 164, West (510 8911/first aid 510 8161). Tram 13/ bus 19, 47, 80, 82, 97.

VU Ziekenhuis
De Boelelaan 1117, Zuid (444 4444/first aid 444 3636). Metro Amstelveenseweg/bus 142, 147, 148, 149, 170, 171, 172.

Banks

There's little difference between the rates of exchange offered by banks and bureaux de change, but banks do tend to charge less commission. Dutch banks will buy and sell foreign currency and exchange travellers' cheques, but bear in mind that few of them will give cash advances against credit cards.

ATMs

Cash machines are only found at banks here: as yet, no bank has been resourceful enough to set any up in shops or bars, as is increasingly the case in the UK and parts of the US. If your cashcard carries either the Maestro or Cirrus symbols then you should be able to withdraw cash from ATMs, though it's worth checking with your bank a) that it's possible and b) what the charging structure is.

Customs

EU nationals over 17 years of age may import limitless goods into the Netherlands for their personal use. Other EU countries may still have limits on the quantity of goods they permit on entry. For citizens of non-EU countries, however, the old limits continue to apply as before. These are as follows:

- 200 cigarettes or 50 cigars or 250 grams tobacco;
- two litres of non-sparkling wine or one litre of spirits (over 22 per cent alcohol), or two litres of fortified wine (under 22 per cent alcohol);
- 60cc/ml of perfume;
- 500 grams coffee or 200 grams coffee extracts or coffee essence;
- 100 grams tea or 40 grams tea extracts or tea essence;
- other goods to the value of €175.

Dentists

For a dentist (*tandarts*), call 0900 821 2230. Operators can put you in touch with your nearest dentist, and lines are open 24 hours for those with more urgent dental emergencies. Otherwise, make an appointment at one of the following.

ESSENTIALS

AOC

*Wilhelmina Gasthuisplein 167,
Oud West (616 1234). Tram 1,
2, 3, 5, 6, 12.* **Open** 9am-noon,
1-4pm Mon-Fri.

Emergency dental treatment. They
also have a recorded service in
Dutch on 686 1109 that tells you
where a walk-in clinic will be open
at 11.30am and 9.30pm that day.

TBB

570 9595/0900 821 2230
A 24-hour service that can refer
callers to a dentist.

Disabled

Winding cobbled streets in the
older areas, poorly maintained
pavements and steep canal house
steps can present real problems to
disabled visitors, but the pragmatic
Dutch can generally solve problems
quickly. Most large museums,
cinemas and theatres have disabled
facilities (but little for the partially
sighted and hard of hearing). The
Metro is accessible to wheelchair
users with 'normal arm function'
but most trams are inaccessible to
wheelchair users due to high steps.
The AUB and Amsterdam Tourist
Board produce brochures listing
disabled-friendly accommodation,
restaurants and other attractions.

Electricity

The Netherlands uses the standard
European 220V, 50-cycle AC voltage
via two-pin continental plugs.
Visitors from Britain will need
an adaptor; American visitors may
need a transformer.

Embassies

American Consulate General

*Museumplein 19, (575 5309/0900 872
8472 preemiumrate/www.usembassy.nl).
Tram 3, 5, 12, 16.*

Australian Embassy

*Carnegielaan 4, The Hague (070 310
8200/0800 0224 794 Australian
citizen emergency phone/www.
australian-embassy.nl).*

British Consulate General

*Koningslaan 44 (676 4343/
www.britain.nl).*

British Embassy

*Lange Voorhout 10, The Hague
(070 427 0427/www.britain.nl).*

Canadian Embassy

*Sophialaan 7, The Hague
(070 311 1600/www.canada.nl).*

Irish Embassy

*Dr Kuyperstraat 9, The Hague
(070 363 0993/www.irishembassy.nl).*

New Zealand Embassy

*Eisenhowerlaan 77N, The Hague (070
346 9324/visas 070 365 8037/www.
immigration.govt.nz/ Branch/TheHague
BranchHome).*

Gay & lesbian information

COC Amsterdam

*Rozenstraat 14, the Jordaan (626
3087/www.cocamsterdam.nl). Tram
13, 14, 17.* **Open** *Telephone enquiries*
10am-4pm Mon-Fri.
The Amsterdam branch of COC
deals with the campaigning side
of gay life.

Gay & Lesbian Switchboard

*Postbus 11573 (623 6565/www.switch
board.nl).* **Open** noon-10pm Mon-Fri;
4-8pm Sat, Sun.
Whether it's regarding enquiries
for general information or advice
on safe sex, the friendly English-
speakers here are well informed.

Helplines

Alcoholics Anonymous

625 6057/www.aa-netherlands.org.
Open 24hr answerphone.

A lengthy but informative message in English/Dutch details times and dates of meetings, and contact numbers for counsellors. The website is in English and you can locate meetings per day or per town.

Narcotics Anonymous

662 6307. **Open** 24hr answerphone in English/Dutch with phone numbers of counsellors.

SOS Telephone Helpline

675 7575. **Open** 24hrs daily.
A counselling service – comparable with the Samaritans in the UK and Lifeline in the US – for anyone with emotional problems. English isn't always understood at first, but keep trying and someone will eventually be able to help you.

Internet

All global ISPs have a presence here (check websites for a local number). Most of the local hotels are increasingly well equipped, whether that means dataports in the rooms, a terminal in the lobby, or laptop-friendly Wi-Fi throughout the entire hotel.

Easy Internet Café

Damrak 33, Old Centre: New Side (no phone/www.easyinternetcafe.com). Tram 4, 9, 14, 16, 24, 25. **Open** 9am-10pm daily. **Rates** vary.
No credit cards.

Freeworld

Nieuwendijk 30, Old Centre: New Side (620 0902/www.freeworld-internet cafe.nl). Tram 1, 2, 5, 13, 17, 20. **Open** 9am-1am Mon-Thur, Sun; 9am-3am Fri, Sat. **Rates** €1/30min.
No credit cards.

Internet Cafe

Martelaarsgracht 11, Old Centre: New Side (no phone/www.internetcafe.nl). Tram 4, 9, 16, 20, 24, 25. **Open** 9am-1am Mon-Thur, Sun; 9am-3am Fri, Sat. **Rates** from €1/30min.
No credit cards.

Left luggage

There is a staffed left-luggage counter at Schiphol Airport (601 2443/www.schiphol.nl) where you can store luggage for up to one month, open daily 7am to 10.45pm (€5/item/24hrs, €3.50/item/each 24hrs after). There are also lockers in the arrival and departure halls, while in central Amsterdam there are plenty of lockers located over at Centraal Station with 24-hour access (from €4/24hrs).

Lost property

Centraal Station

Stationsplein 15, Old Centre: Old Side (0900 321 2100/www.ns.nl). Tram 1, 2, 4, 5, 9, 13, 16, 17, 24, 25. **Open** 8am-6pm Mon-Fri; 7am-5pm Sat. Items found on trains are kept here for three days (it's easiest to just go to any window where they sell tickets and ask), after which time they are forwarded on to **Centraal Bureau Gevonden Voorwerpen** (Central Lost Property Office), 2e Daalsedijk 4, 3551 EJ Utrecht (030 235 3923, 8am-5pm Mon-Fri). Items are held for three months. If you pick it up personally it costs €10; having it posted costs €15 and up.

GVB Lost Property

Arlandaweg 100 (0900 8011/460 6060). Tram 12. **Open** 9am-4pm Mon-Fri. Wait at least a day or two before you call, describe what you lost on bus, metro or tram, and leave a number. They will call you back if it is found. Alternatively, there is also an online form (in Dutch) for lost property at www.gvb.nl.

Police Lost Property

Stephensonstraat 18, Zuid (559 3005). Tram 12/Metro Amstel Station/bus 14. **Open** *In person* 9.30am-3.30pm Mon-Fri. *By phone* noon-3.30pm Mon-Fri. Before contacting here, check the local police station.

Opening hours

Banks 9am-5pm, Mon-Fri (Postbank 9.30am-1pm Sat). Most bars open at various times throughout the day and close at around 1am Mon-Thur, Sun, 2am or 3am Fri, Sat. Shops open 1-6pm Mon (if they open at all; many shops stay closed on Mondays); 10am-6pm Tue-Fri (some open until 9pm Thur); 9am-5pm Sat.

Pharmacies

Dam Apotheek

Damstraat 2, Old Centre: Old Side (624 4331). Tram 4, 9, 14, 16, 24, 25. **Open** 8.30am-5.30pm Mon-Fri; 10am-5.30pm Sat. **No credit cards**.
This central pharmacy has extended opening hours. Outside these hours, customers can phone **Afdeling Inlichtingen Apotheken** (694 8709), a 24-hour service that will gladly direct you to your nearest late-opening chemist.

Police stations

For details and contact information on local stations, look under '*Politie*' in the *Gouden Gids*.

Amsterdam Tourist Assistance Service (ATAS)

Nieuwezijds Voorburgwal 104-108 (625 3246). Tram 1, 2, 5, 6, 13, 17. **Open** 10am-10pm daily.

Hoofdbureau van Politie (Police Headquarters)

Elandsgracht 117, the Jordaan (0900 8844). Tram 7, 10. **Open** 24hrs daily.

Post

Post offices are usually open 9am-5pm Mon-Fri; 9.30am-1pm Sat. The postal information phoneline is 058 233 3333. The main post office is at Singel 250, Old Centre: New Side (0900 7678526). It's open 9am-6pm Mon-Fri; 10am-2pm Sat.

Safety

Amsterdam is a relatively safe city, but do take care. The Red Light District is rife with undesirables who, if not violent, are expert pickpockets; be vigilant, especially on or around bridges, and don't ever make eye contact with anyone who looks like they're up to no good, drug dealers especially.

Be extra careful of thieves on the Schiphol train; if you cycle, lock your bike up well. Keep valuables in your hotel safe, don't leave bags unattended, and make sure cash and cards are tucked and preferably zipped away in your bag.

Smoking

Smoking is restricted to designated areas in stations and airports but is common in bars and restaurants. As for cannabis, locals have a relaxed attitude to soft drugs, but smoking it isn't acceptable everywhere in the city: use discretion and if in doubt, ask before you spark up in public.

Telephones

Amsterdam's dialling code is 020; to call within the city, you don't need the code. If you're dialling from outside the Netherlands, dial the country code, 31, then the number; drop the first '0' of the area code; for Amsterdam you would use 20 rather than the full 020.

US mobile phone users should be sure to contact their provider before departure to check compatibility issues with GSM bands.

Public phones

Public payphones take cards rather than coins, now available from the Amsterdam Tourist Board, stations, post offices and tobacconists. Many also take credit cards.

Time

Amsterdam is an hour ahead of Greenwich Mean Time (GMT). All clocks on Central European Time (CET) now go back and forward on the same dates as GMT.

Tipping

Service charges are included in hotel, taxi, bar, café and restaurant bills, but it's still polite to round payment up to the nearest euro for small bills or the nearest five for larger sums, though tipping ten per cent is becoming more common (this is done by leaving the extra in change rather than filling in the blank on a credit card slip). In taxis, most people now tend to tip ten per cent.

Tourist information

Amsterdam Tourist Board (VVV)

Stationsplein 10, Old Centre: New Side (0900 400 4040/www.visit amsterdam.nl). Tram 1, 2, 4, 5, 9, 13, 16, 17, 24, 25. **Open** 9am-5pm daily. The main office is right outside Centraal Station. English-speaking staff can change money and also provide you with info on transport, entertainment, exhibitions and day-trips in the Netherlands. They also arrange hotel bookings (for a fee), excursions or car hire for free. There is a good range of brochures for sale detailing walks and cycling tours, as well as plenty of cassette tours, maps and a useful monthly listings magazine, *Day by Day*. The info line features an English-language service (€0.40/min). **Other locations**: Leidseplein 1 (9.15am-5pm Mon-Thur, Sun; 9.15am-7pm Fri, Sat); Centraal Station, platform 2B 15 (8am-8pm Mon-Sat; 9am-5pm Sun); Schiphol Airport, arrivals hall 2 (7am-10pm daily).

Translators & interpreters

Amstelveens Vertaalburo

Ouderkerkerlaan 50, Amstelveen (645 6610/www.avb.nl). Bus 65, 170, 172. **Open** 9am-5pm Mon-Fri. No credit cards.

Mac Bay Consultants

PC Hooftstraat 15, Museum Quarter (24hr phoneline 662 0501/fax 662 6299/www.macbay.nl). Tram 2, 3, 5, 12. **Open** 9am-7pm Mon-Fri.

Visas

EU citizens do not require a visa to visit the Netherlands; citizens of the USA, Canada, Australia and New Zealand only need a valid passport for stays up to three months long. Citizens of other countries should apply in advance for a tourist visa. EU nationals with a resident's permit can work here; non-EU citizens will find it difficult to get a visa without a job in place. Either way, jobs are very hard to come by.

When to go

Climate

Amsterdam's climate is extremely changeable. January and February are cold, with summer humid. If you know Dutch, try calling the weather line before leaving on 0900 8003 (calls charged at €0.60/min).

Public holidays

Called 'Nationale Feestdagen' in Dutch: New Year's Day; Good Friday; Easter Sunday and Monday; Koninginnedag (Queen's Day, 30 April); Remembrance Day (4 May); Liberation Day (5 May); Ascension Day; Whit (Pentecost) Sunday and Monday; Christmas Day; and Boxing Day.

ESSENTIALS

Vocabulary

Almost every person you'll come across in Amsterdam will speak good English, and you'll be able to get by without a word of Dutch during your stay. However, a bit of effort goes a long way, and locals are appreciative of those visitors polite enough to take five minutes to learn some basic phrases. Here are a few that might help.

Useful expressions

Hello *hallo/dag*; **goodbye** *tot ziens/ dag*; **yes** *ja*; **yes please** *ja, graag*; **no** *nee*; **no thanks** *nee, dank je*; **please** *alstublieft*; **thank you** *dank u*; **excuse me** *pardon*; **do you speak English?** *spreekt u Engels?*; **sorry, I don't speak Dutch** *het spijt me, ik spreek geen Nederlands*; **I don't understand** *ik begrijp het niet*; **I am ill** *ik ben ziek*; **good** *goed*; **bad** *slecht*; **big** *groot*; **small** *klein*; **nice** *mooi*; **tasty** *lekker*; **open** *open*; **closed** *gesloten/dicht*; **entrance** *ingang*; **exit** *uitgang*; **the bill** *de rekening*; **shop** *winkel*; **hotel room** *hotelkamer*; **single/twin/double bedroom** *eenpersoonskamer/ tweepersoonskamer met aparte bedden/tweepersoonskamer*; **I want** *ik wil graag*; **how much is** *wat kost*

Getting around

Bus *bus*; **car** *auto*; **tram** *tram*; **train** *trein*; **ticket/s** *kaart/kaarten*; **street** *straat*; **square** *plein*; **canal** *gracht*; **left** *links*; **right** *rechts*; **straight on** *rechtdoor*; **far** *ver*; **near** *dichtbij*; **here** *hier*; **there** *daar*; **where is** *waar is*

Places

Shop *winkel*; **bank** *bank*; **post office** *postkantoor*; **pharmacy** *apotheek*; **hotel** *hotel*; **bar** *bar*; **restaurant** *restaurant*; **hospital** *ziekenhuis*; **bus stop** *bushalte*; **station** *station*

Time

Now *nu*; **later** *straks*; **morning** *ochtend*; **afternoon** *middag*; **evening** *avond*; **night** *nacht*; **today** *vandaag*; **yesterday** *gisteren*; **tomorrow** *morgen*; **what time is** *hoe laat is*; **what's the time?** *hoe laat is het?*; **noon** *middag*; **midnight** *middernacht*; **at eight o'clock** *om acht uur*; **quarter past eight** *kwaart over acht*; **20 past eight** *tien voor half negen*; **25 past eight** *vijf half negen*; **half past eight** *half negen*; **25 to nine** *vijf over half negen*; **quarter to nine** *kwaart voor negen*

Numbers

0 *nul*; **1** *een*; **2** *twee*; **3** *drie*; **4** *vier*; **5** *vijf*; **6** *zes*; **7** *zeven*; **8** *acht*; **9** *negen*; **10** *tien*; **11** *elf*; **12** *twaalf*; **13** *dertien*; **14** *veertien*; **15** *vijftien*; **16** *zestien*; **17** *zeventien*; **18** *achttien*; **19** *negen-tien*; **20** *twintig*; **21** *eenentwintig*; **22** *twee 'ntwintig*; **30** *dertig*; **40** *veertig*; **50** *vijftig*; **60** *zestig*; **70** *zeventig*; **80** *tachtig*; **90** *negentig*; **100** *honderd*; **101** *honderd een*; **200** *tweehonderd*; **1,000** *duizend*; **1,000,000** *een miljoen*

Days & months

Monday *maandag*; **Tuesday** *dinsdag*; **Wednesday** *woensdag*; **Thursday** *donderdag*; **Friday** *vrijdag*; **Saturday** *zaterdag*; **Sunday** *zondag*; **January** *januari*; **February** *februari*; **March** *maart*; **April** *april*; **May** *mei*; **June** *juni*; **July** *juli*; **August** *augustus*; **September** *september*; **October** *oktober*; **November** *november*; **December** *december*

Menu Glossary

Basics

Bestek cutlery; **brood** bread; **broodje** bread roll; **glas** glass; **lepel** spoon; **menukaart** menu; **mes** knife; **peper** pepper; **de rekening** the bill; **vork** fork; **wijnkaart** wine list; **zout** salt

Snacks

Bitterballen round, mini-croquettes filled with meat and potato; **borrel/bittergarnituur** sharing platter of snacks to accompany drinks (usually sausage, salami, cheese and *bitterballen*); **borrelnoten** crispy-coated nuts; **frikadel** a very popular deep-fried skinless sausage with ingredients best left a mystery; **kaassouffle** cheese fritter, only tasty when very hot; **kroket** croquette filled with meat and potato; **oliebollen** deep-fried dough balls traditionally served around New Years, either plain or supplemented with raisins, currants and/or diced apples; **pannekoek** pancake; **patat** French fries/chips, also called *frites*; **patat met** French fries/chips with mayonnaise; **pindas** peanuts; **saucijzenbroodje** hot sausage roll made with puff pastry; **snert** a thick pea soup, also called *erwtensoep*; **tostis** grilled ham and/or cheese sandwiches; **uitsmijter** cheese and/or ham on bread topped with three fried eggs

Meat

Bal/gehaktbal meatball; **biefstuk** steak; **bio** organic; **eend** duck; **kalf** veal; **kalkoen** turkey; **kip** chicken; **lam** lamb; **rund** beef; **scharrel** free-range; **spek** bacon; **struisvogel** ostrich; **varkensvlees** pork; **vlees** meat; **worst** sausage

Fish

Ansjovis anchovies; **gambas** prawns; **garnalen** shrimps; **gerookte** smoked; **haring** herring; **maatjesharing** first herring of the season; **makreel** mackerel; **mosselen** mussels; **oesters** oysters; **paling** eel; **tong** sole; **tonijn** tuna; **venusschelpen** clams; **vis** fish; **zalm** salmon; **zeeduivel** monkfish; **zeevruchten/zeebanket** seafood

Fruit & vegetables

Aardappel potato; **aardbei** strawberry; **appel** apple; **bosbes** blueberry; **champignons** mushrooms; **citroen** lemon; **druiven** grapes; **framboos** raspberry; **fruit/vruchten** fruit; **groenten** vegetables; **kersen** cherries; **knoflook** garlic; **kruiden** herbs; **limoen** lime; **rauwkost** coleslaw; **rijst** rice; **sinasappel** orange; **zuurkool** sauerkraut

Puddings & cakes

Flensje crêpe; **gember** ginger; **griesmeel** semolina; **hangop** strained thick yoghurt; **honing** honey; **koek** cake; **koekje** biscuit; **roomijs/ijs** ice-cream; **slagroom** whipped cream; **stroop** syrup; **suiker** sugar; **toetje** dessert; **vla** custard

Dairy

Blauwe kaas blue cheese; **boter** butter; **geitenkaas** goat's cheese; **kaas** cheese; **magere/halfvolle/volle melk** skimmed/semi-skimmed/full milk; **oud/extra belegen** mature; **roomkaas** cream cheese; **schapenkaas** cheese made from sheep's milk

Index

Sights & Museums

ESSENTIALS

Eating & Drinking

ESSENTIALS

ESSENTIALS

Step into the World of Heineken

Stroll through the former brewery, learn about the company history, the brewing process and experience the international dimensions of Heineken. The world's best brew in the green bottle. *Cheers!*

Stadhouderskade 78 Amsterdam The Netherlands

Visit our website for opening hours. Visitors under 18 years must be accompanied by an adult at all times.
Phone +31 (0)20 523 96 66 www.heinekenexperience.com

Heineken
experience